DOCTRINE AND RACE

D1712872

DOCTRINE AND RACE

African American Evangelicals and Fundamentalism between the Wars

Mary Beth Swetnam Mathews

The University of Alabama Press
Tuscaloosa

The University of Alabama Press
Tuscaloosa, Alabama 35487-0380
uapress.ua.edu

Hardcover edition published 2017.
Paperback edition published 2018.
eBook edition published 2017.

Typeface: Minion

Cover image: Members of the congregation of Bush Chapel African
Methodist Episcopal Zion Church on the chapel steps on Easter Sunday,
Barrow County, Georgia, 1920; courtesy of the Georgia Archives, Vanishing
Georgia Collection, brw115
Cover design: David Nees

Paperback ISBN: 978-0-8173-5918-8

A previous edition of this book has been catalogued by the Library of Congress as
follows:

Library of Congress Cataloging-in-Publication Data

Names: Mathews, Mary Beth Swetnam, author.
Title: Doctrine and race : African American evangelicals and
fundamentalism between the wars / Mary Beth Swetnam Mathews.
Description: Tuscaloosa : University of Alabama Press, [2017] | Series:
Religion and American culture | Includes bibliographical references and index.
Identifiers: LCCN 2016023986| ISBN 9780817319380 (cloth : alk.
paper) | ISBN 9780817390723 (e book)
Subjects: LCSH: African Americans—Religion—History—20th
century. | Baptists—History—20th century. | Methodist Church—History—
20th century. | Evangelicalism—United States—History—20th century. |
Fundamentalism—United States—History—20th century. | United States—
Church history—20th century.
Classification: LCC BR563.N4 M294 2017 | DDC
286.089/9607309042—dc23
LC record available at https://lccn.loc.gov/2016023986

To Jim and Lydia

Contents

Acknowledgments   ix

Introduction   1

1. "Too Frequently They Are Led Astray": White Fundamentalists and Race   11

2. "What Is the Matter with White Baptists?": African Americans' Initial Encounters with Fundamentalism   41

3. "We Need No New Doctrine for This New Day": African Americans Adapt Fundamentalism   68

4. "Only the Gilded Staircase to Destruction": African American Protestants Confront the Social Challenges of Modernity   98

5. "And This Is Where the White Man's Christianity Breaks Down": Race Relations and Ecclesiology in the Era of Lynchings and Jim Crow   126

Conclusion   153

Notes   159

Bibliography   187

Index   195

Acknowledgments

While my name appears as the author of this book, I am indebted to numerous people whose support was crucial to the completion of this project. I thank them here, collectively and singularly, and hope that I have managed to mention all of them.

Fellow travelers in the field of fundamentalism studies have provided me with insightful observations, debated me when they thought I was wrong, and celebrated when I brought new ideas to the conversation. Matthew Avery Sutton, in particular, read multiple drafts and challenged me to refine my argument. Kathryn Lofton assembled a veritable who's who of the field and organized a 2012 colloquium at Yale. There I had the wonderful experience of hashing out ideas in person with Katie Lofton, Matt Sutton, Darren Dochuk, Brendan Pietsch, Mike Hamilton, Tim Gloege, David Harrington Watt, Seth Dowland, and Dan Vaca. Every scholar should have the benefit of such talented minds.

Beyond the smaller circle of fundamentalism historians, Paul Harvey read chapters and offered excellent suggestions in terms of organization and content. Edward J. Blum cheered on my insistence that the historiography of American Protestant fundamentalism has all but ignored the question of race, and his enthusiasm lifted me when I thought I was not up to the task. Randall Maurice Jelks read portions and offered useful advice on how to link the work I was doing to studies of the next two decades of civil rights activism. Doug Thompson gave me important feedback on the middle chapters. And the anonymous reviewers for the University of Alabama Press greatly improved the manuscript with their comments.

Without the assistance of numerous librarians, I would never have written this book. Carla Bailey, the maven of all Interlibrary Loan librarians, managed to find and bring to campus multiple primary and secondary sources. The staff at the Howard Divinity School Library graciously endured my overuse of their microfilm readers and located periodicals I did not know were in their collections. Bill Sumners, director of the Southern Baptist Historical Library and Archives, and archivist Taffey Hall guided me to materials that were crucial for my research.

Closer to home, Mike Utzinger and the members of the Southeastern Colloquium for American Religious Studies kindly allowed me to present an early draft of the first chapter. Two colleagues here at the University of Mary Washington—Krystyn Moon and Susan Fernsebner—took time out from their busy schedules to read drafts and provide feedback. The university itself provided me with a Jepson Fellowship, multiple research travel grants, and a sabbatical semester, all of which meant the difference between an unfinished, languishing manuscript and a completed book.

Finally, but most importantly, I thank my husband, Jim, and daughter, Lydia, both of whom were supportive of the project, even if it meant long periods away from home and countless hours writing in the attic "tree house." I dedicate this book to them.

DOCTRINE AND RACE

Introduction

In 2008, as the United States elected Barack Obama to the presidency, the voters of California also approved Proposition 8, a ballot initiative that defined marriage as the union of one man and one woman. National media outlets expressed surprise that African Americans in California would support what appeared to be two diametrically opposed positions: the elevation of the Democratic nominee—a black man—to the presidency and the limitation of the rights of a minority group, a position that also enjoyed the support of conservatives in California and nationwide. How could a minority group, especially one that itself had benefited from civil rights legislation and tended to side in recent elections with proponents of liberal causes, vote to limit the options of another minority, the pundits asked.[1] Inherent in their confusion was an assumption that black voters would support all causes deemed as civil rights issues, including gay marriage.

But the black Californian voters who helped boost Obama into the White House and who reversed a previous statute on marriage in their state were not necessarily exhibiting a new electoral trend, nor were their ballots contradictory. Instead, they were embracing twin ideals of African American life—racial identification and overwhelmingly Protestant church allegiance—to reshape the world around them. By supporting the son of a Kenyan immigrant and the legal language to deny gay marriage, they continued a tradition that dates back at least to the start of the twentieth century. This book is an attempt to explain the interaction of black theology and black culture through the eyes of black Baptists and Methodists in the years between 1915 and the start of World War II. In order to confine the work to a single volume, I have chosen to use the lens of fundamentalism, an emerging religious movement started and run by white Protestants. The use of fundamentalism, both white fundamentalist outreach to black congregations and black ministers' understanding and appropriation of it, casts new light on the field of African American religious history, as well as the topic of fundamentalism itself.

African Americans created their own traditionalist conservative evangelicalism. It drew heavily from what they perceived as traditional Protestant doctrines but could also include more progressive notions as well. They engaged in this discussion because fundamentalism had posed a question that demanded a response from Protestants in the United States: are you with us or against us?[2] Fundamentalists viewed the Christian world as bifurcated into right and wrong, orthodoxy and heresy, with no middle ground. African Americans heard this and responded in their own way— they refused to side entirely with a single group. African Americans would not join a movement that employed new methods of understanding eschatology and that lacked social justice, nor would they cast their lot with those Protestants who appeared to reject the very source text of Christianity and the crucial notion that it was divinely inspired. With one they would be safe in inspiration but not in life; with the other they could gain the world but lose their soul.

Present in both fundamentalist writings and African American responses was the issue of race, but not always in direct and central ways. Race mattered to fundamentalists, but it was not their primary focus. Early fundamentalist gatherings were of white Protestants, and they viewed themselves as contending for the fate of the Christian church in an embattled world. African Americans were simply not members of their circle. In large part, this fundamentalist segregation stemmed from the segregation of Christian churches nationwide as well as a general indifference to the plight of American Americans by white Americans, but when confronted with African Americans, white fundamentalists relied on racial interpretations that marginalized them. White fundamentalists like John Roach Straton and A. C. Dixon constructed their racial notions on the twin pillars of black inferiority and white paternalism, pillars that were common beliefs among whites in general. Present in their sermons and letters are references to their beloved Negro mammies, as well as their abiding belief that African Americans were an impressionable race of people. This impressionability meant that blacks were easily led, either astray by the disreputable elements of society or to virtue by the uplifting power of white Protestant thought. That Protestantism, these men argued, had to be a conservative one. These white fundamentalists who had moved north in their own version of the Great Migration sought to position themselves as authorities on race relations in the urban North. So the general self-declared role of white fundamentalists on race relations was that of spokespeople for blacks, not necessarily as evangelists seeking to bring African Americans into the fundamentalist fold. Perhaps as a consequence of fundamentalists' apathy toward race relations in general, historians of the movement have not engaged fully with how fundamentalists understood race and race relations, nor whether or how they sought interaction with African Americans.[3] On the other side of the racial divide, the extent to which African Americans interacted with white fundamentalists, who had no specific denomination, and with fundamentalist theories in general has also received scant attention. Instead, historians have done yeoman's work in charting the myriad ways in which African Americans interacted with white Protestants on a denominational, general level.[4] *Doctrine and Race* attempts to address at least one of these deficiencies, by analyzing how African Americans understood and appropriated fundamentalism for themselves. The book also begins to examine white fundamentalism's views of African Americans, both racially and spiritually.

The topic of fundamentalism itself has become more contested in recent years. Delineating the tenets and membership of the fundamentalist movement is increasingly difficult, and some scholars now argue that the very term fundamentalism has no real meaning. As recent scholarship has shown, the fundamentalist movement consisted of several competing factions, and the divisions they had were over doctrinal and organizational matters. The notion that fundamentalists were militantly anti-modern is useful, but only to a certain degree. In the first few decades of the twentieth century, many evangelicals, indeed many Christians of all types, saw trouble all around them—from wars to saloons to fashions to immigration. Those troubles mattered to the traditionalist evangelicals and the progressives alike, as well as to those somewhere in between. While the term fundamentalism may someday become outdated, *Doctrine and Race* assumes it still has usefulness and can be defined as the militantly anti-modern evangelical movement that championed notions of biblical inerrancy, the deity and Virgin Birth of Christ, an insistence on holy living, as well as an emphasis on the literal return of Jesus. This final characteristic could include apocalyptic tendencies, but it could also be an emphasis on the Gospels' inerrant message that Christ would return.[5] The term fundamentalist differs from the term evangelical in that the former is a subset of the latter, with evangelicals in general holding to notions of the need for a personal conversion experience by the individual, a reliance on the Bible as a guide for both faith and daily living, and a divine requirement to spread the gospel far and wide. Fundamentalists held evangelical notions and battled mightily for them in a world they saw as turned against God and the saving power of evangelical Christianity.

While white fundamentalists largely ignored African Americans, African American pastors and laypeople were acutely aware of fundamentalism. Their denominational newspapers carried extensive coverage of the fundamentalist/modernist controversy in the early 1920s, and reprints of columns and articles by fundamentalist writers continued to appear into the 1930s. In many of these discussions, black Protestants, especially black Baptists, but to some extent African Methodist Episcopal (AME) and African Methodist Episcopal Zion (AMEZ) leaders, voiced support for the fundamentalist positions. They used portions of its doctrinal emphases and discourses to delineate their own interpretation of evangelical Christianity. Like the white fundamentalists, African American Baptists and Methodists were concerned primarily with preserving the "old time religion" and spreading the gospel message in what they saw as a fallen world. Like the white fundamentalists, African Americans writers applied racial labels to "deviant" religion, accusing white modernists of being infidels and apostates. For these writers, the notion of modernists even beginning to downplay a traditional evangelical doctrine such as the divine authorship of the Bible was patently ridiculous. More than once, African American commentators observed that white denominations, not black ones, were having wrenching debates over doctrine. Clearly, they argued, white people had left behind the foundations of Christianity, but African Americans had not. The distancing these writers employed helps revive historian Timothy L. Smith's contention that evangelicalism in America most closely resembles a kaleidoscope, with different tenets and different actors merging together at certain times, then finding themselves far apart at others.[6] In this case, black religious writers positioned themselves as the guardians of orthodoxy and frequently, but not always, portrayed white modernists as the heretics. It also calls into question the fundamentalists', and indeed subsequent historians', assumption that Christians had to choose one side or another during this theological debate. Adding further depth to the situation, black Baptist and Methodist writers, unlike white fundamentalists, also rotated the lens of biblical message to include an emphasis on social justice. This emphasis was not, however, innovative for these interwar black evangelicals. As Christopher Z. Hobson has documented, the prophetic tradition runs deep and wide in black religious history.[7] For the subjects of this study, combining biblical inerrancy, for example, with social justice was a traditional way to interpret the Bible, an adherence to the faith of the generations before them.

The complicated status of African Americans in US society, however, meant that black intellectuals, like W. E. B. DuBois and Kelly Miller, called

on them to embrace scientific progress and leave behind the "old-time religion" that many African American denominational leaders and white fundamentalists were unwilling to abandon, although historian Edward Blum's
work questions how much DuBois would have rejected religion.[8] Historian
Barbara Dianne Savage has written insightfully about how African Americans in the early to mid-twentieth century debated the efficacy of black
religious institutions in the battle for political rights, while Moses Nathaniel
Moore has written about black liberals and their use of liberal Protestant
theology to further the agenda of racial equality.[9] My work confirms Savage's argument that the debate existed long before the civil rights movement and complicates it by demonstrating that these Baptist and Methodist
ministers were also determining which type of religion would best advance
racial progress and concluding that it was conservative evangelical religion.
In that respect, I offer another dimension to Moore's liberals—those "conservatives" who wanted to hold onto the traditional evangelical religion
while also elevating the status of all African Americans. My work also com-
plements that of scholars Dennis Dickerson, who describes the efforts of
men like Howard Thurman, and Randall Maurice Jelks, who has charted
the life of Benjamin F. Mays. Both Dickerson and Jelks have aptly demonstrated the connection between black intellectuals of faith in the 1930s and
1940s and the early leaders of the civil rights movement.[10] I contend that
this interconnection had earlier roots, roots that stretch all the way to the
interwar years, when African American evangelicals were examining a variety of methods to advance civil rights and improve their brethren's lot
in life. Their decisions to employ progressive and traditionalist notions of
religion were carefully considered and allowed them to remain true to their
faith while advancing social justice. Intellectualism, faith, and traditions
wove themselves together in these clergy's lives and influenced several generations of leaders after them.

To complicate the matter further, in this book I argue that fundamentalism itself was a racialized term. The men who coined the term were white,
and in their worldview, and indeed in the worldview of most white Americans of the era, Christianity was defined by the goals and aspirations of
white, middle-class, educated Protestants. For fundamentalists, Christianity represented the highest achievement of white civilization, and their
understanding of the purest form of Christianity—conservative evangelical
Protestantism—was a reflection of that viewpoint. Because they occupied a
place of relative privilege in American society, they could afford to assume
that their theological positions were the norm, rather than the exception,
and the highest ideal, rather than an interpretation. Indeed, virtually all
white Protestants, whether they supported fundamentalism, opposed it, or

ignored it, assumed that white Protestant thought was normative and superior, so in that respect, fundamentalists were no different than non-fundamentalist whites. But it was the fundamentalists' challenge to define Christianity in stark terms that triggered a response among black evangelical clergy, a response this book examines. In some complicated ways, African Americans often bought into this notion of white normative religion, although they also sought to replace it with their own ecclesiology.

But even if they had self-identified as fundamentalists (and not all people whom later scholars call fundamentalists would have agreed with the label), African Americans would have been excluded from the definition of fundamentalism and full fellowship with the fundamentalists. The movement's leaders had so racially coded fundamentalism as the purest form of Christianity that their racial inclinations could not allow African Americans the ability to confess it for themselves. Indeed, white fundamentalists frequently worried that modernism and liberal theology were making inroads among African American denominations. That concern was seldom if ever accompanied by an acknowledgement of theological orthodoxy on the part of African Americans. Black Protestants, in the eyes of white fundamentalists, could not be trusted to stay the biblical course and were seen as theologically gullible and weak. And so we return to the racial presuppositions of fundamentalism's white migrants, like Straton, Massee, and Riley, as well as the racial presuppositions of most white Americans. Religious life in America was segregated and racially coded. Moreover, our understanding of the distribution of the formative books—*The Fundamentals*—needs an asterisk. While the current narrative holds that oil baron Lyman Stewart financed their distribution to all American ministers and missionaries, black Baptists and Methodists appear not to have received them. The adjective "white" should precede "American" in our telling of the *Fundamentals* creation story.[11]

For their part, African American Baptists and Methodists did not explicitly embrace or reject fundamentalism, in part because they were actively forming their own interpretation of evangelicalism and in part because they were also wary of the movement, especially as intellectuals, both black and white, disparaged it. With "race leaders" like DuBois and Carter Woodson making the argument that African American religious institutions were obstacles to black progress, as Savage chronicles, these ministers needed to make a careful argument in favor of what was fast becoming known as "old-fashioned."[12] To change and improve their society, these actors needed to look beyond the past; they needed to embrace change. Yet change was anathema to parts of their doctrine and belief. And so the black encounter with fundamentalism was, like so many other facets of their experience, a complicated one. They were caught between the push/pull forces of religion and racial equality.[13]

The study of African Americans' interaction with fundamentalism and evangelicalism demands new nomenclature for the actors involved. The terms "liberal" and "conservative" are too binary to be of assistance in understanding the myriad positions black denominational writers took on subjects ranging from biblical inerrancy to Prohibition to questions of ecclesiology. Both the "liberal" and the "conservative" ends of the spectrum were represented, but there were countless points in between these two extremes. Because the term "conservative," when applied to evangelicals, carries the presumption that the group opposes changes to the social and political status quo, it does not fit the subjects of this book, who desperately sought racial equality in all facets of life. Conversely, "liberal" does not apply entirely either, as most of the people quoted here would not have self-identified as liberals, largely because they did not embrace what they understood as "liberal" religion. That term meant an abandonment of evangelical doctrine, a reading of the Bible as a human work produced in a specific context, and an endorsement of changes in courtship, interpersonal relationships, and gender roles. Their politics, too, were not necessarily liberal. Black Baptists and Methodists supported limits on dancing, drinking, and dressing. More often than not, they embraced a traditional stand on religion and a progressive stand on race relations. These two terms, "traditional" and "progressive," are more helpful in describing the hopes and aspirations of black Methodists and Baptists. Moreover, these terms were not used as widely during the period in question, which allows us to classify the actions on a scale of our own device, rather than being captive to notions of the time, notions that have carried a certain amount of baggage into the present day.

Historian Mary R. Sawyer has already written about the "'both/and'" nature of African American Protestantism. I concur with her general observations, but I take exception to her contention that Jim Crow black religion was "conservative/passive."[14] The Methodists and Baptists in this study spoke out about a wide variety of issues, including the segregated social order. Some African American Protestants were both theologically and socially traditional, with occasional forays into progressive social territory, and the lens of fundamentalism allows us to understand the ways in which they shifted from traditional to progressive stances, depending on the matter at hand. There was an ongoing debate about how to be a black Christian in a segregated and hateful world. The editors, ministers, and laypeople who wrote for denominational papers were interested in selecting a course for black Christians in the twentieth century, a course that necessarily avoided the perils of modernity in society.

The voices in the debate were not unanimous on which track to take. Some tended to sympathize slightly more with more liberal theologies, while many others landed on the side of what the fundamentalists would have defined as the true interpretation of evangelical Christianity. This debate itself demonstrates that African American Protestants were never theologically uniform and that they had their divisions, just like any other group. The social constructs of race did not define their theology except when it came to understanding how Christians should treat each other. For the ministers in this book, Jesus preached an integrationist message, not a discriminatory message. True Christianity did not include a Jim Crow heaven, they often observed. Their overwhelming concern was how to preach the gospel in a changing, challenging, falling, and fallen world.

Prevailing notions of race did more, however, to define their understanding of social and political issues, and, unlike what some present-day commentators might believe, African Americans in the early twentieth century were more socially traditional than progressive. Black people needed to hew to a careful reading of social behavior, including avoiding the perils of dancing, drinking, and promiscuity, not only because these behaviors imperiled their immortal souls, but because these behaviors reflected poorly on the race. Black commentators were constantly aware of and warning about the ways white racists would use black missteps to punish not just the transgressor but all black people. The here and now mattered just as much as, and sometimes even more than, the hereafter. In this respect, my work confirms and amplifies what historian Anthea Butler has shown, that uplift movements had both a biblical and a racial basis.[15]

The significance of *Doctrine and Race* is multifold. First, it demonstrates the racial coding of two different terms present in the religious discourse of the day. White fundamentalists made the term fundamentalism apply only to white people, while African American Protestants defined modernism as a white-only term. Both races were creating boundaries around their faith. Second, the book provides a window on how black Christians actively grappled with the various theological questions of the day in a way that showed their construction of an evangelicalism with both traditionalist and progressive elements. While most scholars today would avoid the term "the black church" as a singular construct, we tend to clump black religious belief together into singular units. By shining a light on the internal debates of black Methodists and Baptists, we can see the lively differences, as well as the unifying similarities. Complementing the work of historian Lerone

A. Martin, *Doctrine and Race* complicates our understanding of how much control black denominations had over their constituent members and black interpretations of Christianity overall.[16] Finally, the book explains that African American Protestants (in this case evangelicals but not Pentecostals) were socially conservative for reasons of both theology and self-preservation. They could be both traditional and progressive at the same time. If they could split the difference between opposing religious ideologies, so too could other contemporary groups.

For this research, I relied primarily on the publications of four African American denominations: the National Baptist Convention, Incorporated; the National Baptist Convention, Unincorporated; the African Methodist Episcopal (AME) Church; and the African Methodist Episcopal Zion (AMEZ) Church. These four denominations did not and do not comprise a majority of African American Protestants, but they do provide a manageable means to examine the workings of black religious institutions in the early twentieth century. Their differing polity—congregational for the Baptists and hierarchical for the Methodists—allows for a sufficient contrast in organizational styles, while the fact that they were already organized, rather than emerging during this period, ensures that they had worked out their organizational issues and were more focused on theology and culture. The denominational quarterlies and weekly papers afford the best opportunity to observe the debates and discussions going on in the communities. Editors often held long tenures, which hints at the esteem they were held in by readers in their respective communities. By no means could they be considered absolute spokesmen for their denominations, yet their longevity and their frequent concurrence with denominational leaders, whose speeches they often featured, lends further evidence to their representative nature. Three of the four editors of the AME Zion's *Star of Zion* during the interwar period left the position because they had been elevated to the office of bishop within the denomination, a certain sign of their orthodoxy in the eyes of their peers.[17] While Pentecostal churches would make a fine complement to the study, their relative newcomer status and their less structured polity made me decide to omit them from the work at hand. Even though *Doctrine and Race* omits Pentecostals, the contributors to black denominational publications were very much aware of the growing charismatic movement. They made infrequent mention of it directly, but they often stressed the need to hold to the "old time religion," a religious expression that they believed excluded both modernism's influence and that of the liminal religious expressions of Pentecostal and Holiness adherents. Black evangelical writers faced a new landscape, both in northern cities and in the South, but for the sake of the larger argument, I focus only on the black Methodists and Baptists. Where available, I made use of the papers and publications of white fundamentalist leaders.

Because the denominations studied here often faced financial hardships, their extant sources are difficult to locate. Anthea Butler's observation that "much of African American religious history is crumbling before our eyes" is truer with every passing day.[18] Perhaps this book can help spur more investment in archives for these and other denominations, as letters, journals, and other archival material would provide even more detail. The people who appear here deserve to have more of their stories told.

Doctrine and Race contains five chapters. The first examines the racial assumptions of the men who founded and promoted the fundamentalist movement. Their worldview meant that African Americans could only be recipients of mission activities, and passive recipients at that. In Chapter 2, I document the close watch black Baptists and Methodists kept on the fundamentalists in the 1910s and 1920s. Chapter 3 explores the ways in which and the degrees to which fundamentalist doctrines resonated with black Protestants. Chapter 4 delves into how black views on a variety of topics, from dancing to Prohibition, mirrored and only occasionally opposed those of white fundamentalists. In the final chapter, African American Protestants use damning hermeneutics to expose the racial implications of Christianity as practiced by white Christians. While white fundamentalists and African American evangelicals appear segregated by the chapter organization, their ideas and their conversations were never completely partitioned, and white and black voices appear in each chapter. The public domain of ideas and theologies could never keep the conversation as divided as Jim Crow proponents would have wanted to believe.

As of this writing, neither fundamentalists nor black Protestants have realized their aspirations. Fundamentalists still continue to predict and hope for the imminent return of Christ, while African Americans—Protestant and non-Protestant alike—await a society that will value them for the content of their character rather than the color of their skin. A century ago, both groups waited and hoped. They continue to wait today.

1

"Too Frequently They Are Led Astray"

White Fundamentalists and Race

"Cuff was a negro slave who lived in the South before the war," the 1929 article in William Bell Riley's *The Pilot*, told readers. "He was a joyful Christian and a faithful servant." But Cuff's master, greedy for money, sold him to "an infidel," who insisted that Cuff not pray. Cuff persisted, despite repeated whippings. The "infidel" master, suddenly taken ill and believing himself to be on his death bed, insisted that his wife not call the doctor but instead bring Cuff in from the fields. Cuff, naturally, came to the man's bedside and when asked to pray for him, responded, "'Yes, bress de Lord, Massa, I'se been prayin' for you all de night,' and at this he dropped on his knees, and like Jacob of old, wrestled in prayer." The master and mistress both converted, Cuff "embraced" the master, and "race differences and past cruelty were swept away by the love of God, and tears of joy were mingled."[1]

This anecdote illustrates the complicated racial views of many white fundamentalists in the early decades of the twentieth century. Cuff, as a "faithful servant" in more ways than one, embodies for the unnamed author the honorable yet childlike faith of slaves. Slavery and its attendant cruelties are compartmentalized in the past, even as a certain nostalgia pervades the brief piece. Cuff serves as a model slave, and a model evangelist, for the white editor and his readers—a man who rendered unto Caesar his labors and to his heavenly master his witness. Cuff's appearance in a 1929 fundamentalist paper provides a window into white fundamentalists' racial views. These leaders created a definition of fundamentalism that was white but relied heavily on African Americans in their storytelling, discussions, and performances to legitimate and underscore the "whiteness" of the fundamentalist movement.

The formal movement of fundamentalism was primarily a white phenomenon. Defined and debated by white men, it grew during a time of racial segregation and white hegemony. As such, it should come as no surprise that, in the words of Joel Carpenter, "fundamentalism, like other historical evangelical movements, has tended to attract Anglo-Americans and Northern European immigrants of Protestant background."[2] While Carpenter declined to elaborate on why this attraction was so strong for whites, an investigation into the words and deeds of the early fundamentalists reveals both reasons for the appeal as well as means by which these leaders sought to place themselves firmly in the white Protestant power structure of the early twentieth century.

Why these men felt a need to argue their case for a return to the "old-time religion" has received much attention from scholars. The changing theological climate, brought about by new methods of biblical criticism and a perceived conflict with Darwinian evolution, combined with large internal migrations by both black and white southerners, as well as an influx of millions of foreign immigrants, led many white Protestants to believe that the world they had grown up with was fast fading. America's entry into World War I and the subsequent riots and labor disputes following the armistice only provided additional proof that their worst fears were coming true.[3]

Pivotal eras often produce cultural changes. But while both the white men who were to lead the fundamentalist movement and whole families of African Americans moved northward, they did not abandon their notions of race. Nor did the North and its inhabitants embrace a view of race that could be construed as divergent. Instead, the migrants, both white and black, found that racism pervaded all sections of the nation.[4] Historian Edward J. Blum has convincingly chronicled the methods by which white northerners and white southerners explicitly embraced themes of white supremacy and marginalized African Americans in the late nineteenth century. Protestant leaders were no exception to this rule, and Dwight L. Moody "accepted race-based segregation at his revivals and thereby offered religious legitimacy to Jim Crow," to name but one example from Blum's research.[5]

For white ministers, including those who would become fundamentalists, the prevailing sentiment was one of segregation and racial differentiation. That prevailing sentiment, however, was by no means a monolithic front. Rather, various fundamentalists embraced similar themes but with different interpretations of the role of African Americans in public life, the religious beliefs of African Americans, and the proper interactions between the races. In general, fundamentalist leaders did not advocate that African Americans could be a particular mission field for them, and none proclaimed a possible alliance with their black Protestant counterparts. Instead, these white leaders tended to ignore race except when the use of racial paternalism benefited their narratives. In those instances, they relied on paternalism and a belief in black inferiority to argue for white agency as spokespeople and guardians of African Americans. They repeated these arguments in private and in public, in letters and in sermons, adding a fundamentalist layer of support for the continued subjugation and segregation of African Americans.

The prevailing mores of race prevented white fundamentalists from reaching out to African Americans for several reasons. First, white Americans who considered African Americans as intellectual and social equals were few and far between in the general US population, let alone in a group of men who wished to return the country to what they saw as traditional values. In other words, fundamentalists had no interest in challenging established racial norms in their quest to return America to those norms. Instead, they chose to reify and even sanctify the racial constructs of the day. In this way, the fundamentalists were not advocates of change; they were proponents of the status quo. Second, any overt outreach to African Americans was not in the strategic interest of early fundamentalists. Cross-racial movements were risky politically, both in secular and church politics, and the fundamentalists would be less likely to gain a national audience for the balance of their goals if they included outreach to minority populations among them. Third, most white Protestant leaders, whether liberal or conservative, were largely unaware of developments and events within the African American denominations. Indeed, the black Protestants of the South had walked out of white churches in the late nineteenth century, and white southerners had done little to invite them back.[6] Black denominations in the North were already well established. White Protestants, because they could not control these groups, had for the most part abandoned dialogue with them, substituting in lieu of dialogue monitoring and mission outreach. Despite the fact that fundamentalism had challenged all segments of Christianity to meet their orthodoxy or be labeled as hopelessly erroneous, white fundamentalists did not realize that African Americans had heard their challenge and were in the process of debating the matter in response. Finally, fundamentalism itself had a built-in mechanism that limited social outreach—the attention to conversion rather than amelioration of social ills meant that, once fundamentalists saw a group as being squarely in the "saved" column, they were less likely to work to assist that group in any social and political challenges they faced. In short, in their expectations of Christ's imminent return, they did little to improve the social problems of their day, including those of racial segregation and discrimination.

White fundamentalists frequently commented in letters, journals, sermons, and articles about the racial differences between whites and blacks, and they sought to preserve and reinforce those differences and the attendant segregation of the races. When they spoke publicly, these fundamentalists situated themselves as experts on the construction of divinely sanctioned racial boundaries in American society. One such example was J. C. (Jasper Cortensus) Massee, a northern Baptist who was born in Georgia but eventually pastored churches in the Northeast.[7] While his biographer, C. Allyn Russell, saw in Massee a tendency toward individualism, in race relations, he displayed no such trait. In a sermon entitled "How Did the Negro Get His Skin?" Massee argued that the only answer to the difference in color among humans was "that God made them so." The sermon survives only in outline format, but despite its brevity, it suggests conformity with racial ideals of the time, with an occasional turn of phrase that, while hinting at new ideas, served only to return the outline to the straight and narrow. The line "God made them so" occurred before another notation in which Massee appeared to argue for racial distinction—"we should not let a previous condition of servitude prejudice . . . or provoke to discontent"—but then added "let us recognize that God has set this difference . . . and strive to preserve the purity of the race to which we belong . . . and make it worthy of God."[8] Massee clearly wanted whites and blacks to maintain their races as separate and in this way continue the racial division God had created. Here was a minister in a prominent northern city giving his benediction to segregation and discrimination.

Like Massee, Amzi Clarence (A. C.) Dixon gave religious favor to segregationist views, which should come as no surprise considering Dixon's background (he was born in the South before the Civil War) and his family ties (his younger brother was Thomas Dixon, author of *The Clansman*, the book that inspired the famous movie *The Birth of a Nation*).[9] Indeed, Texas fundamentalist J. Frank Norris praised Dixon, saying that he had "been through many battles, being a member of the original Ku Klux Klan and a brother of Thomas Dixon, Jr., who wrote the '*Clansman*.'"[10] In an undated manuscript, Dixon outlined what appears to be a sermon entitled, "Our Brother in Black." Dixon noted that "our brother in black [as] a man" could go one of two different directions, "grace of God can make a good man. Sin makes a bad man out of him." Dixon then observed that "more of them [African Americans] want to be preachers," adding "older men [in] particular." He commented that African Americans are "emotional" in their "sermons," and "like it warm." After dispensing with the religious propensities of African Americans, Dixon added that blacks have good imaginations, citing the Brer Rabbit stories as evidence of how black southerners create tales from animals, "all but cats. Don't like them." Blacks were also "humorous without intending it," and given to "good natural humor." He even mentioned the "eloquent" preachers, with John Jasper as his particular example.[11] Jasper, a former slave from Virginia, was most famous for his sermon, "The Sun Do Move," a literal interpretation of the biblical account of Joshua 10:12–14, in which God stopped the sun so that Joshua could defeat his enemies. The text of Jasper's sermon was made famous by William Hatcher, who published it in 1908.[12] The sermon would remain a contentious point for African American preachers in the 1920s and 1930s, many of whom were both proud of the ex-slave's accomplishments and repulsed by his lack of education. That lack of education, the unintended humor of blacks, and black emotionalism were ways for Dixon to reduce African Americans to religious novices, people who needed white guidance because they lacked the ability to discern the gospel for themselves. Dixon's racism meant that there could never be a full-fledged dialogue between whites and blacks on religion or any other issue.

For Dixon, the concern with African Americans was more of a political issue than a theological one. Indeed, in this sermon and in his extant papers, he discussed African American religious beliefs only in passing. Far more important was Dixon's concern about the black vote. In an article he wrote for *The Living Word*, Dixon argued that "ignorance, whether black or white, has no right to the ballot."[13] He echoed this sentiment in his "Our Brother in Black" sermon, posing the issue in the form of a question: "As citizens, do they have their rights?" He answered it with, "All that the same class of whites have [*sic*]. Ignorance should not be allowed to vote."[14] While Dixon's opposition appears to be class-based or education-based, his argument was disingenuous. Most affluent white men of his time would have supported poor white male rights long before they would embrace equal civil rights for African Americans. His use of education may have been an attempt at making his position appear more moderate for his audience. Like many other members of his family and his acquaintances, Dixon stood firmly against black enfranchisement.

In another undated manuscript, Dixon addressed the "Future of the Educated Negro." Setting the tone early, Dixon proclaimed that "the educated negro, like the educated white man, needs to know that manual labor is honorable, and however classical and thorough his education, it does not raise him above the dignity of toiling with his hands for daily bread." Dixon told the story of a black man, imprisoned and facing execution for "a capital offence," who had told Dixon's father, "'I am going to be hanged tomorrow because I was educated. I got above work.'"[15] Dixon's conclusion was that education had spoiled the man, who had turned to crime rather than "return to the drudgery of his former life." According to Dixon, "he should have been taught that education was not intended to raise him above the necessity of manual labor, but rather to dignify such toil by enabling him to do his work better." Dixon's words are reminiscent of John Calvin's opinion that the reprobate belonged in church because it taught them why they were worthy of damnation. For Dixon, African Americans could never escape the content of their character, to borrow a phrase from Martin Luther King Jr., because they were doomed by the color of their skin. Here was scientific racism, the use of data to prove racial differences and to justify discrimination, at its worst.

Dixon argued that African Americans needed to remember that they were, indeed, black and should be "willing to remain a negro, and give to posterity only negro children." While he tolerated African American claims that Adam was "a colored man" and other statements of racial pride by black orators, he drew the line at intermarriage. "For [an African American] to assert and practice the right to intermarry with the whites," Dixon argued, "is to doom his race to extinction." Citing Frederick Douglass, whom Dixon claimed had confessed to making "the mistake of his life in marrying a white woman," Dixon warned of "race antagonism" against blacks should intermarriage occur. According to his second wife and hagiographic biographer, Helen Cadbury Dixon, A. C. Dixon was troubled when President Theodore Roosevelt invited Booker T. Washington to the White House in 1901. She quoted her husband as saying that he doubted Roosevelt's "'political sagacity in so doing, and Booker Washington's wisdom in accepting the invitation. . . . The South looked upon it as an effort to force upon them social equality with the negro. Social equality means inter-marriage, which would portend the extinction of the Anglo-Saxon race, and its transmutation into a race of mulattos.'"[16] Like so many white Americans (and many black Americans), Dixon opposed intermarriage, stating, "'I do not want the negro, or the Mongolian, to marry my daughter nor my son to marry his daughter. 'They twain shall be one flesh'; and to my thinking, the one flesh includes one skin.'"[17]

In making his case for racial separation, Dixon drew on a classic dichotomy of southern whites: the distinction between political rights and "social privileges." For such proponents, the ballot was a political right, but equal and integrated accommodations were a "social" concern, one that the US Constitution had no control over. In language that would be echoed by Texas fundamentalist J. Frank Norris and Arkansas Baptist Ben Bogard in 1928, Dixon told his congregation that "a man may demand his political rights, but, if he comes demanding social rights, he will find that what he claims as a right, others regards as a privilege, and if he persists in his demand even privileges are apt to be withdrawn."[18]

The threat of intermarriage and racial equality played a role in the 1928 presidential campaign, as J. Frank Norris and Ben Bogard used New York governor Al Smith's record while he was mayor of New York City to incite southern Democrats to break party lines and vote for the Republican, Herbert Hoover. While some historians have noted the concern that many southern Democrats and Protestants nationally had about Smith's Roman Catholicism, the race question among Protestant ministers has not yet received much scholarly attention.[19]

In the case of Norris and Bogard, the role of white Protestant ministers moved from writing letters to actively campaigning against Smith's candidacy because, to them, it threatened the social order in the American South. Norris voiced his concern in a telegram to Democratic Party chairman, Senator Pat Harrison. Norris was outraged that Al Smith, while mayor of New York City, had failed to dismiss Ferdinand Morton, a black man appointed to the position of chief of the Civil Service Commission by Smith's predecessor, Mayor Hyland. According to Norris, Smith was "the power that controls both Tammany Hall" and the current mayor, Mayor Walker. Additionally, Norris listed offenses such as "negro men teaching white girls and boys in public schools of New York," that Al Smith "blocked the legislation preventing inter marriages of negroes and whites," that Al Smith supported "fines" for "white owners of restaurants or cafes for refusing to serve negro customers with white patrons," that Al Smith and Tammany Hall supported sending "negro bishops and ministers through south lining up negros for Al Smith," and that the "negro boss of Texas negros Gooseneck Bill McDonald" was supporting Al Smith and working to get blacks to vote for Smith.[20] In subsequent exchanges with Harrison, Norris repeated these charges and provided additional details to back his claims.[21]

In addition to the public debate with Harrison, Norris worked behind the scenes to bolster opposition to the New York Democrat on racial grounds. In a letter to Glenn L. Gill, of Whon, Texas, Norris solicited information on Smith, stating that "I have been told that gov. [sic] Smith of New York appointed a negro named Ferdinand Morton to a very high position in New York City and that you have at hand positive proof of this." Norris enclosed "a stamped envelope for reply," asking that Gill "give complete and accurate information as I plan to give the matter publicity and it would be embarrassing to be misled."[22] The files give no indication whether Mr. Gill provided the requested proof, but Norris's public demands met with the approval of at least one member of his church, who wrote that her family ties to Mississippi, the home state of Senator Harrison, demonstrated the party chairman's less than perfect record on race. She cited the race of the state's postmaster general, "a negro," and related a story of corruption. Her conclusion: "these and like circumstances exist in the state of Mississippi.

No wonder the majority [of African Americans] are for Al Smith and Pat Harrison."[23] Her words were mild compared to those of Miss Sarah B. Balfour, a self-described "very old Lady" from Nebraska. Miss Balfour alleged that blacks would be thrown out of office after the 1928 race as "whites will not be controlled by the Negro and if any one of them votes for Al Smith he should be thrown back into slavery." She reminded Norris that "no democrat none other than own good President Abe Lincoln" had "set them free" and that "they should be reminded of that fact before it is to [sic] late."[24]

In his opposition to Smith, Norris found common ground with his one-time adversary, Ben Bogard, a Landmark Baptist minister from Arkansas who had once described Norris and his fundamentalist allies as "funnymentalists."[25] Bogard, editor of the *Baptist and Commoner*, informed his readers in September 1928 that "negroes and whites ride on the same seats in trains and street cars, EVEN IN SLEEPING CARS," adding that "negro children go to school with white children and sit in the same classes and the white children are sometimes under negro teachers in New York." But that was not the worst of it, as Bogard relayed that Al Smith had not taken action even though "NEGROES AND WHITES MARRY EACH OTHER IN NEW YORK."[26]

In October, Bogard alerted his readers to misinformation about Hoover and set the record straight about Smith. The Democrats, he charged, were "declaring that Hoover favors negro equality. Of course they know this is false but they are using it for all it is worth." Instead, Bogard alleged, "negro equality is a social and not a political question and the bunch that has put Al Smith into office are [sic] negro equality people and Al Smith is himself a negro equality man." Bogard listed a set of charges against Smith, including:

> Al Smith meets on a level every Sunday his negro brethren in the church where he worships the Pope and Romish relics. Negroes and whites attend school together in the State of New York where he has been so long governor. He has never recommended the segregation of whites and negroes. When that infamous bill was introduced in Congress to force a state in which a negro rapist is caught and mobbed to pay the negro's family ten thousand dollars, thus putting a premium on rape, Governor Smith was appealed to use his influence to prevent the passage of the bill and he refused. If that bill had passed it would have meant that when a negro lays his black hands on your daughter and succeeds in outraging her and the negro is caught and mobbed, that we must pay out of the state treasury ten thousand dollars to the rapist's family.[27]

By connecting Al Smith's views on racial equality with the old southern concern over blacks' supposed hyper-sexuality and the need for protection of white southern women and their virtue, Bogard drew on a familiar theme for his readers and made it easier for them to contemplate bucking the party line and voting for a Republican.

But Bogard clearly did not trust this argument alone and augmented it with what he saw as photographic proof of the dangers of a Smith presidency. In the October 10th issue of the *Baptist and Commoner*, he included a "disgusting picture" over the headline, "WHAT WE SEE IN TAMMANY HALL: STARTLING, DISGUSTING FACTS, AL SMITH AND TAMMANY HALL NEGRO EQUALITY." The subtitle read, "Seeing is Believing. Here is the Buck Negro With His White Stenographer. This Is Only One of Many Such Cases of This Thing." The picture in question shows a black man, seated behind a desk. A white woman to his right appears to be taking dictation. Bogard identified the man as "F. Q. Morton, and his stenographer is Miss Florence Eckstein." This juxtaposition demonstrated that Al Smith supported racial equality, and Bogard would have none of it. "If you vote for him," Bogard railed, "you will be voting for negro equality. . . . It is enough to make the blood of any true southern white man boil with indignation. What are YOU going to do about it?" He then answered his own question: "I think I know what the great majority of southern white men will do. For one, I intend to vote for the Lily White Republican, Herbert Hoover."[28] Bogard had transported the southern white fear from the South and into the office buildings of New York City; the migration of blacks north meant that those migrants would forget their place and demand equality. Not content to demand workplace equality, they would then transgress the gendered lines of behavior and destroy the virtue of white women. In an article on the eve of the election, Bogard reminded his readers of Smith's views on race and their effect on women: "Southern social and racial ideals are menaced by Smith, who is an officer of Tammany which has many negro officials, and has now a high-salaried negro (with a white woman for stenographer), who passes on all white applicants for office. Smith was reared among negroes and believes in social equality. He approves of marriage of negroes and whites. He ran for office on a ticket with negroes. His Tammany puts negro teachers over white children. Smith knows nothing of the fine ideals of the South."[29] Bogard and Norris together were fighting to protect the honor of southern white women and the South in general. For them, Smith's candidacy meant a break from what they and many other fundamentalists believed: that African Americans occupied a certain place in the social world and that place must never alter. But while Norris and Bogard were virulent in their racial views, their fellow fundamentalists largely agreed with the broader notion that they advanced. White fundamentalists like Massee, Dixon, and others were no advocates of integration.

At the same time that men like Norris and Bogard were working to keep blacks separate, white fundamentalists extolled the value of Protestantism for the same African Americans they sought to marginalize. Underlying many of the fundamentalists' assumptions, and those of many white Americans, was the notion that Protestant Christianity had been a benefit to those who received it and that it went hand in hand with the general improvements whites brought to other races, even as they kept their social and physical distance. Writing in the Denver Bible Institute's monthly, *Grace and Truth*, L. J. Fowler outlined the role of the white missionary, regardless of place. "In the wisdom of God," Fowler wrote, "He has seen fit to use the Anglo-Saxon race in an outstanding way during the past few centuries in the great missionary advances."[30] For white fundamentalists, and white Protestants in general in the United States, Protestant Christianity was the chief weapon available to civilize the various races. Such a trusting belief in the positive power of Protestantism was not confined to conservative evangelicals or fundamentalists. Josiah Strong's *Our Country*, published in 1886, lauded the civilizing effects of "true spiritual Christianity."[31] Indeed, for many white Protestants in the United States, the benefits of converting various immigrants and minorities to Protestant Christianity were myriad and far-reaching. Black, Jew, Roman Catholic—all could improve themselves through religion, and all required it to be considered "American."

White Protestants had no trouble voicing their opinion about the salvific effects of their religion on African Americans, and they often did so in the pages of fundamentalist-friendly publications. According to Dr. A. M. Moore of Durham, North Carolina, the "Negro minister is often inefficient, but he is a loyal leader of an important group of our citizenship and should be helped by a white congregation."[32] W. D. Powell, DD, echoed these sentiments in the *Watchman-Examiner*, calling on his fellow Baptists to "place [blacks] on their feet and not on their backs. We want to help them to develop Christian manhood and womanhood, and not contribute to their delinquency."[33] The *Watchman-Examiner*, edited by Curtis Lee Laws, who would later coin the term "fundamentalist," ran a steady stream of such articles.[34] According to John W. Bradbury, Laws's successor as editor of the Northern Baptist publication, Laws was born shortly after the end of the Civil War in 1868 in Loudoun County, Virginia. He studied at Richmond College (now the University of Richmond) and Crozer Theological Seminary, before settling in New York City.[35] In editing the publication, Laws often filled his pages with articles about the South and race relations. They reveal an abiding belief that blacks were religiously willing but deficient in understanding and leadership, deficiencies that white southerners could address and remedy.

For example, in March 1917, Howard Wayne Smith voiced concerns in the *Watchman-Examiner* about the ongoing Great Migration and concluded that "neglected, these black brothers become a menace to the community in which they live; cultivated, they become an asset."[36] That cultivation meant proper religious guidance. The next month, A. T. Robertson praised the work of "Negro Baptists" who had persevered in their loyalty and religion despite the fact that the "South could not after the [Civil War] in its dire poverty care for the white churches and schools, let alone those of the negroes." Their loyalty, Robertson continued, meant that African Americans would not "play into the hands of Germany during this current crisis." Instead, blacks "will be ready to do their bit in the war" if necessary.[37] A 1919 advertisement by the American Baptist Home Missionary Society in the *Watchman-Examiner* reminded readers that its work "looks forward to the time . . . when the Christian morality and spirit and ideas inculcated in these schools shall permeate the colored people, and protect them against superstition and the multiform enticements of evil conduct and false teaching."[38] Frank Sullivan, writing in the paper about a 1922 visit to Olivet Church in Chicago, Illinois (the church of L. K. Williams, head of the National Baptist Convention, Incorporated), remarked that the churches in the area "are doing their best to make Christians and good citizens of their own people." The congregation "was an inspiring sight that morning—1,800 well dressed, well behaved, devout worshipers on time."[39] Common among these various pieces was the notion that whites could assist blacks in ridding themselves of the defects inherent in their character by virtue of their race. While it was an optimistic point of view, it was racist nonetheless and reduced African Americans to recipients of instruction rather than fellow travelers on the road to salvation.

Laws himself saw evangelization as the way to maintain the standards that he had come to associate with being American, and he both argued this view himself and gave voice to other writers' articles in support. In "American Blood in 1975," he warned that to "Christianize the people of many lands before they intermingle their blood is the surest way to safeguard a second, third, and every generation of ideal Americans." By converting all minorities to Christianity, evangelicals of his day could ensure "the enforcement of law and the perpetuity of American ideals."[40] Not only was Christianity a means to civilize African Americans, it was also a way of alleviating racial tensions. Writing about the Reverend Eugene E. Smith's address to the annual gathering of Northern Baptists, Homer DeWilton Brookins explained that Baptists needed to help spread the Gospel to blacks to "help to Christianize the rising tide of race consciousness on the part of the negro."[41] Without the influence of Protestant Christianity, Brookins and Laws predicted a dire situation ahead for white and black Americans.

With African Americans safely segregated from white society and with the supposed uplift of Protestant evangelization eradicating any danger posed by blacks, white fundamentalists, like their society at large, could turn to stereotypes to confirm their view that African Americans were intellectually and culturally deficient. The use of dialect served to further marginalize blacks as residents of the United States who could not speak proper English. The emphasis on the perceived musical propensity of African Americans allowed whites to compartmentalize any contributions blacks may have made or were making to American culture.

A leading proponent of using stereotypes to marginalize blacks was William Bell Riley, born in Indiana but raised in Kentucky and pastoring a church in Minneapolis. Riley organized the World Christian Fundamentalist Association meetings in the 1920s and included African Americans in the proceedings as comic relief and entertainment.[42] Riley used his platform as WCFA leader to advance racial stereotypes through the use of music and minstrelsy, as African American musicians performed for white fundamentalist gatherings lampooning evolution while also reinforcing white views of blacks' racial and linguistic inferiority. The *Toronto Mail and Empire*, covering the 1926 WCFA gathering, noted that the "The Cleveland Colored Quintette rendered religio-comic songs and choruses" for the attendees. One such song was entitled, "'The Devil's No Relation of Mine'" and included the lyrics:

> Oh I'm so glad I don't believe in evolution
> That my ancestors once lived in a tree
> The Bible tells me God is my Creator
> And that is plenty good enough for me.
> Oh glory hallelujah, my heart is filled with joy.
> I'd have you to know, both one and all
> That God is my Creator, and I'm a baboon-hater,
> And the monkey's no relation at all.[43]

The *Mail and Empire* went on to say that "these happy colored minstrels have been a popular feature for all the sessions of the Fundamentalist Convention." Referring to the Quintette, Riley "challenged the audience to find better entertainers in any show in the city. 'If you can tell me where I can see a better show, I'd like to go and see it.'"[44]

That appreciation for the Cleveland Colored Quintette continued into the 1930s. In his call to fundamentalists to attend the WCFA conference in Columbus, Ohio, in 1932, Riley wrote in May that the music would likely include the "'Cleveland Quintette,' composed of the best colored singers we've ever heard."[45] In June's issue of *The Christian Fundamentalist*, Riley reminded his readers that "one of the biggest features will be the world-famed *Cleveland Colored Quintette*. We have heard many singers in our time, but these five men we have never heard surpassed." He went on to praise not only "their wealth of tone and perfect harmony," but also "their repertoire, including as it does, the greatest negro spirituals, [and] the most marvelous renditions of the white man's great songs." He was also sure to get in a plug for the Quintette's "musical ridicule of such false philosophy as Darwinism in such numbers as 'The Monkey's No Relation of Mine.'"[46] In the issue following the meeting, Riley noted that "Saturday night was given over largely to the Cleveland Colored Quintette, and was concluded by a Consecration meeting led by Mr. Lacy, a quintette leader, with Mr. Jones of the quintette presiding."[47] Apparently, the meeting's participants were so moved by the music that they allowed themselves to be led by the black musicians.

But when Riley wrote an article for Curtis Lee Law's *Watchman-Examiner* about the very same event, he omitted all mention of the Cleveland Colored Quintette. Instead, he described the Saturday evening event as "a great consecration service" in which "160 young people volunteered for life service." "On Sunday night," he added, "about fifty more volunteered."[48] Whether Riley had included the Quintette in his submission to the *Watchman-Examiner* or not is impossible to know, but the text of the Northern Baptist paper omitted the mixing of the races, as well as the mention of a black man leading a white audience in praise and worship. The meeting's events even made the pages of *Time* magazine, which commented that during the meeting "the Cleveland Colored Quintet sings 'The Monkey's No Relation of Mine,'" but did not mention members of the ensemble leading the prayer services.[49] The moment must have been a powerful one for those attending, and the use of a black musical group, members of a "less educated" race, to ridicule the "educated" teaching of evolution was no accident. By employing the talents of the Cleveland Colored Quintette, Riley and his fellow fundamentalists were using minstrelsy and racial stereotypes to combat the advance of a scientific subject they saw as directly contradicting revealed scripture.

Riley was not the only conservative evangelical to embrace the group. The Quintette itself had interactions with other white evangelical leaders, including Paul Rader, former pastor of Moody Church, in Chicago in 1922, and a continuing affiliation with the Christian and Missionary Alliance, of which Rader was the president.[50] According to the members (Alexander E. Talbert, J. W. Parker, H. D. Hodges, Spurgeon R. Jones, and Floyd H. Lacy), the Christian and Missionary Alliance was responsible in many cases for their conversions, and it hosted their concerts on more than one occasion.[51] The benefits for conservative evangelicals of using a black singing group to attack Darwinism were too many to pass up. The audience got a chance to see the musical talents supposedly inherent in the race, and they were treated to the irony of hearing black men, often caricatured as apes, poking fun of Darwin's theory, which many fundamentalists alleged meant that humans were descended from apes.

Other fundamentalists employed black singers during revivals and church services. Harry A. Ironside, pastor of Moody's Memorial Church in Chicago, visited his friend W. B. Riley for a series of services in late October 1930. According an article in the *Pilot*, "Mr. A. E. Greenlaw, Negro baritone, was here to sing to us at each meeting." Mr. Greenlaw's "marvelous voice and his friendly attitude won our hearts."[52] Further south in Texas, John R. Rice wrote enthusiastically of Elbert T. Tindley, son of gospel hymn writer Charles A. Tindley, who would be singing at Rice's Dallas Bible School in May 1937. A caption under Tindley's picture read, "Nationally known negro soloist, sweet voiced, dramatic Spirit-filled. He will make you laugh and weep and revive your heart. He sung all over America with leading white evangelists. He will sing solos two days during the Bible School and will be one of the outstanding features such as you may never hear again."[53] Reporting during the meeting, Rice continued his effusive praise of Tindley. "Brother E. T. Tindley," he wrote, "has been the sensation of the Bible School." People attending the event "begged and begged for more!" Rice related the story of a woman who told him that she had arrived at the meeting "prejudiced against Brother Tindley whom she had never seen." Telling Rice that initially she had "said to herself, 'I don't care to hear these colored singers. They do not say their words plainly enough for me to understand them,'" she reversed her position once she heard the musician. "'Before he was half way through the first verse I was "squalling." I think I will not be a backslider any more after hearing him sing,'" she explained. Rice then claimed that he was not using Tindley "merely as entertainment," but asserted that "we want him back with us again whenever possible," suggesting that he employed the singer as a means to provoke conversions, though not necessarily that he viewed Tindley as an equal.[54] Indeed, when Rice advertised his Dallas Bible School session for later that year, he promised that Tindley would be there, a "SPIRIT-ANOINTED COLORED GOSPEL SOLOIST, WHO I BELIEVE SINGS WITH THE GREATEST BLESSING

OF ANY MAN, WHITE OR BLACK, I EVER HEARD."[55] Tindley's skill for Rice was music, a common theme in white fundamentalist views of blacks.[56]

While Rice may appear to have been granting some agency to African Americans, his accommodation was quite slim. For him, as for other white fundamentalists who enjoyed black music, the music itself was a reinforcement of their views on blacks in general, especially in their belief that black religion was emotional. Because it came from black traditions, the music they produced was, in the eyes of whites, emotionally provocative, which allowed whites to continue their stereotype that blacks were caught in a religious childhood. The use of African American musicians reinforced whites' racially coded ideas of black inferiority rather than provoking them to engage in a religious dialogue with the musicians and their pastors.

Northern Baptist Curtis Lee Laws also employed the stereotype of blacks as preternatural musicians. In an article entitled, "The Editor Afield: Morehouse College and Spelman Seminary," he told readers of *The Watchman-Examiner* of his trip to Georgia and his encounters with students at the above schools. At Morehouse, "the densely packed negro audience listened to the sermon [ironically by Brown University president W. H. P. Faunce, no friend of fundamentalism] with rapt attention and proved its capacity to appreciate fully a sermon that would have proved acceptable in the college chapel at Harvard, or Yale, or Columbia." But Laws could not leave his account of Morehouse without including a mention of a concert he heard there, lapsing into the familiar white descriptions of blacks' supposed innate musical aptitude. "These negro students," he explained, "are at home alike with plantation melodies, Gospel hymns, and the finest classical music." He added, "we rejoice that as these young men become trained musicians they do not forget the weird fantastic melodies which are the peculiar contribution of the negro race to the world of music."[57] Within his praise for the Morehouse musicians was an assumption that the men were progressing on a musical trajectory that aimed for Euro-American hymnody, not the musical traditions of their ancestors. Uplifting the race could happen musically, as well as theologically and socially. But uplift was not really the point of listening to black men sing. Rather, for white fundamentalists, the use of African Americans as entertainers once again allowed them to marginalize and subjugate blacks. Laws, Riley, and others used black singers largely as performance material rather than treat them as evangelical equals. In these very public forums, black musicians and black music were performative art that white fundamentalists employed to other African Americans and sanctify this marginalization.

In addition to black music, white fundamentalists often commented on black conversation, and they used dialect to lampoon both African Americans and the proponents of modernism. In the February 1928 issue of the *Moody Bible Institute Monthly*, readers could see an advertisement for Dr. French E. Oliver's "Famous Negro Sermons!" It promised that the sermons in question were in "Charming Negro Dialect" and an "Actual Reproduction of the Style and Material Used by the Old Time Negro Preachers of the South." The volume was "Bound in Red Leatherette" and promised to be a "Marvelous Christmas Gift for Pastors, Laymen, Lecturers, Platform Men and Women." The publishers included a few helpful testimonials from various experts, including the praise of one Alexander A. Murray of New Zealand who said it was "'a masterpiece in Negro dialect, subtle humor, and sound theology.'"[58] One wonders about the expertise of New Zealand ministers in assessing the authenticity of African American speech patterns. The book was pocket-sized, and contained such dialectic misconceptions of biblical texts as "'De Lawd Am No Respecka'able Pussun,'" "'Whip Yo' Chilluns,'" "'Frow Down Jezybell,'" and "'Bo'ned in Zion!'"[59] A year later, the *Moody Monthly* ran an advertisement for "Seven Unanswerable Books" by B. H. Shadduck, PhD, which included the title, "Rastus Agustus Explains Evolution." Rastus, from the illustration on the cover, is a crouching African American man, clad in overalls and clutching a book in his left hand while he extends his right hand upward in a form of a salute. The light cast upon him, however, shows an ape-like shadow behind Rastus. Historian Ronald Numbers has called the Rastus books "some of the most tasteless tracts of the time," and notes that Shadduck was a minister in the Pilgrim Holiness Church, not a fundamentalist organization but with ties to the Holiness movement.[60] Much like the Cleveland Colored Quintette, Rastus Agustus was a projection of whites and their inclination to tie African Americans to lower primates. For the Cleveland Colored Quintette, the connection was musical, but for Rastus Agustus, it was visual.[61]

The use of dialect to caricature African Americans was common among white fundamentalist writers. They employed it in a folksy manner as a way of introducing readers or listeners to a common truth, one so obvious that even those of limited intelligence could understand it. Returning to the theme of evolution, the *Christian Fundamentalist* published what appears to be either a poem or a song, signed by "Anon.," in which the writer pondered how anyone could believe Darwin over the Bible:

Let dem what thinks dey's kin to apes/ Be classed among dat race
De Lo'd made all de cullud folks,/ An neahly all de white
But dem what thinks dey cum fum apes/ It may be dey am right.
Dey oughter know dey own kinfolks/ If anybody do
An' so we'll let dem think deir way/ I spec' dat's best, don't you?[62]

Implicit in the prose is the white assumption that if even African Americans can see the folly of evolution, no one should believe in it. And while the text appears to extol the common sense of blacks, it also ridicules their reasoning ability and leaves them asking for approval.

Dialect as a measure of black folksiness and dependence on whites was common in white fundamentalist prose. For William Bell Riley, an allusion to Uncle Remus, a fictional character created by white southerner Joel Chandler Harris, was particularly useful in showing the flaws in the theological arguments of the modernists. "To quote from the language of Uncle Remus," Riley wrote, "'Truth ain't never been hurt yit by folks not believing in it.'"[63] A. T. Robertson, correspondent from the South to the *Watchman-Examiner*, reported that the drought in the South in 1930 was bad but "the old negro's philosophy that 'it mount be wuss' [it might be worse] has a core of solace in it."[64] Curtis Laws, warning new preachers not to pad their vocabularies in an effort to sound erudite, quoted the reaction of "an old negro" to a sermon the famous (and white) Virginia Baptist John A. Broadus had preached: "'He ain't no great preacher, fo' I could understand every word he said.'"[65] In this case, the "old negro" had conflated complicated speech with good preaching and in "contemptuously" reacting to Broadus had revealed his own ignorance. Such jibes at African American speech could serve as humor, as a small item in the *Watchman-Examiner's* "Just for Fun" column illustrated, using the words of Jesus to the disciples after they saw him walking on water:

> A professor attempted to teach a class of little negroes to memorize, "Be not afraid, it is I."
> Professor (following day) "Sam, what was the quotation I taught you yesterday?"
> Sam (after thinking): "Don't get skeered, 'taint nobody but me—"[66]

Queried about the new radio program, "Amos and Andy," Laws mused that "these entertainers are white men, posing as negroes who spread abroad through the radio delightful dialogues always humorous and genial and generally wholesome." He found no issue with their use of dialect, or even the secular nature of the program in question, but instead admitted that "we occasionally feel ashamed that when we get pleasure from their frolicsomeness that we do not use the tooth paste which stands behind their radio efforts."[67]

Other fundamentalists made use of dialect in their conversations with friends and coworkers. J. Frank Norris, in a letter to the Reverend J. H. Bradley of Arlington, Texas, explained a difficult political choice this way: "Your inquiry with reference to the District Attorney's office to hand. My position in the present race is very much like the negro preacher's text. He said to his congregation: 'Bredren, my text tonight is two roads. One of dem leads to hellfire and damnation, and the other leads to torment. As for this nigger he is gwin to take to de woods.'"[68] In a letter to his assistant, Jane Hartwell, Norris also boasted of pranks he had played on African Americans working in his church. Describing himself as "feeling the holiday spirits still on," Norris snuck "upstairs over the choir and began to drop some papers through." He then "would watch the negroes as they looked up and hear them as they argued—one saying that nothing fell and the other that it did." Having unsettled the men, Norris then "dropped a couple of song books through the opening, that is, where the curtain goes up." He described the result as "too funny to describe to see those three negroes jump straight up, each one jerk off his hat and hold it in his hand. They argued as to whether they would stay there or not, one declaring there were spooks and 'haints' and the other said there was nothing to it." Not content with this reaction, Norris proceeded to "drop a folding chair through the opening and you could hear it all over the block as it hit the floor full and square." He described the result as "too much." The men ran from the building, bumping into each other. "After Bum [one of the men] got clear outside, eyes all bulging out," Norris continued gleefully, "he just vowed and declared there were 'haints' in the church and they wouldn't go back in until Fred took them in." Ever the practical joker, he wrote of his plan to visit a local store and "get one of those big cannon crackers and come back and watch where the negroes are working and then go down in the basement right under them and touch them off." Norris justified his cruel antics by adding that he wanted "to see to it that these negroes earn their money. I think in the meantime I will get in conversation with them about the end of the world and when they are going to be earthquaked." Norris assured Jane Hartwell that he would not "tell my wife anything about it for she thinks it is sinful to treat them that way." He saw it instead it as "really a righteous act to shake them up and have them forget their troubles—I know it has that effect on me, that is to watch them."[69] Norris used these men for his own amusement, so he could forget his own "troubles," and was willing to use his fundamentalist belief in a premillennial tribulation to further agitate and ridicule them. But while Norris's actions are the most morally repugnant of the preceding examples of white use of dialect, music, and superstition among African Americans, he and his fellow white preachers marginalized and demeaned blacks on a more regular and socially acceptable basis.

For all of their discussion of African Americans' social status, musical exceptionality, and dialect, white fundamentalists did not take black commitment to Protestant thought for granted. Indeed, they often worried about the backsliding they attributed to African Americans, whether personally witnessed, read of in press accounts, or heard through rumor. They both pined for the days when African Americans were dependent upon white ministers and looked warily about themselves for evidence that the modern world, or possibly worse yet, the Roman Catholic Church, was making inroads among African Americans.

For example, W. B. Riley took the time to note other white ministers' efforts to evangelize among and counsel African Americans. In an editorial about his 1931 trip to Texas, Riley reported on his appearance before "a large company of colored people in one of the colored churches of Beaumont, a fine assembly of preachers being in the same." The black preachers in his audience, he reported, assured him that "in spite of the earnest attempts to bring them to be modernists, they still believed in God and His holy Word, and were standing steadfastly for the faith once delivered." As if to underscore their devotion to conservative theology, Riley noted that "several of them ordered our entire series of forty volumes."[70] The "series" to which Riley referred was "The Bible of the Expositor and the Evangelist," which the back cover of *The Christian Fundamentalist* advertised at $1 for cloth or 50 cents for paper binding, plus appropriate postage costs. A twenty- to forty-dollar outlay for the series would be a significant expenditure during the Great Depression and speaks either to the devotion of the preachers in the audience, their relative affluence, or Riley's pride in authorship.

The idea that modernism, which stood as the single largest enemy of and threat to fundamentalism, might be creeping into African American churches found expression elsewhere in fundamentalist circles. In April 1931, the *Moody Bible Institute Monthly* reprinted an article from the *Western Recorder* on the religious and social forces that might cause blacks to stray from evangelicalism. Beginning with the claim that "the Negro, in some quarters, is drifting away from the white man and the white man's religion," Charles T. Alexander outlined two distinct threats to African American adherence to Christianity: the rise of Islam (Alexander is unclear whether this is Islam or the nascent forerunner to the Nation of Islam—the Moorish Science Temple) and the modernistic tendencies of secular universities. The first problem, that of the advance of "three Mohammedan mosques in Chicago, and the present claims already of approximately 300,000 Mohammedan Negroes in America" forced white conservatives to "take heed to what is going on quietly in our midst":

He is breaking from the old moorings of his historic Christian faith as given him by the Protestant and evangelical people. That is all the "religion" he has known in America. It took many centuries to free the Hebrew race from pagan idolatry. It was never burned out of those people till the Babylonian captivity. The Negro race in America is not far removed from the centuries of their bondage to pagan idolatry in Africa. With confidence in the white man and his religion gone, he will drift rapidly from his historic faith in America. And when the drift gains momentum, they will turn upon their own Christian leaders as but puppets and imitators of the "white man's" religion. It will then be too late for us to talk about the "evangelization of the Negroes of America." The work will then be hard sledding indeed.[71]

The *Western Recorder* attributed this willingness of blacks to stray from Christianity to the increasing secularization of black leaders, "who have been educated in the large universities of the land, which are now saturated with the cult of Modernism and destroying the only faith the Negro has known with a pagan philosophy of human life and human destiny."[72] The situation was dire, and the implications of the *Recorder's* argument were that evangelical Christianity had saved the slaves from their African idols, but that this new generation faced a return to equally dangerous idols—humanism and secularization. Central to Alexander's argument was the presumption that, under the old guidance of white, anti-modern leaders who trained black preachers and their parishioners to follow the very tenets of Christianity that fundamentalism fought to protect, African Americans' souls were safe. The new social and political trends in black society threatened to undo centuries of work. In 1930, J. Frank Norris voiced this sentiment in a telegram to Texas senator Tom Connally, warning "against negro socialistic element defeating high class man like Judge Parker" for a seat on the US Supreme Court. He elaborated that he "considered that northern element most menacing and dangerous factor in American life . . . issues nonpolitical and moral."[73]

Like other fundamentalists, Curtis Laws remained concerned about the influence modernism could have on African Americans, especially those who attended universities where such thought was considered to be rampant. Commenting on an affiliation among Morehouse College, Spelman College, and Atlanta University in 1930, Laws expressed his confidence that Dr. John Hope, the president of the new university comprised of the affiliated schools, would maintain "the integrity of the colleges" and warned that when blacks attended schools outside the South, "too frequently . . . they are led astray."[74] On a trip to the South almost a decade earlier, Laws had commented on how well Benedict College, a black institution, trained its students. "The big assembly room was an interesting sight," Laws explained, "when the students began to march in with perfect decorum and orderliness. They were as neat as wax, and the behavior throughout was admirable." Laws said the school and its educators were "blessing a race, a Nation and a world."[75] The civilizing benefits of education, coupled with Protestant thought, would uplift the black race, according to Laws, and white Protestants, especially those in the South, with their racial "expertise," were best equipped to take on the task.

That civilizing effort had its enemies, however, as Laws explained in a warning about the inroads Roman Catholics were making among African Americans. Turning to the standard notion that African Americans were easily controlled and less educated, Laws warned that "there is much in Roman Catholicism that has an appeal to the average uncultured Negro. Priestly authority, the mystery of an unknown tongue, the secrecy of the confessional, and the gorgeous ritual of spectacular worship are all calculated to work on the credulity of one who is naturally superstitious." Laws went on to reprint a call from Dr. George Rich Hovey in *Missions* for an "'educated Baptist ministry.'" According to Hovey, "'the menace of false teaching promulgated by well-trained men compels us to provide an educated colored Baptist ministry. Shame on us if we are not as wise in the things of the kingdom as are the promoters of error in their work.'"[76] For both Hovey and Laws, blacks were still quite susceptible to "false teachings" and "superstition," despite Laws's earlier claims of respect for African Americans. Moreover, the strength of the color line meant that Hovey, and, by reprinting, Laws, would not cross it themselves to preach the Baptist gospel to blacks. Instead, the ministry must come from people of the same race. This insistence on separate ministry begins to hint at why white fundamentalists did not call for a mission among American blacks. Rather, they preferred to maintain their distance, calling for white-controlled seminaries to train black men to prevent the tide of modernist, socialist, communist, or Roman Catholic thought among African Americans nationally.

As they raised the alarm over the social and theological perils facing African Americans, white fundamentalists often relied on the argument that they—as white southerners—were best suited to speak for African Americans. While not all early fundamentalists were from the American South, a fair few were, including W. B. Riley, J. C. Massee, J. Frank Norris, Curtis Lee Laws, and John Roach Straton. These men used their familial backgrounds to make the case that they, and not the African Americans themselves, could speak to questions facing the race.

Many of these writers emphasized their relationship with their childhood mammy, a kindly black woman who was a moral foundation for them—a trope of white southern nostalgia.[77] According to Helen Cadbury Dixon,

A. C. Dixon spoke fondly of his black mammy, saying "'she was black as to body, but white as an angel in soul. She taught us to pray and to sing Gospel hymns. Our mother had such confidence in Aunt Barb's piety that she gave us over largely to her teaching. I learned many a lesson of trust from the pious negroes as they lived and died in their simple, child-like faith.'" "Aunt Barb," according to Helen Dixon, "remained with" the Dixon family after Emancipation, "until her death a few years later." Clearly, Helen and A. C. Dixon believed, the former slave was loyal to the family who had "fed and clothed [her] just as well as" they had fed and clothed themselves."[78] Dixon's nostalgic memories of his mammy were not alone. W. D. Powell, writing in the *Watchman-Examiner*, remembered his black mammy fondly, crediting her with orchestrating his conversion to Christianity. "By her prayers and counsels," he reminisced, "and with that strong black hand placed upon my head, she finally led me to that lonely place where I met my Saviour face to face." Not one to be ungrateful, Powell asserted that on trip home to Tennessee he hired someone to tend to his mother's grave, and he "arranged for the contractor to render the same service to the grave of my black mammy, whose spirit has gone to the heavenly home and whose body awaits the resurrection morn."[79] There was no word in Powell's account of whether his black mammy would enjoy an integrated afterlife.

Fellow southerner W. B. Riley preserved a clipping in his scrapbooks in which his friend, Texan J. Frank Norris, made the case for his concern for and protection of African Americans. The clipping, dated May 25, 1926, provided coverage of the Baptist Bible Union's meeting, ending with an exchange between the Reverend J. Frank Norris, who spoke "on the subject of immersion," and an audience member over the treatment of African Americans:

> "How can a man practice race hatred toward the black man and follow Christ?"
> [Norris] replied:
> "The black man is not on trial tonight," adding
> "'There is a colored delegate here who will tell you that the Southern white man is the best friend the black man has on earth."[80]

Why Riley chose to preserve this particular article is a mystery, but its inclusion is most likely a tacit approval of J. Frank Norris's public display of paternalism.[81] Riley also collected articles on "Educating the Negro," about efforts by the Baptist Home Mission, and "The Southern People and the Negroes," which addressed the proposed reunification of northern and southern Methodist churches.[82] Riley maintained a watchful eye over the possible racial ramifications of several different denominations' actions.

While Curtis Lee Laws, like Riley, did exhibit a certain amount of paternalism toward African Americans in the South, he seemed less strident than his fellow southern fundamentalists when he addressed the issue of race relations. In an editorial entitled, "Race Prejudice," he warned readers that anyone who claimed to be without "race prejudice" was likely wrong. "Race prejudice," he admonished, "is practically universal among grown-up folks." Laws defended whites from the charge that they were the worst offenders, citing the Japanese "contempt for all others . . . [and the Chinese] profess to dislike the white man . . . because of his disagreeable odor." Moreover, Laws added, "some members of the dark races are not slow in these days to remind us that the white race has had its innings in running the affairs of the world, but that now the colored races are to have their change." He concluded with a warning, "the races must come to a better understanding with one another or we shall have another period of chaos on earth compared with which the World War would seem but a boys' quarrel." If Christians did not address the problem, "racial Armageddon" could occur.[83] While these comments appear inflammatory, Laws was not merely a prophet of doom. The next month, March 1925, he wrote about the Great Migration and the "recent movements of the negro population" which had "filled people with astonishment and struck many with dismay." With an apparent disregard for the existence of the continent of Africa, Laws claimed that "never in the world's history have so many negroes been brought together in one community." According to Laws, the mass movement of African Americans to New York and other cities was worth "cheering." "Every Christian and every true American," Laws explained, "will rejoice in the negro's progress. There are problems attending all this but with patience and Christian courage the problems can be solved."[84] By 1931, he was even more sanguine about race relations in the United States. "In some places there is still friction, but broadly speaking," Laws wrote, "there is no country on earth in which two races as different from each other as Negroes and white people live together so peacefully."[85]

At first blush appearing more progressive than Laws was John Roach Straton, pastor of New York's Calvary Baptist Church. But despite his intervention against New York City screenings of *The Birth of a Nation*, Straton harbored many of the same racial conclusions as his fellow fundamentalists. Born and raised in Georgia, Straton attended Mercer University and the Southern Baptist Theological Seminary. He headed north in 1905 to Chicago, then returned south in 1908, first leading a church in Baltimore and then one in Norfolk. In 1918, however, he was called to Calvary Baptist Church in New York City.[86] In moving to the Big Apple, Straton joined many thousands of southern migrants, both white and black.

Straton quickly gained a reputation as a preacher willing to speak out on the evils of the day. Although most of his press coverage came in the form of outright ridicule of his opposition to public dances, baseball games on Sundays, and other social activities in New York, he also tackled race relations. Straton addressed both the showing of the controversial film, *The Birth of a Nation* and the founding of a chapter of the Ku Klux Klan in the city. D. W. Griffith's motion picture, *The Birth of a Nation* elicited a warning from Straton to Mayor John F. Hylan, arguing that the film was "nothing short of a dark and deadly menace to our safety and peace." According to Straton, "the play [*sic*] is dangerous even in peaceful times," but was even more dangerous "in these times when many minds are already inflamed by racial prejudice." More than just a threat to law and order in the city, the film's portrayal of African Americans was incorrect. Drawing on his own southern roots as his reason for authority on the matter, Straton told Hylan that "the type of Negro, for one thing, that this picture portrays is not a true type. Such Negroes are no more representative of the colored race than a white degenerate is representative of the white race."[87]

Straton did not just write to the mayor; he also preached a sermon at Calvary within the week to correct what he perceived as the film's incorrect portrayal of African Americans. The sermon, with the tantalizing title, "How to Fight the Negroes, the Foreigners, the Catholics, and the Jews— The More Excellent Way," reads as a paean to the New South's understanding of African Americans: easily manipulated, intellectually simple, and relatively harmless when handled properly. After reminding his congregation of the role of slaves in building the country and how the freed slaves overcame "all the handicaps of race and former slavery," Straton emasculated African Americans in his description of them: "As a race, the Negroes are peculiarly lovable. They are naturally industrious, good natured, obliging, warm-hearted, hospitable, friendly, and loyal. They have a humor that is almost universal among them, that is quaint and original to a remarkable degree, and that has added, especially in the South, immeasurably to the brightening and enjoyment of our American life. As a race, they are naturally inclined to music. Instead of getting together, like some other backward peoples, for wild orgies that frequently end in feuds, and blood-shed, and that lead to social disturbance and rebellion against all government, these simple minded people come together in their gatherings and, among the more ignorant of them, nothing more harmful than a banjo or accordion is the center of attraction."[88] Having assured the good people of Midtown Manhattan's Calvary Church of the gentle nature of this "backward" and musical people, Straton gave a nod to black "talent for oratory," referring to "many great preachers and such orators as the late Booker T. Washington," all of whom were "being used of God to bless them as a people and even to inspire our own white ranks." Straton declared that "'the vast majority of them [African Americans] are as harmless human beings as exist on this earth.'"[89] In his efforts to defuse a potentially volatile situation, he removed from African Americans all political agency, as well as any character development or internal moral compass. His identification of African Americans as docile and his self-identification as an expert demonstrates that, like many white southerners described by historian Grace Elizabeth Hale, Straton "confused slave and ex-slave masks with black selves."[90] The audience from Manhattan (and indeed all four other boroughs of New York) could now take part in white gullibility or self-delusion.

When he was not proclaiming the relative timidity of African Americans, Straton returned to the southern memory of the Negro mammy, who selflessly cared for her white charges while ignoring, one presumes, her own kin. Historian Kimberly Wallace-Sanders has observed that the early years of the twentieth century saw "a startling urgency in the need to document an acceptable version of domestic interaction between slaves and slaveholders."[91] For men of A. C. Dixon's age, that need for acceptability was a concern, but for younger men, such as Straton, who was born in 1875, the need was more appropriately described as one of class and racial superiority. By hearkening to the days of his mammy, Straton could tie himself to the more affluent levels of southern society even as he sought to connect the Old South to the New South. In his 1922 remarks to the National Law Enforcement Conference in Nashville, Straton paid homage to the religious dedication of his "'Negro Mammy,'" saying he thought "she was the noblest Christian woman that ever lived except my own mother."[92] In an undated sermon, he preached, "I can never get away from the fact that as a helpless babe I was nursed by the faithful arms of old Aunt Tilly, my Negro mammy, and almost the first human face that ever made an impression on my childish memory was that black face. Equally with the white and beautiful face of my mother, there lingers in childhood's picture gallery the black and yet, too, beautiful face of old Aunt Tilly." Straton bore witness that Aunt Tilly was "one of the best and most consistent Christians" he "had ever known," despite the fact that she "was only an old black woman" who "could not write her name." An earlier draft of the sermon includes Straton's note to himself to "tell story of my old Negro mammy, Aunt Millie," rather than Tilly, which begs the question how important this woman was to Straton's personal history. More likely, she served as a trope that connected Straton's southern heritage to an image of benign blacks who, although streaming into northern urban areas by the thousands, could be controlled and domesticated. In the earlier draft, Straton even used the words of a black preacher in Harlem to reify the mammy image. In his notes, Straton reminded himself to "tell story of my visit to the mass meeting of New York preachers in Harlem when, following my address, one of their most eloquent preachers got up and in referring to my having been nursed by a black mammy and to the fact that Dr. George Truett, Henry Grady, and many other men of today had been so nursed, said, "Dey is still our white folks. We oughta be proud of 'em and help 'em, because we nursed 'em and made up what dey is."[93] In the draft, Straton called on his fellow Christians to refrain from "going to [the African Americans] at night with a fiery cross to terrorize their souls, [instead] let us go to them carrying the blood stained cross of Jesus Christ to save their souls."

While Straton's sentiments may have seemed noble, he was trapped in the very model of race relations his southern childhood and contemporary societal connections embraced, that of the docile Negro who could be a boon if met with the kindness his or her simple heart needed, or a bane if treated with violence. Indeed, his repeated mentions of hiring "an old negro" or "an old-fashioned negro mammy" to cook for him and his house-mates during their years at Mercer underscored his public declaration of first-hand knowledge about African Americans.[94] For Straton, the African Americans of his childhood became the African Americans who were moving north into his adopted city. He prided himself as an expert on them, and as such, counseled a paternalistic approach to the new migrants. Treat them with kindness, yes, but do so the way you would also treat a child, or even an animal, with kindness. Nowhere in Straton's extant papers does there appear an effort to engage in dialogue with African Americans over theological issues, yet there is not outright hatred in his prejudice. Even in a 1900 article for the *North American Review* entitled "Will Education Solve the Race Problem?" Straton, while clearly racist in his assumptions, displayed no overt hatred or hostility. Taking refuge in crime statistics and the questionable assumption that because there was less black crime during slavery it meant that African Americans were better suited to the segregated and controlled life of slaves, he couched his position as one of caring for blacks. "If racial contact is seen to prove disastrous to the weaker," he wrote, "then segregation must be effected."[95] Almost three decades later, he was clearly cognizant of black preachers in New York City and had met with them, but he left no evidence of what that outreach entailed. Most likely it was not in his best interests to do so, and his experience as a southerner and a Baptist had led him to believe that a well-trained group of African American evangelists, trained by white men, was best equipped to engage in such work.

Straton's views that black religious leaders needed white guidance was shared by other fundamentalists. Indeed, the Reverend Edmund H. Iron-

side, with considerable assistance from his father, Harry A. Ironside, founded the Dallas Colored Bible (now Southern Bible) Institute in the mid-1920s
to train black men for the ministry. Its founding was very much in keeping
with other Bible colleges that were a part of what became the fundamentalist movement, but DCBI had a particular charge to improve black understanding of the gospel. Its very existence was credited to Jim Crow laws, but
its founders and supporters clearly saw African Americans as in need of
white assistance to find salvation.

Histories of DCBI tend to agree that Edmund Ironside began the school
after interested black men requested further instruction in theology and
homiletics, although who reached out to whom initially remains unclear,
with black authors crediting black initiative while white authors stress the
presence of a glaring need. Regardless, Ironside, the son of the Moody Memorial Church's pastor, decided to found a theological training school in
Dallas for African Americans.[96] The initial purpose of the school, according
to its "Articles of Incorporation," was "'to provide and maintain the highest standard of instruction possible, for the Negro of the South, leading
to a diploma or degree, when sufficient number of hours and credits are
obtained.'"[97] A decade later, the Articles of Incorporation were revised to
add "It is the further purpose of this school to teach and defend that body
of conservative truth which has been held by Evangelical Protestantism,
believing in inerrant authority of the Scriptures, which are interpreted according to the premillennial system of doctrine as set forth in the doctrinal
statement of the school drawn up by its founder and adopted by the Board
of Directors."[98] Given the extant sources, it is difficult to determine whether
the premillennialism included in the updated articles was the hook that
drew the first black students to the street preachers Ironside knew, but its
addition to the school's purpose a full decade after the founding begs the
question whether there was some event that precipitated the need to add
an explicit mention. Once the school started, Ironside was the only faculty
member, and the curriculum was drawn from Cyrus Scofield's *Rightly Dividing the Word*, James Gray's *Synthetic Bible Studies*, and "'H. A. Ironside's
commentaries from Joshua to Revelation,'" so there was from the start a
clear emphasis on fundamentalist doctrine, including premillennialism.[99]

White discussion of DCBI emphasized a larger deficiency than just the
absence of premillennial teaching among African Americans. Instead, the
primary impetus was a concern that black preachers lacked the proper understanding of evangelical doctrine and could be corrupted by modernist influences. An undated fundraising pamphlet circulated by Ironside
emphasized the need for better trained ministers who would benefit their
communities, "imparting the truth as they learn it to those to whom they

minister." Indeed, the pamphlet underscored the inadequacy of facilities available, noting that the prospective students were "anxious to see a Bible institute started for colored students, to which people of their race may come to learn more accurately the way of the Lord."[100] The *Christian Fundamentalist* reported that the school was needed, that a "Bible institute for colored boys is eminently desirable," because "the denominations that have been working in the South with the colored boys are almost without exception imposing upon the minds of colored candidates for the ministry, modernistic ideas." It was time to "save the rising colored ministry from that rationalism which practically repudiates revelation, and presents other than Christ as the way of salvation."[101] In the eyes of white fundamentalists, Ironside's work among African Americans was necessary to prevent modernism from gaining even more of a bulwark among them. It was not, however, a relationship of equals. Implicit in the descriptions of DCBI's founding is the notion that whites had to assist blacks in finding the true path to salvation. The "boys" DCBI trained were grown men, but to white fundamentalists and most white Americans, they would never be equals.

Like many other black educational institutions, DCBI faced financial hardships. Any record of donors "has been lost over the years," but white contributions were probably the bulk of its funding.[102] A hagiographic biography of H. A. Ironside notes that Edmund Ironside "was greatly discouraged" by the "hardships encountered." According to fundamentalist biographer E. Schuyler English, "Ed felt that the ministry was eminently worthwhile," even if the operation of the institution was a constant challenge. Apparently Edmund's health was not good, and he died in 1941 of a heart attack. English returned to the trope of the faithful black in describing the younger Ironside's funeral. "More than two hundred friends, both colored and white, attended the service," he wrote, adding, "no higher compliment to Edmund's understanding of and interest in these colored folks could have been paid than was spoken by one of the race that he had loved much and served well, who said: 'Edmund Ironside was the blackest white man I ever knew!'"[103] While Edmund likely did touch many lives with his service, the larger white fundamentalist community would continue to relegate African Americans to the category of "these colored folk," rather than embrace them fully.

DCBI survived its many difficulties and continues to operate today as the Southern Bible Institute. Its website describes the school's approach as "non-denominational" and lists among its "Biblical and Theological Distinctives" many fundamentalist doctrines, including biblical inerrancy and dispensational premillennialism. It also, however, teaches what could be described as more Pentecostal tenets, among them the appropriation of the

Holy Spirit to live without sin in daily life and an endorsement of glossalalia and healing.[104] The institution's history, though, illustrates the patriarchal relationship white fundamentalists had with African Americans.

That patriarchy was expressed in other forums as well. A pair of letters written to "Perplexing Questions" columnist Dr. C. W. Foley, "instructor in Christian Evidences, Exegesis, and Analysis" at Riley's Northwestern Bible College, frame the estrangement of white fundamentalists from African Americans. Foley's column in Northwestern's *Pilot* offered readers a chance to have their biblical questions addressed by an expert in fundamentalist doctrine. In March 1930, "C. L. E., Windom, Minn." asked Foley to "explain the origin of the races." Foley's response began with the origin of the "nations . . . found in Genesis, chapters 9–11," which included "what we may call 'the table of nations'" in chapter 10. "The history of the race," he ended, "has here its new beginning. Our present nations all begin here."[105] The passage to which Foley referred his reader explicates the sons of Noah—Shem, Ham, and Japheth—and their subsequent children. As scholar Stephen R. Haynes has documented, the use of Genesis 9–11, with its attendant table of nations, was central for white southerners' biblical justification of slavery.[106] While Foley did not elaborate and appeared to conflate the terms nation and race, a subsequent question regarding Noah's curse elucidated from Foley a response that had its roots in antebellum theology and would appear in later segregationists' religious justifications. An inquirer asked, "Was Ham's color changed when the curse was pronounced upon him?" After first confessing that "frankly, I do not know one thing about [the color of Ham's skin]," Foley gave a legalistic answer—that the curse was not pronounced on Ham but on Ham's son, Canaan. But he then added that the curse, "this doom," as he called it, "has been fulfilled in the destruction of the Canaanites, and the slavery of the Africans, the descendents of Ham."[107] Foley's reliance on the antebellum justification of slavery seems out of place in 1930, but when one considers the continued interpretations of the text by Southern Presbyterian minister Benjamin M. Palmer and later use by white segregationists in the 1950s, the response appears less anachronistic. Foley employed the curse of Ham (or Canaan) to legitimize past mistreatment of Africans, and he implied that contemporary notions of racial inferiority were just as biblically based. Sixty-five years after the Civil War, even as most of its veterans were dying off, some white fundamentalists could still trot out the theological argument for slavery.[108]

Throughout the 1920s and 1930s, white fundamentalists hewed closely to prevailing and long-held views of race, especially when those views restricted the social access and political power of African Americans. A religious movement based in large part upon both the preservation of nineteenth century Protestant thought and the expectation of Jesus's return within their lifetimes gave white fundamentalists little interest in direct contact with African Americans or in improving their lot in life. Indeed, to do so would have made the movement, already on the margins of American culture by the end of the 1920s, countercultural in a way that did not appeal to these conservative white evangelicals. Moreover, the white fundamentalists demonstrated little interest in the actual workings of African American churches beyond those conclusions they had already drawn about worship, music, and dialect. But while white fundamentalists were busy thinking of reasons to continue the established boundaries of race, their African American counterparts were monitoring their every move and distancing themselves from the white fundamentalists, not theologically, but by racial identification.

2

"What is the Matter with White Baptists?"

African Americans' Initial Encounters with Fundamentalism

Just weeks after the United States entered the Great War, Jonathan H. Frank, editor of the *National Baptist Union-Review*, described another struggle underway, a struggle between different factions of white Protestants over doctrine. This battle, however, was far from the churches of black Americans, he assured his readers. "The upheavals and readjustments of mental processes that have unsettled so many white people are not challenging the attention of colored Baptist preachers," he wrote. "Thus far colored folks are not engaged in the unholy task of explaining away the Scriptures because of scientific thought, so called." Frank also excluded the black faithful from engagement in atheism, biology, philosophy, and sociology as attempts to understand the world. White people might rely on "'The Spirit of Modern Progress,'" and they might not fear "'a new religion.'" But, he assured his readers, "Colored folks are not ready as yet to discard Christianity for civilization. Thank God."[1]

As white fundamentalists prided themselves over their knowledge of the nature of African Americans, their religious inclinations, and their ability to comprehend the saving power of Protestant Christianity, black religious leaders, both in Baptist and Methodist denominations, kept a watchful eye on the fundamentalists and their theological dispute with modernist leaders. Long familiar with the fundamentalists, both black religious writers and black secular reporters recorded their observations and interpreted the meaning of the debate for their readers, often declaring their sympathy for fundamentalist theology and opposition to modernism. They engaged in this discussion because they correctly perceived that the fundamentalist movement had demanded that Protestants provide an accounting of their theology and a defense of its soundness. The first step in that response was a careful examination of the warring factions and their positions.

Although there is no hard evidence that African American ministers received copies of *The Fundamentals*, the books that defined the beginning of the fundamentalist movement and which were, according to accepted historiography, mailed to every minister in the United States using Lyman Stewart's vast oil fortune, African Americans nonetheless were aware of the areas of debate as well as the various organizations doing battle. For the most part, black Baptists and Methodists favored the traditionalist position they believed that the fundamentalists were championing. It was, for them, a set of beliefs that had deep roots in the Protestant tradition, and those roots were vital to keeping the message of Christianity alive in a challenging world. While the next chapter will explore more fully the ways in which traditionalist notions of evangelicalism appealed to African Americans, this chapter highlights one important distinction that they made in watching white debates—that modernism was a white phenomenon.

For these black religious writers, modernism was a danger white people had created, and white people would reap what they had sown. African American evangelicals' reactions to modernist theology tend to support historian William R. Hutchison's definition of modernism as the "conscious, intended adaptation of religious ideas to modern culture," with its attendant focus on the notions that "God is immanent in human cultural development and revealed through it" and that "society is moving toward realization (even though it may never attain the reality) of the Kingdom of God."[2] While Hutchison contends that modernism has deep roots in the nineteenth century, he admits that the cultural developments following World War I and the presence of a concerted response to modernism—fundamentalism—forced a crisis with which churches grappled in the interwar period. Black Protestants offered a steady resistance to the perceived threat of modernism in the 1920s and 1930s, even as they continued to turn the term into a racial one. In their view, black denominations, largely immune to the problem, had a duty to the larger Christian message to fight theological modernism wherever they found it. As noted earlier, fundamentalists were well known for their opposition to this modernism, and black Baptists and Methodists commented frequently on their racially based understanding of the movement. As they observed white Protestants debating the merits of fundamentalism and modernism, black Protestants made the term "modernism" a white term. White denominations were more prone to this contagion than black denominations, they argued. But they did not confine their commentary to what was happening in the white religious world. Instead, black Methodists and Baptists declared their own staunch position as anti-modernists. Yet modernist ideas, or at least progressive Protestant language, did appear in their denominational papers. This chapter examines the black use of the blanket term "modernism." Chapter 3 will explore the ramifications of modernism's association with evolutionary theory.

Within black Baptist and Methodist denominations, there were clear lines between supporters of fundamentalism and skeptics of it. While black denominational papers did debate the merits of the basic tenets of fundamentalism, as well as the accompanying concerns over Darwinism and societal changes, their disputes rarely descended into the bitter battles that so often characterized the discussions in white denominations. Moreover, those publications that expressed doubts about the wisdom of fundamentalism almost never condemned it outright. Instead, they sought a middle ground between the strict constructionism of the fundamentalists and the more liberal interpretation of the modernists.

Much like their white counterparts, African American Baptist groups in particular were drawn into the debate over biblical interpretation. The publications of two groups in particular, the National Baptist Convention USA (or Incorporated) and the National Baptist Convention, Unincorporated, diverged on the notion of Christianity as a progressive, developing religion, while at the same time repeating their confidence in and agreement over such tenets as the divinity of Jesus, the reality of sin, and the general notion that the Bible was the inspired word of God. The varying stances of these two newspapers, whose parent denominations had only just separated from each other in 1915, suggest that the schism may have been at least in part theologically motivated. Extant scholarship on the split is scarce, but all sources agree that the divide started over the control of the National Baptist Convention's Publishing Board. According to historian Clarence M. Wagner, the dispute arose as a result of a legal ambiguity in Tennessee, where the Publishing Board and Convention operated. This ambiguity did not allow the Convention itself to elect the Publishing Board's members, but rather stipulated that only members of the Publishing Board could vote on membership and leadership of the Publishing Board itself. Since the Publishing Board was both a successful venture and the means by which the Convention disseminated information, the division between Elias Camp Morris and Richard H. Boyd, "two strong men," was a high stakes battle. In the end, the original NBC split into the two groups—Incorporated and Unincorporated. While Wagner hints at other causes of the strife, including the idea that "disunity . . . was an advantage to some white Baptists," he tends to side with the consensus that the split was a leadership issue.[3] Lillian B. Horace, biographer of Incorporated pastor and president Lacey Kirk Williams, also attributes the divide to the question of control over the Publishing

Board, calling it a "sad day for thinking Baptists."[4] More recently, histori-an Bobby L. Lovett also credits the control of the Publishing Board as the cause of the schism.[5]

While the legal issues and leadership divisions certainly contributed to the split, the paths the two papers took following it suggest that there were divergent perspectives on theology. During the years following the emer-gence of fundamentalism, the *National Baptist Union-Review* (the publi-cation of the Unincorporated body) regularly favored the fundamentalists, echoed much of their language, and lambasted modernism at almost ev-ery opportunity. At the same time, however, the *National Baptist Voice*, the Incorporated body's paper, shied away from consistently traditionalist evangelical language and frequently employed terms used by Social Gospel advocates. A clear dichotomy between the two conventions, however, is im-possible to identify or defend. Both organs of the Incorporated and the Un-incorporated groups stressed the need for social justice for African Ameri-cans, and both called into question the validity of a white Christianity that could encourage or even permit racial oppression. But the *Voice*, the organ of the National Baptist Convention, Incorporated, did trend more strongly toward a Social Gospel message, while the *Union-Review*, the paper of the National Baptist Convention, Unincorporated, took a more traditionalist prophetic stance, predicting dire consequences for white racism and more consistently employing conservative evangelical positions. These topics will be discussed more fully in future chapters.[6]

Although white fundamentalists may have not embraced African Amer-icans publicly, they were well known to readers of both African American denominational and secular newspapers. Even before the formal inception of fundamentalism in 1919, its leaders garnered their attention. A cursory examination of secular papers reveals frequent mentions of the men who would become associated with the movement. In 1908, for example, the *Washington Bee* reported on a "national conference of presidents of institu-tions for the education of the negro." Among the men tasked with consider-ing the topic of the "'Negro as a free man,'" was "the Rev. Jasper C. Massee, pastor of the First Baptist Church, Chattanooga, Tenn."[7] Two years later, Massee's involvement in uplift efforts again gained attention as he spoke in Durham, North Carolina, to a meeting of the "advisory board of the Na-tional Religious Training School." The event was covered by the Chicago *Broad Axe*, the *Washington Bee*, and the *Savannah Tribune*.[8] Massee con-tinued his relationship with the school, and the *Washington Bee* was able to note his expected participation at the "Second Annual Summer School at the National Religious Training School" (now North Carolina Central University) in August 1911.[9]

While Massee was engaged in uplift measures and efforts to ensure that African Americans were protected from secular threats, the Reverend John Roach Straton, fundamentalist pastor of New York City's Calvary Baptist Church, earned attention from the *Chicago Defender* for his public denunciation of racial violence. The *Defender*, noting Straton's roots in a "prominent southern family," carried the partial text of his condemnation of the 1919 Washington riots from his pulpit in the "fashionable Calvary Baptist Church." In the excerpt, Straton stayed true to his role as spokesperson for race relations, noting that "'[t]hough I have lived most of my life in the south, I raise my voice in most earnest protest against the awful injustice that exacts a vengeance on a whole people because of the crimes of a few individuals.'" Given the source, the *Defender* argued, Straton's stand was "significant."[10] As mentioned in Chapter 1, Straton prided himself on his ability to speak on behalf of African Americans, but his mammy rhetoric and his association with allies of the Ku Klux Klan, including, as historian Michael Lienesch notes, appearing "at [KKK] chapter meetings across the South," would later lead many African Americans to believe in his guilt by association, if not outright participation.[11]

Despite his questionable ties to the KKK, Straton received praise from a variety of black denominational newspapers. For example, the *A.M.E. Christian Recorder*, the publication of the African Methodist Episcopal (AME) Church, told its readers about his efforts to ban dancing: "Dr. John Roach Straton, preaching last night in Calvary Baptist Church attacked the modern dance as 'a bait of the devil.'" As further proof of Straton's fine work, the article noted that, in response to a recent meeting of the National Association of Dancing Masters, which Straton said had stated it wanted to "'purify the dance,'" Straton railed, "'You cannot purify a pole-cat!'"[12]

When Straton traveled to Nashville to deliver the "closing address at the National Law Enforcement Conference in the Ryman Auditorium," the *National Baptist Voice*, published by the National Baptist Convention, Incorporated, reprinted his remarks, complete with condemnations of "modern dances" ("a 'hugging match' set to music"), the "dress of the young woman today" ("shameful"), the "New Theology," "socialism" ("which leads to idolatry"), "Bolshevism," "Darwinism," and—possibly the reason why the *Voice*, which did not lean towards the traditionalist position often, quoted him this time—"the Ku Klux Klan."[13] The praise for Straton's stand on race relations, however, was not uniform. Later that same year, for example, the secular African American newspaper *The Appeal* (St. Paul, Minnesota) called Straton, "a vaudevillian reactionary . . . pastor" and accused him of cooperating with the New York Klan in its attempts to recruit members.[14] When Straton espoused traditionalist evangelical positions, African American Protestants could happily support him. Indeed, it is difficult to find in the black denominational press a sustained argument against restrictions on dancing or one in support of higher hemlines and shorter hair on women, as Chapter 4 will explore further. But when these same papers learned of Straton's too cozy relationship with Ku Klux Klan members, they swiftly rebuked him.

That the African American writers, both religious and secular, were cognizant of and interested in fundamentalist leaders like Norris, Straton, and Massee should come as no surprise. The twin forces of uplift and self-preservation demanded that blacks in the United States, especially those who were upwardly mobile, both know and understand the white majority, its spokespeople, and its debates. The first concern educated black leaders had was the uplift of the race. To proponents of uplift, who ranged from Booker T. Washington to W. E. B. DuBois, African Americans needed to emulate the social behaviors and expectations of white society. The legacies of slavery included illiteracy and poverty, and the way to alleviate these problems, they argued, was to inculcate in African Americans a desire for self-betterment and upward mobility. According to proponents of uplift, the combination of hard work, thrift, sobriety, and education would allow African Americans as a race to claim their proper place in society. For African American ministers, who were often the leaders and most well educated members of their communities, the need to stay current with developments in theology and practice was especially pressing. Black pastors needed to keep a weather eye on religious developments, both as a way of changing with the times and as a way of sounding the call when theological developments departed from accepted traditions.[15]

The goal of uplift dovetailed well with the need for self-preservation, especially in the American South. With the increase of lynching in the late nineteenth century and the enactment of Jim Crow laws, African Americans faced segregation and discrimination at every turn, and racism in the South, and in the North as well, could turn deadly at a moment's notice. Unlike white fundamentalists, who were part of the white majority and who could afford to employ stereotypes and misconceptions when dealing with minorities, blacks in early twentieth century America, North and South, were better served by knowing what the white community was debating, what it said about them, and what it had planned for them. As historian Evelyn Brooks Higginbotham so eloquently notes, "In the closed society of Jim Crow, the church afforded African Americans an interstitial space in which to critique and contest white America's racial dominations."[16] From their parsons' studies and from their newsrooms, African American leaders closely monitored white fundamentalists and their activities. They sought both to maintain traditional theology while also keeping up with chang-ing times around them. But the latter presented its own set of challenges. What should a church or denomination or pastor adapt, adopt, or reject? Questions like these elicited few uniform answers, as black Baptist and Methodist writers reflected the fundamentalist/modernist debate as a way of expressing a traditionalist evangelical theology that could speak to the spiritual and social needs of African Americans.

As fundamentalism formally emerged in 1919 with the first World's Christian Fundamentalist Conference in Philadelphia, it made its presence known in a variety of secular African American publications. In a column dealing with the activities of prominent members of the Kansas City black community, the *Kansas City Advocate* made note of Mrs. M. C. Matthews, Mrs. F. Morris, and Mrs. Rogers's recent attendance at a Bible conference, during which "they heard the great Dr. Riley of Minneapolis, Dr. Massee of Brooklyn, N.Y.," who "talked fine on Christian Fundamentals."[17] Funda-mentalism appears to have moved Mrs. Matthews to speak on its behalf. A few years later, the same paper noted that she gave "Advice on Fundamen-talism" at the Western Baptist Convention of 1925.[18] That women attended these talks and had their remarks reported in the secular press indicates that both men and women were aware of the white fundamentalists. But no articles exist in the denominational press of black women reporting on their attendance at fundamentalist talks, raising the point that denomina-tional editors may not have sought to give women such a religious platform. Indeed, black denominational papers were generally opposed to women taking a leadership role, as Chapter 4 will document.

Some coverage of fundamentalism in the black secular press was nega-tive. In 1922, the San Jose *Evening News* compared I. M. Haldeman's lan-guage in discussing the Second Coming of Christ to "the fiery crusading doctrine Mahomet [Mohammed] preached of old" and likened Haldeman's imagery of Christ as the head of a victorious army as "a 'Kaiser Jesus.'"[19] The *Cleveland Gazette* noted that the "fundamentalist-modernist battle that is going on in certain quarters indicates a wider cleavage than that of one church denomination." The paper went on to describe the two sides as "radical and conservative, progressive and reactionary, flapperism and old-timeism, the pace that kills and the simple life."[20] This sampling of cov-erage in many ways mirrors the ways in which white print media reported on fundamentalism at the same time—a mixture of curiosity, interest, and rejection.[21] These papers also bought into the fundamentalist premise that there was a clear dichotomy on theological positions, a dichotomy their black religious counterparts did not always recognize or embrace.

The general debate between fundamentalists and modernists attracted attention not only in secular newspapers, but also in African American denominational publications, especially discussions of theological modernism, which black writers tended to identify as a white phenomenon. Most of the publications stated firm opposition to notions of reading the Bible as a historical source rather than a divinely revealed text, of adapting Protestant theology to reflect the views of the society in which it lived, and other tenets supported by modernists. To that extent, editors ran reprints of white fundamentalist articles against modernism, and they added their own editorials and coverage of the controversy. But they complicated the discussion by accusing the white Protestants of having created the monster of modernism in the first place. In doing so, African American evangelicals racialized the term modernism just as fundamentalists had racialized fundamentalism. Ironically, both terms described white Protestants, while African Americans tended to argue that neither described black Protestants.

Black denominational writers often supplied their readers with synopses of the fundamentalist/modernist debate. African Methodist Episcopal Zion (AMEZ) bishop W. J. Walls, in a *Star of Zion* editorial, informed his subscribers to the church's official paper that "there is afloat in the world today a new current of religion and religious discussion. The two terms modernist and fundamentalist signify the groups which are at war with each other." Walls described the fundamentalists as those who "stand by the old ecclesiastical dogma, and the modernists approach everything with an open mind and critically pass the word around that nothing in religion, any more than in science, is a closed matter." Presciently commenting on the battle to define the church, Walls predicted that "it appears that if the agitation keeps up . . . there will be a new church of the Modernists collected out of the dissenting ones who favor an open church and an open creed in all the Protestant churches." He expressed his hope "that when the storm is blown over, that which remains will be stronger than ever before."[22] While Walls gave a summary of the debate, he took a rather distant stand on it, neither committing himself entirely to one side nor delving deeply into the "dogma" he said divided the two sides.

Providing a more thorough discussion of white Baptist debates over fundamentalism and modernism, Joseph A. Booker, DD, told the readers of the *National Baptist Voice* about the 1922 meeting of the Northern Baptist Convention (white). According to Booker, the lines were "tightly drawn between the Fundamentalists and the Liberals [which] made things look warlike for most of the week." He noted that the "Fundamentalists were led by such men as Dr. J. C. Massee, Dr. Curtis Lee Laws, Dr. W. B. Riley, et al." The "Liberals," he added, "had such men as President Harding's pastor and John D. Rockefeller's pastor identified with them." Booker concluded that the liberals won the battle, "and the war seemed to end and the war did end. From that time onward both factions in all sections of the country moved forward in a good order of faith and fellowship."[23] His conclusion that the debate was ended in 1922 was, as history has shown, too optimistic. Both Booker and Walls were not overly concerned about the controversy, which may indicate that they were more progressive—indeed both looked to the future in their predictions with hopeful eyes—or that they did not perceive the matter as one of concern for black Methodists or Baptists.

In contrast and in the same issue of the *Voice*, the Reverend Robert A. Ashworth gave a more thorough analysis of the history and goals of the fundamentalist movement. Correctly noting that the fundamentalists had "manifest[ed] themselves as a distinct group within the denomination slightly after the war," Ashworth observed that the "Baptists of the North are largely conservative in their views of doctrine, but only a fraction of the conservatives are affiliated with the fundamentalists and very many conservatives are wholly out of sympathy with their methods and propaganda." A more succinct and accurate description of the "come outer" effort within the Northern Baptist Convention would be difficult to find in contemporary sources. The debate within the Northern Baptist Convention included a dispute among conservatives, some who wished to reform the denomination from within and others who felt that separation, or to come out, from the denomination was the only viable option.[24] Ashworth listed J. C. Massee, W. B. Riley, John Roach Straton, and Curtis Lee Laws as the "most conspicuous leaders," and noted that they were "pronounced pre-millennarians," and highlighted the propensity of Northern Baptist "pre-millennarians" to become "ardent Fundamentalists."[25] Ashworth's observation that premillennialists tended to make the most vocal fundamentalists illustrates that African American ministers were cognizant of the divisions within the fundamentalist camp and that these same African American ministers were not wedded entirely to the notion of dispensational premillennialism. Indeed, as we shall see in future chapters, premillennialism and apocalypticism meant less to black Baptists and Methodists than did other doctrinal matters.

Just as the National Baptist Convention, Incorporated writer Robert Ashworth had seen modernism as dangerous, National Baptist Convention, Unincorporated president J. Edmund Wood saw the movement as a threat and warned his body in his 1925 annual address. According to Wood, a small girl "was shown a picture of Jesus Christ standing in Pilate's hall, with His hands tied behind Him, and the cruel soldiers were whipping Him with knotted whips as the blood spurted out from His quivering flesh. As this little girl looked, her eyes filled with tears and she exclaimed, 'Oh mama, why doesn't someone untie His hands?' When I contemplate the big task before the Master; and the assaults made upon Him by the infidel, the atheist, the agnostic, and the modernist; and how the disloyalty and indifference and worldliness of His professed followers tie His hands, in sadness my soul cries out: 'Why don't you untie His hands?'"[26] Wood echoed these concerns in his next two annual addresses, suggesting that, at least within the National Baptist Convention, Unincorporated, there was strong sentiment in favor of the fundamentalist position against modernism.[27] His use of his national platform, at annual meetings of hundreds of Unincorporated Baptists, helped spread the word about modernism as a theological threat.

The fundamentalist/modernist debates continued to interest the black denominational press for many years, even after secular papers had turned away. Assessing the situation in the Southern Baptist Convention, the *National Baptist Union-Review* told its readers in 1928 that "in Texas the denominational war still goes on" over fundamentalist issues and the editorial control of Baptist newspapers. The editorial also mentioned the concerns SBC leaders had over the decision of the World Baptist Alliance to allow "modernists" like Harry Emerson Fosdick and Shailer Mathews to speak at the meeting in Toronto.[28] The next month, the editor grudgingly admitted that as the World Baptist "Congress" was "broadly for all sorts and conditions of Baptists, I suppose that they have as much right to be there and to speak as have the orthodox class."[29] Editor J. H. Frank's patience and notions of congregational polity were sorely tested by those Baptists he perceived as having departed from "correct" path.

Like the black Baptists, the black Methodists kept tabs on fundamentalist/modernist battles. The AME Zion's *Star of Zion* also railed against the theological changes. A 1923 editorial by W. J. Walls noted that "every educational system, every great ideal has either been revamped or shakened [*sic*] alarmingly." Even the Bible was not immune, as "the doctrines of the Bible have not been spared in this renaissance of the 20th century free lancing and mental soundings." Comparing the two sides to "two gigantic cocks with feathers bristled and spurs sharp and ready," the editorial warned, "in some quarters, the spurring has actually begun." Meanwhile, "our poor world is dying for Christian principle in practices."[30] A few months later in the same paper, the Reverend A. Ellison agreed, asking "Has Christianity Lost Its Place in These Modern Times?" In response to his own question, Ellison answered, "Some say that the world is growing better, but to my mind, we are growing worse. We have left the old land mark. There should be less trouble in the Church today than it was in days gone by, because we claim to know." He continued, "but I fear that the trouble is when one knows so much, he denies the Divinity of Jesus Christ."[31] Walls added his concerns. Speaking on the topic of "Meeting Modernisms" to the AME

Zion's Board of Bishops, he saw the church "passing as we are through a new explosive state in the Church and world . . . [and that] the A.M.E. Zion Church cannot exist in the midst of the perilous times when men are erring." His answer was simple: "We therefore preach more strongly than ever the sufficiency of the Holy Scriptures, the supernatural origin of the Church, the absolute credibility of miracles, the reality of an old-fashion, sound conversion, and that 'Jesus Christ according to the will of the flesh, is the son of David and declared to be the son of God with power.'" Walls saw the need to engage in evangelism, noting that "we shall continue to teach that our hope is in Jesus and not theory, in the practice of God's presence in works of brotherly love and soul redeeming rather than in word battles over biological and metaphysical tommyrot."[32]

Continuing the coverage, the *Star of Zion* questioned whether "Protestant Christianity [was] in a Schism, a Battle, or a Split?" Attributing the fighting to factions within the "Episcopal and Presbyterian Churches," the *Star* noted that the "Presbyterian General Assembly of the northern Church was well nigh rent by the fight over Rev. Dr. Raymond D. [*sic*] Fosdick, a Baptist minister occupying a Presbyterian pulpit in New York City." While the new editor, W. H. Davenport, did not get Harry Emerson Fosdick's name correct, he did know that John Roach Straton was "engaged in a series of public debates on the question of the infallibility and divine origin of the Bible" with "Dr. Chas. F. Potter, the Young pastor of the Unitarian Church of the West side of New York." For the *Star*, "the real crux of the discussion seems to be not as much the divinity of Christ and the infallibility of the Bible, as the questions of whether it is the right of the Church to interpret Divine revelation for all or the right of the individual to interpret for himself, the revelation."[33] Davenport did have a point that there were larger questions at stake in the debates between Straton and Potter, but he also proved that black observers did not always fully understand the battle between white modernists and fundamentalists. Modernists thought religion could and often should adapt to culture, and they saw part of that adaptation as both the ability to reject the inerrancy of the Bible and to interpret the Bible individually. Davenport, however, had cast the debate in terms of a Protestant Reformation battle against the Roman Catholic Church rather than a struggle over the limits of Enlightenment thought. In the role of the Roman Catholic Church, he placed the fundamentalists, and in the role of Luther and the Protestants, modernists. Luther and most Protestants, though, would not have embraced the notion of individual biblical interpretation. Moreover, Luther and most Protestants would have endorsed notions of biblical inerrancy. Whether Davenport's identification with modernists as twentieth century Lutherans was one of sympathy to their cause or merely an anachronism is hard to tell. He did, however, write numerous editorials for the traditionalist position.

Entwined with their critiques of modernism, African American Methodists and Baptists also indicted white people as the source of the controversy. The *National Baptist Union-Review* (*NBUR*) tended to take this position more often than did other denominational publications. All were fascinated by white debates, and their assessment of them did not acknowledge the presence of modernism in black churches. Yet despite their lack of acknowledgement, almost all of the denominational papers in this study had modernist terms, language, and occasionally arguments in their pages. Only the *Union-Review* held most closely to the anti-modernist position and led the charge that modernism was a whites-only phenomenon.

The *Union-Review*'s editor, J. H. Frank, got an early start in tying modernism to whites. In 1918, he questioned the theological credentials of liberal Baptists from John D. Rockefeller to Shailer Mathews. Almost a century before the Republican Party would begin to refer to certain members as Republican in Name Only (RINO), the *NBUR* published an editorial, "Baptists in Name Only." According to the editorial, Rockefeller and the Reverend Johnson Myers, pastor of Emmanuel Baptist Church in Chicago, were both "saturated with the church federation idea," which would lead only to "aping Rome, episcopalizing Baptist churches, holding 'Union Meetings' with Methodists," among other dangerous acts. These ideas clearly meant that "not every man marching with Baptists is a Baptist; a number of the marchers are Baptist in name only." Employing dialect to make his point, the editor said, "Thank God colored Baptists 'hasn't sense 'nough to 'splain away de Scriptures'" Indeed, black Baptists were so theologically sound that it "has been well said, 'When you see a colored man not a Baptist, take it for granted some white man has been tampering with him."[34] Adding race to the question of orthodoxy, the *Union Review* held that black Baptists were doctrinally correct, while white Baptists ran the risk of straying from the path of truth.

The paper continued its critique of white liberal Baptists two months later, noting that Shailer Mathews taught at "the Chicago University," and cited him as saying "recently: 'I am a Baptist, and am proud of it.'" But, the editor explained, Mathews had dismissed the notion of denominational differences, claiming, "'There is, said, he, 'no more difference between us than there is between branches of the army.'" Not so, the *NBUR* countered. "Long time ago," the paper argued, "Job said, 'Great men are not always wise,' Prof. Mathews is one of the unwise great men."[35] Frank held Mathews, Myers, and Rockefeller in disdain. Their theology was suspect, and their efforts to promote it dangerous.

By early 1926, Frank regularly referred to the modernists as "White Infidels." Combining race with his charge of religious heresy, he used the pages of the paper to ridicule their beliefs and call upon his readers to stand against the threat to orthodox religion. Reporting that "certain white folk have chartered, incorporated, a society in New York with the expressed purpose to destroy Christianity," he accused "Dean [William] Pickens," the dean of Morgan College and an NAACP organizer, of having the "aim to oppose the truth and the movements that give us Christian homes, Christian society, Christian institutions and that aim at Christianizing the world." But, Frank added, "we are laughing at the folly of people engaged in a fight against God. Of course we pity their ignorance." Historian Sheldon Avery has chronicled the "feud" Pickens started with black ministers, accusing them of "'ignorance and bigotry'" for their "literal interpretation of the Bible." In Pickens's attempt to move African Americans away from traditionalist religion, Frank predicted that a "little handful of Colored Americans, followers of Tom Paine, Vaoltare [sic], Hume, Ingosol [sic], modernist preachers like Slater, Potter, ungodly scientists, evolutionists, and religious bolsheviei, now have their chance to again demonstrate their chronic tendency to imitate the ungodly white people." For Frank, white theologians of the modernist bent were misguided, and those African Americans who followed them were heading down the slippery slope to unbelief. In this case, belief and unbelief were closely aligned with race. Whites tended toward heresy, while blacks appeared to Frank as the "true" Christians. In answer to the whether the "infidels" would ultimately be successful, he claimed that the Christian believers of the country would not let that happen. "As for destroying Christianity and razing the churches," he wrote, "stopping religious movements and throwing a monkey wrench into the Christian printing outfit, eradicating from the hearts of the people their thirst for God, we believers are not at all uneasy." Instead, Frank calmly predicted that "Christ will never fail."[36] But in an editorial in April 1926, Frank again raised the same arguments, so the threat still remained.[37] The claim by black writer Kelly Miller that he was an "avowed evolutionist," invoked Frank's scorn, and he quickly associated Miller with H. L. Mencken, "white publisher, and of course, Sinclare [sic] Lewis. What a crowd of agnostics, infidels, atheists!"[38] Frank had placed Kelly Miller outside the pale of true Christians.[39]

For Frank and for other black writers, theological modernism was a racial term, a means of making whites the "other," while emphasizing the theological soundness of African Americans. Blacks were the mainstream; whites were the outsiders. Frank had, as a member of what whites considered the "other," turned the argument back against them and "othered" the white "mainstream." In doing so, he engaged in the same racial labeling of religious beliefs that white fundamentalists had used when they called blacks religiously immature and in need of guidance. While both black Protestants and white fundamentalists could agree that modernism was their enemy, each believed the other was more susceptible to it.

Even as he linked modernism to race, Frank said certain white preachers were immune to the heresy. In "White Baptists," he predicted a big "explosion" in the "May [1926] meetings of white Baptists." "The *Union-Review*, of course," he wrote, is "fundamentalist. All colored Baptists are fundamentalists except a half-dozen imitators of Ingersoll, Darrow, Fosdick, and Dieffenback [sic], the so-called 'Intellectuals' of our race." This unequivocal statement of alliance with the fundamentalists meant that the *Union-Review*'s editor considered the vast majority of African American Baptists as allied with truth and that blacks who sided with modernists were misguided. But Frank did not tie truth in religious beliefs to one race. Instead, he cited the fundamentalists as "Stalwarts named Riley, Norris, Goodchild, Straton, Shields, Stealey, Porter, Ragland, Leavels, Massie [sic], Wilson, . . . Haldeman" and claimed that they, along with "thousands of others [were] determined and active against modernism, its infidelity, evolution, its rejection of the supernatural and over-emphasis on the natural." While he was at it, Frank took aim at E. Y. Mullins and his allies in the white Southern Baptist Convention, saying that neither their beliefs nor fear of a fight at the convention "should be allowed to hinder an out-going declaration as to what Baptists believe."[40] A few months later, Frank charged that "were the white Baptists, both south and north, better Christians, they would have less internal strife." Indeed, their infighting was leading them to ignore the plight of African Americans, as "neither convention is doing anything on a large scale for Colored Americans."[41] The next month, he noted that the Northern Baptist Convention, among its meeting results, had "nothing done for the Colored people."[42] And in 1929, he outlined a hierarchy of Protestant orthodoxy, with "Colored Baptists of the United States" at the top because they were the most "intensely biblical in their faith and practices," but "Southern White Baptists" came a close second, handicapped by an "offset to their orthodoxy," by which he most likely meant their racism. Following them were the "Northern White Baptists," who were more liberal in doctrinal beliefs."[43] In Frank's view, not all white Protestants were susceptible to modernism, but the monster of racism preyed upon those who were immune. Race and ecclesiology will be further explored in Chapter 5.

While the white conventions failed to meet Frank's expectations in assisting their brethren of color, he championed the orthodoxy of black Baptists. "The infection of false teachings afflicting white Baptist churches, schools, and homes," he claimed, "balks at the color line because Colored Baptists will have none of it. Colored Baptists are basically sound, and they are ever singing—'the old time religion is good enough for me.'" But white Baptists, he maintained, were "honey-combed with false teachings, anti-Scriptural doctrines." Black Baptists, he contended, were not party to such heresies—"Colored Baptists sin more from ignorance than from knowledge. They know nothing and care little for 'the new' in theology."[44] Here Frank was speaking both to his Baptist audience and to black sociologists, who, as Barbara Dianne Savage has demonstrated, were engaged in a lively debate about how much the "black church" could advance African Americans as a race. Both Savage and historian Curtis Evans argue that part of the debate included an essentialist discussion of how religious African Americans were.[45]

Union-Review editor J. H. Frank had set up a clear and, to him, convincing dichotomy between the forces of biblical inerrancy, on which side he placed the majority of African Americans, as well as the leaders of the fundamentalist movement, and the forces of modernism, in which camp he included black intellectuals like Kelly Miller and William Pickens, as well as the majority of white Americans. The publication of *Elmer Gantry* in 1927 brought further charges in a column entitled, "Among White People." According to Frank, Sinclair Lewis had written a book "in which he degrades preachers." This act of hostility against the church was akin to Bruce Barton's *The Man Nobody Knows* (1925). In that book, Frank argued, "Barton, like Lewis, has manufactured a lot of stuff, written unfair, unjust criticisms and made bold assertions against proven facts to the contrary."[46] But while Frank condemned fictional portrayals of religion, he further commended the efforts by fundamentalists and their allies to keep the faith. In an editorial about the Canadian Baptist Convention, he lauded T. T. Shields and the "faithful, loyal Baptists standing with him in leadership." Frank continued, likening the debate to the American Revolution, "there are times in the political progress of a government when actual revolution is in order, times when that is the last step in defense of liberty, the protection of life, and the conservation of property, not otherwise when the devil is leading entrenched foes of Christ and his revealed will and purpose."[47] Whether Frank believed that Shields could bring American religious exceptionalism to Canada or serve as a model for Shields's American fundamentalist brethren, he did not say, but clearly the struggle was of the utmost importance.

Frank's linkage of modernism to whites extended from Canada to the American South. Telling his readers of Southern Baptist publisher Clarence P. Stealey's efforts against modernists in the SBC, Frank relayed Stealey's announcement that he would "issue a southwide paper known as the Southern Baptist, subscriptions for which we understand are pouring in." This new publication would be welcome, Frank argued, because "the South needs a paper of that style and stamp—a paper fundamentalist to the core, to equal for the backward South the Watchman-Examiner, leader of the fundamentalist north, a truly great paper." He concluded that "Colored preachers should subscribe by the thousands."[48] As an addendum to the article, Frank relayed that "reports come to this office that the white Baptist war has split the ministers meeting in Chicago and a new organization of fundamentalist ministers has formed. In that, white Chicago Baptists are like their brothers of color. Colored Baptists divided because of short-sightedness, white because of ignorance (smile)." Again he condemned the schismatic tendency of fundamentalists, as he advised, "White Baptists ought to have remained in the old conference where they met those who teach false doctrines, an opportunity they would have to preach and teach the misled preachers the right way."[49] The problem continued, and he was reduced to wondering in a headline, "What is the Matter with White Baptists?" Frank contended that the years of infighting over doctrinal issues, combined with financial problems, caused the leaders of the denomination to "bird like, hide their heads in the sand, figuratively speaking, and pretend that there is nothing discouraging in the situation." The "situation" was the result of "all the unfortunate happenings of the last twenty years."[50] As late as 1929, he was still declaring the traditionalist position of black churches and referring to black secular intellectuals as "following the path marked by white infidels and atheists, named Fosdick, Darrow, Manchen [sic], Ingersol, 'modernists,' 'Liberalists,'" as well as labeling Fosdick individually as "Judas."[51] Indeed when the Laymen's Foreign Missionary Report was released in 1933, Frank joined the chorus of outraged traditionalists who feared that American missionaries were spreading liberal theology overseas at the expense of their denomination's financial support. Describing an address about the report by a "gentleman" who defended it, Frank railed, "this is modernism with horns on." He concluded that the "AVERAGE AUDIENCE WILL NOT NEED A COMPANY OF SOLOMONS TO 'DIVIDE' IT, BUT ONLY A FEW DAVIDS TO 'SLAY' IT."[52] Whether the entire denomination of National Baptist Convention, Unincorporated churches agreed with Frank is hard to tell, as the paper tended not to print letters to the editor, but Frank's longevity in the position and his vehemence in denouncing modernism as a white invention do indicate that there was a receptive audience for his views.

In contrast, the AME Zion Church's *Star of Zion* expressed more sympathy for the fundamentalist position than the modernist, and it linked modernism to whites, but it did so with far less gusto than did J. H. Frank and the *Union-Review*. A 1922 editorial, for instance, asked, "Is Civilization Sinking?" It cited a "recent remarkable statement" by H. G. Wells, who said that the "'vital, intricate mechanism of modern civilization [was] falling to pieces.'" According to the editor J. Harvey Anderson, Wells had "pessimism and not faith." Instead, the massive debts and movement of peoples across the war-ravaged countries of Europe was possibly "God's way of purging the world for His own. We think it is the white race Mr. Wells is fearing for. In so far as we know, God's world will go forward, and He always will have some people to run it on towards the perfect day, scientists and philosophers to the contrary irrespective."[53] If the tone of the editorial seems less strident than those of the *National Baptist Union-Review*, it reflects the sympathy the paper's editor and writers had to the fundamentalists but also their tendency to align more with black intellectuals. For men to become Methodist ministers, they had to train at a seminary and complete an approved course of study. While many Baptist ministers, both white and black, pursued advanced degrees, the overall composition of the Methodist ministry, again both black and white, was more highly educated than were their Baptist counterparts and exposed to a wider variety of intellectual perspectives. Thus the *Star of Zion* maintained leanings toward the fundamentalists while also publishing contributions from, among others, Kelly Miller, whom *Union-Review* editor Frank had pilloried.

One example of this attempt at balance was a small item in the *Star's* January 8, 1925, editorial page. Untitled, the piece noted the "rejection of Dr. Harry Emerson Fosdick from the pulpit of the First Presbyterian Church of New York City" and that that event had "renewed interest in 'The Modern Use of the Bible,' written by Dr. Fosdick." "While one may not agree with all of Dr. Fosdick's conclusions," the editorial continued, "and to some of them there may be risk in agreement, yet he writes with fascinating charm and convincement." For editor William H. Davenport, Fosdick was not a "white infidel," as he was to J. H. Frank, but he was, nonetheless, in error in portions of his theology. "The iconoclasm of some chapters will prove offensive to many of the orthodoxy," Davenport concluded.[54]

But by the 1930s, the *Star* was less interested in balance and compromise. Reprinting "Modernism's Fruits" from the *World Evangel* in 1930, the *Star of Zion* told its readers that "in proportion as the people have accepted the teaching of modernism, there has also been an increase in immorality and crime of all kinds."[55] Modernism in this case became a cause of lawlessness, with the paper associating the loosening of theological restrictions with the loosening of moral codes. In July 1930, editor Davenport blamed low attendance at churches in general on modernism. According to him, "the disposition of the church to surrender its principles and cater to a liberalism which is growing weary of its own liberalism . . . empties the pews of the Protestant Churches."[56] For Davenport, the rudderless direction of modernist theology failed to inspire the faithful because modernist theology itself was uninspired. In contrast, he argued a few months later, "'the old time religion' was good enough for our fathers and it did them nor their children any harm. They were not disturbed by the theories of atheistic and skeptical scholars." He added, "they were willing to be laughed at and ridiculed, but they had as their possession a sterling Christian character which shone resplendently in their communities."[57] The nostalgia for the past, with its fond images of full pews and upstanding citizens, may well have sustained Davenport during the early 1930s, although it was a nostalgia for what happened inside and not what happened outside the church's sanctuary.

Modernism could be blamed for more than just crime and empty churches. Protesting a report that a University of Kansas historian had debunked the story of John Smith and Pocahontas, Davenport asked where the line would be drawn. "In religion, these iconoclasts," he railed, "are called 'Higher Critics,' more recently, 'Modernists;' and one is called an old fogey if he doesn't believe the stories as written by the only persons who were in a position to know what they were talking about." Davenport held fast to the notion of divine inspiration of scripture and embraced the notion that the biblical authors were who they purported to be—eyewitnesses to revelation. Modernism had unleashed for him a flood of attacks on the veracity of witnesses, whether to the divine or to the mundane. "A thousand years from now," he concluded, "when electricity gets in its perfect work there will arise 'scholars' who will dispute that coal oil lamps were ever used, and that locomotives were ever propelled by steam. It will be mythical."[58]

Despite the turn against modernism in the early 1930s, the *Star of Zion* never damned modernism with the vitriol of the *Union-Review*'s J. H. Frank (although admittedly that would be difficult to equal). The paper instead sought to achieve some sort of moderation or compromise between the warring factions, and it associated modernism with white denominations rather than black ones.

But the propensity to oppose modernism vocally was not uniformly a Baptist phenomenon, as the National Baptist Convention, Incorporated's paper, the *National Baptist Voice*, illustrates. While the Baptist *Union-Review* proclaimed its general and enthusiastic support of the fundamentalist leaders and their efforts to preserve "that old time religion," the *Voice* had a much less enthusiastic response. It generally ignored developments in the fundamentalist/modernist battles, but when it did comment, it was more interested in calling for consensus and unity than promoting the doctrinal beliefs of one side or another. In 1925, J. G. Jordan reported that "the Northern Baptists are seemingly going to pieces over what Baptists stand for," while the Southern Baptists were debating how to describe the creation of humanity, whether to say simply that God created people or to clarify that evolution had no role. "Let us all pray," Jordan wrote, "that the right will triumph as our God goes marching on."[59] Here the debate was clearly one of white denominational manufacture, but Jordan did not necessarily condemn the more progressive forces in the debate. They were instead evidence of the need for reconciliation rather than condemnation.

Other contributors to the *Voice* also urged diplomacy. The Reverend Robert A. Ashworth's previously discussed article, "The Rift in the Baptist Lute," observed that the white fundamentalists in the Northern Baptist Convention displayed an aggressive nature and that their insistence upon combating the teaching of evolution had "aroused misgivings in many minds that the movement is hostile to modern learning and would place fetters upon free inquiry." For Ashworth, the issue for Baptists was a reconciliation of the "two influences [that had] been at work among Baptists very diverse in their nature and very difficult to harmonize":

> One has come from the Calvinistic tradition, with its strong emphasis upon theology and correctness of doctrine, and the other from the Anabaptists, who put their emphasis upon a Christian experience, and were the champions of freedom and conscience, the right of private interpretation, "the inward light," the separation of Church and State, and the application of the Gospel to the problems of society. Some of us have always leaned toward one ancestral inheritance and some to the other. The only way in which they can be reconciled and live together in contentment is through the application of that principle of toleration and reciprocal recognition of one another's points and liberty which Baptists in the past have thought to be in a special degree their characteristic.[60]

Ashworth argued that by ignoring the Baptists' heritage of using religion to ameliorate social problems and their tradition of freedom of conscience, the fundamentalists in the Northern Baptist Convention repudiated a portion of their past that they could not afford to ignore. While Ashworth did not condemn them outright, he certainly left the impression that the fundamentalists were making a mistake by appearing intolerant of divergent doctrine. Implicit in his argument is the assumption that Baptist polity allowed for such divergence and, indeed, even welcomed it. While J. H. Frank at the *Union-Review* would have driven the "infidels" out, Ashworth would have fought to keep them in the church community.

That Ashworth would have reservations about the fundamentalists is not surprising, given the evidence of more liberal Protestant thought in the pages of the *Voice*. In 1921, editor J. D. Crenshaw, after lamenting the rising crime statistics and the recent wave of lynchings, managed to express hope for the coming year. Referring to 1920, he wrote that "it was a year of great movements actuated by good and great minds for and in the interest of the betterment of human conditions, as well as it was a year of great unrest, turbulence, violence, lynching, atrocities, and wars. But, despite man's inhumanities to his brother man, the good of the earth are hoping for a greater reign this year of the gospel of the Fatherhood of God and the brotherhood of man."[61] In 1922, echoing this Social Gospel language, the *Voice* reprinted a R. F. Horton piece from the *Christian Work*, entitled, "The New Note in Christianity." Rather than praise the fundamentalists, Horton bemoaned the shift away from discussion of the Kingdom of God, which "dies away entirely in the Church." For Horton, "the Kingdom of God brings a new hope that, as we recover His conception of the Kingdom, the world may begin to change under the mighty influence which entered into it when Christ came." One of the messages of the Gospel, Horton insisted, was that Jesus "left upon the world the impression that it was a practical work to be done here on earth, and that practical work was to bring in the Kingdom of God here." "Thus," he continued, "the essential idea of the Kingdom of God in Christ's view was not a future paradise to be realized after death, but a paradise regained in this world, which had been ruined by the trail of the serpent over everything which God had made good—the reign of God on earth. That is the simplest rendering of the phrase 'the Kingdom of God'—the reign of God on earth—all human life, personal, family, civic, national, international, brought under the will of God."[62] Horton's interpretation of the Kingdom of God employs the emphasis that Social Gospel figures such as Walter Rauschenbusch would have advanced. This rhetoric was decidedly liberal, the language and eschatology against which fundamentalists were reacting. The *Voice*'s use of the reprint implied, if not endorsement of, at least acceptance of the more liberal form of theology that faded from public favor following the Great War and the consequent social upheavals.[63] Indeed, Ashworth's comment that white fundamentalists' "fierce attacks upon 'the social gospel' have not been reassuring" hints that he too was more sympathetic to progressive theology than to traditionalist.[64]

The National Baptist Convention, Incorporated's lenient attitude toward theological liberalism and attempts to bridge the divide between modernist and fundamentalism positions on issues are all the more intriguing in light of the close relationship its president, Lacey Kirk Williams, had in the 1920s with white fundamentalist and fellow Texas Baptist, J. Frank Norris. Norris's name made several appearances in the *Voice*, usually with comments of editorial approval. For example, in 1926, an article detailing a "missionary mass meeting" on foreign evangelization described a sermon Norris "(white)" had delivered to the group. Norris hit the highlights of evangelical homiletics: "(1) Christ died for us. (2) Christ was buried and rose again. (3) Our resurrection is assured. (4) He will return in victory and power." The "sermon," the *Voice* reported, "was a soul thriller—a masterpiece."[65] Given the denomination's propensity for more liberal theological positions and given Norris's stance as a strident fundamentalist, his praise in the pages of the *Voice* hints at a more nuanced understanding of how theological liberalism and conservatism could coexist in a single organization. Williams and Norris were either able to bury the theological hatchet in their dealings with each other, or Norris was unaware of the public stands taken in the *National Baptist Voice*. Obviously Williams was not aware of Norris's cruelty to his black workers. A third possibility may be that Williams was theologically closer to Norris than the *Voice*'s editor was. Williams was not president at the time of the NBC split, but he did rise quickly through the ranks of the NBC Incorporated leadership in the mid-1920s.[66] Indeed, in his address to the 1925 Annual Session of the National Baptist Convention, Incorporated, Williams included a lengthy defense of fundamentalism as he understood it, including its acceptance of "the teachings of the scripture on the Virgin Birth, the Deity of Jesus, his vicarious sufferings, and his bodily resurrection, his ascension and Second Coming." Williams noted that "Fundamentalists, it seems, keep very good company."[67] That same year, the Unincorporated Baptists invited Norris to speak at their Forty-third Annual Session, held conveniently in Fort Worth, Norris's hometown. According to the minutes, Norris "spoke on 'Fundamentalism' and insisted on gospel ministers to genuineness of the Bible. Offering of $313.25 was taken."[68] Both the Unincorporated Baptists' and Williams's relationship with Norris, whose racial views towards African Americans were paternalistic and emasculating, show that Baptists—both black and white—defy easy characterization and categorization. Indeed, when Norris shot and killed a man, D. E. Chipps, in a dispute over Norris's political attacks on the Roman Catholic mayor of Fort Worth, the *Voice* took a cautious tone, arguing the right of any minister to defend himself, voicing confidence that the criminal justice system would determine whether there was just cause in the act, and praising Norris for being the "most outstanding preacher of the Fundamentalist group and the bitterest anti-Romanist in the American pulpit." That superlative, however, was given without aligning the *Voice* with the Norris faction; instead, it merely observed his status among his peers.[69]

Like the *Voice* and unlike its fellow black Methodist paper, the AME Church's *Christian Recorder* leaned away from full embrace of fundamentalism. Rather than side decisively with either the fundamentalists or the modernists, the *Recorder* preferred to call upon the warring parties to lay down their weapons and seek reconciliation. But, interestingly enough, some of the discussion that prompted the *Recorder* to call for a truce seemed to originate within the AME Church itself. How the debate over fundamentalism influenced discussions of white denominations like Methodists has not yet received adequate investigation. The AME Church's situation hints that no Protestant body was entirely immune from the controversy.

In an open letter to the Right Reverend A. L. Gaines, bishop of the Fourth Episcopal District of the AME Church, a trio of writers—George W. Slater Jr., E. H. McDaniels, and P. H. Jackson—quoted another letter, written by a "member of the Episcopal Committee," that described a divided and contentious church. The unnamed Episcopal Committee writer was quoted as saying, "'that the restive spirit which dominates world affairs is also gripping the church." The writer did not name the dispute, but did aver that "'it is far from a healthy sign when people are silent or fail to offer their protestation against evils (real or imaginary) that seem to threaten the very foundations of their most sacred of all institutions, the Church of God.'" Slater, McDaniels, and Jackson, however, were a bit more sanguine in their forecast for the church. "Elijah saw the altars of God torn down and forsaken," they noted, "but even this prophet of God failed to reckon with the facts that there were thousands who had not bowed to Baal. So in the African Methodist Episcopal Church the signs of real virtue are very manifest." Instead of resorting to personal accusations, the writers cautioned that "the spirit of mere vituperative condemnation cannot take the place of intelligent loving efforts for restoration and advancement. Paul's injunction will be found most potent, 'Brethren, if a man be overtaken by fault, ye that are spiritual restore such a one in the spirit of meekness.'" Rather than devoting efforts to gathering damning evidence against a wayward preacher, the writers counseled a prayerful intervention with the unnamed individual, urging that the church "labor to have him reconciled and restored rather than condemned and destroyed."[70] At least among Slater, McDaniels, and Jackson, there was no appetite for accusations and punishment in doctrinal disputes. Instead, they worked to move the AME Church to moderation.

This desire for reconciliation over accusation was also reflected in the Reverend I. W. L. Roundtree's 1925 query, "Do We Need a Reformation in the A.M.E. Church? If So, to What Extent?" Roundtree responded to a call from Bishop W. H. Heard that the AME Church needed a "reformation." In considering such an event, Roundtree first outlined the basic tenets of AME Christianity: "repentance, faith, and holiness . . . justification, adoption and sanctification and the entire system of Biblical truth and doctrines, accepted by the church from its beginning and reaffirmed in her first delegated General Conference in 1816." He argued that any "reformation" would not rearrange or reform but would instead be "a revolution so destructive that it would put the African Methodist Episcopal connection out of Christendom." Rather Roundtree urged an increase in standards for the ministry "so that our preaching may be more exegetical and doctrinal."[71] He did not advocate an outright housecleaning of the AME's theological affairs, but he was amenable to a program that would ensure better and more effective preaching. His willingness to do so suggests that he may well have considered AME preaching to be less "doctrinal" than his expectations. But Roundtree was unwilling to commit entirely to the fundamentalist standards.

Adding to the AME chorus calling for middle ground, the "Committee on State of the Country" reported in the *Recorder* on the fundamentalist-modernist debate and its wide-ranging topics. Among these, the committee listed the "immaculate conception, the virgin birth and other fundamentals truths as taught in Holy Scriptures." While the committee likely did not mean to include the Roman Catholic dogma of Immaculate Conception (that Mary was conceived without the taint of original sin), it did recognize that the overall dispute meant that "Science and the Bible have been arrayed against each other in deadly conflict." But the committee refused to accept the fundamentalist dichotomy of science versus religion. Instead, it called for "freedom of thought," while also maintaining "our most vehement opposition to the teaching of our rising youth at the formative period of their lives those dangerous theories and heresies which would wreck their barks on the shoals of doubt and unbelief."[72] The solution for these men was not to end all scientific instruction but instead to limit it to more advanced students, students who had presumably been inculcated in the faith and would know how to reconcile their religious teachings with those of evolutionary science. The committee did not, however, offer a specific plan on how to accomplish that goal.

In addition to seeking a middle ground between the fundamentalists and the modernists, the contributors to the *A.M.E. Christian Recorder* occasionally displayed opinions that both the fundamentalists and modernists would likely characterize as more liberal than conservative. In November 1924, Richard R. Wright Jr. discussing the topic of "Neighborliness," admonished his readers that "while the theologians may fuss over the Virgin Birth, and other things, God wants a sincere soul, a loving neighbor—that's all."[73] He repeated his impatience with theological hairsplitting the next month, declaring that "we all admit that we do not understand how Jesus raised Lazarus . . . but the chief thing for us is to see the lengths to which Jesus would go for a friend. He has said that he would give his life for his friend. Here he brings back to the bosom of his family the dead brother and friend."[74] Had the fundamentalists been reading the pages of the *A.M.E.*

Christian Recorder and seen this article, they would have added it their proof that modernism threatened African American faith. Here was an African American preacher and editor downplaying the necessity of believing in a literal reading of an account of a miracle and instead interpreting it as a lesson in self-sacrifice. Wright's educational background was similar to that of W. E. B. DuBois and to that of more liberal preachers. He studied under Shailer Mathews at the University of Chicago—a hotbed of theological liberalism—and received his doctorate in sociology at the University of Pennsylvania, working on a similar topic as DuBois had there.[75] Now editor of a denominational paper, Wright had a public platform for his views.

Richard Wright and the *Christian Recorder* were not alone in espousing modernist thought. Reflecting the broad reading interest that had introduced them to white fundamentalism, black Baptists and Methodists occasionally used terms and ideas that were decidedly un-fundamentalist. These instances would have made white fundamentalists howl with rage over what they would have seen as theological liberalism's hold over impressionable black minds. More reasonable explanations include, however, the idea that these writers were using a variety of methods at their disposal and, once again, gathering useful material from disparate sources and that the theology of modernism did have a certain appeal to African American Protestants. All of the papers in this study had some modernist or liberal theological terms in their pages, and these terms coexisted in papers that claimed to oppose modernism at every turn. Moreover, Social Gospel terms also appeared from time to time in various publications. This rhetoric was not wholesale endorsement of the Social Gospel, but it does indicate that while black Baptists and Methodists saw modernism as an enemy of true Christianity, they did not mind some of its antecedent's terminology and goals. This topic will be discussed further in Chapter 5, as black Protestants used their understanding of Christianity to call into question the racist practices of their white brethren, but phrases like "Fatherhood of God" and "Brotherhood of Man," divorced from their racial arguments, did appear in the denominational literature, indicating the pervasiveness of the terms in American Protestant discourse.

Both modernist and Social Gospel terms appeared, for example, in the *National Baptist Union-Review,* the paper edited by anti-modernist J. H. Frank. In 1926, he cautioned his readers to "Remember: The Bible was NOT written to be authority in history, in science, in art, in philosophy—but to teach life and how to live." While this statement was sweeping in its apparent modernism, Frank qualified it by adding, "I do not mean to tell you that the Bible is false when dealing with history, etc, for it is not false but true, true to fact and true to the truth founded upon the facts."

He noted that "Paul tells us 'all Scripture inspired of God is profitable for doctrine, reproof in righteousness.'"[76] Frank's refusal to categorize the Bible as the ultimate historical document ran counter to fundamentalist understanding of the text. By the mid-1920s, white fundamentalists had clearly aligned themselves with the twin ideas that the Bible was both a historic and scientific document, but Frank was not willing to join them. Nor was he willing to say that the Bible had no historical value, but his explanation bordered on the very modernism he so often assailed. Frank also produced two editorials on the notion of the Fatherhood of God and the Brotherhood of Man—subjects that were dear to an antecedent of modernism, the Social Gospel. Both editorials were, however, more of a call to Christ than an expectation that humans could help implement the Kingdom of God on earth.[77] Frank clearly saw no logical inconsistency in opposing modernism and arguing that the Bible could not serve as the sole source of knowledge on ancient history.

Even though it had distanced itself somewhat from modernism, the AME Zion's *Star of Zion* could find something good to say about white modernists. In 1928, the paper labeled Yale undergraduates "fortunate in hearing Dr. Harry Emerson Fosdick discuss the 'Soul, the Human Test.'" The *Star* thought so because Fosdick decried a "rapid rise in agnostics, not atheists, denying God, but agnostics, often reverently saying that they cannot make up their minds." Fosdick also condemned materialism in the address.[78] Two years later, the paper called readers' attention to Fosdick's efforts to ban latecomers from his church sermons, noting "he does not wish to preach to people who come straggling in just before the sermon."[79] White fundamentalists would never have given Fosdick a fair hearing after his theological dispute with J. Gresham Machen in 1922, but black Protestants were more open to the modernist leader when they could find common ground with him. And Fosdick was not the only beneficiary of the *Star*'s praise for white liberals. The Reverends (and brothers) Charles Whitney Gilkey and James Gordon Gilkey, pastors of the Park Baptist Church in Chicago and South Congregational Church in Springfield, Massachusetts, respectively, won praise from the paper for their books and sermons.[80] The *Star* also ran an article by the Reverend D. E. Thompson arguing that the "extension of the Kingdom of God in the world" depended on "men" whose love for god came from "duty" and not "fear." Thompson's use of the Social Gospel notion of the Kingdom of God on earth, and his article, called for a clergy engaged with the culture surrounding it, not isolated from it.[81] His viewpoint was one that combined education and social action, themes common to the liberal strands in American religious thought.

Of all four papers, the *National Baptist Voice* was the most comfortable with both Social Gospel terms and modernist theology. R. C. Barbour, editor of the paper in 1934, called his brethren to help in "building up the kingdom of God on earth," although he likened the effort to reviving the "lost vitality of first Century Christianity." Barbour harnessed the notions of progress and tradition to call for a better world.[82] That same year, he argued explicitly against discarding the Social Gospel and gave voice to that movement's emphasis on interrelatedness. "Everyone is integrated in the social oneness," he wrote, "to which he can no more be indifferent to the leaf to the tree that bears it."[83] That fondness for the Social Gospel's ideas extended to modernist Fosdick as well. Barbour wrote that "no other preacher and pastor in America has been misunderstood as much as Dr. Fosdick." He added, "if there is a greater American preacher than Dr. Fosdick, we would like to know his name."[84] Fosdick's image had certainly been rehabilitated in the intervening years between his 1922 feud with Machen and the Depression years of the early 1930s. But the *Voice* had always been more comfortable with progressive theology.

Absent from the discussions of modernism was any writer's or paper's self-identification as "modernist," although the next chapter will demonstrate that writers and papers sometimes did call themselves "fundamentalist." That these periodicals and authors did not embrace the term modernism indicates both their theological and racial distance from the term. Modernism was white, modernism was a threat, but, at the same time, modernism was present even if not always acknowledged in black Protestant denominations. In fact, modernist notions of religion adapting to culture would prove very alluring for African American Methodists and Baptists when they indicted white churches for their racism.

Fundamentalists and fundamentalism, as well as modernists and modernism, were well known to readers of African American publications. Like many African Americans in the early twentieth century, the white fundamentalists had southern roots and were frequent speakers in the South. More importantly, however, they were waging a battle for the direction of Protestant Christianity. This battle mattered to African American Protestants almost more than it mattered to white Protestants for two reasons— race and religion. Because blacks were so often the victims of a racially oppressive system, they needed to know where they stood in white eyes at every moment. Moreover, because black Baptists and Methodists were heirs to the evangelical traditions of the nineteenth century, they tended to see the fundamentalist/modernist controversy in the same way that white fundamentalists did—as a battle for the future of religion. In their investigation of white evangelical thought, African American denominational papers made cogent observations, came to differing conclusions, and espoused many tenets of fundamentalist theology in their own beliefs, all while proclaiming themselves as the correct arbiters of Christianity.

3
"We Need No New Doctrine for This New Day"

African Americans Adapt Fundamentalism

W. A. Taylor, the pastor of the Florida Avenue Baptist Church in Washington, DC, shared his dilemma with his fellow National Baptist Convention, Incorporated members. In a 1935 article rhetorically entitled, "Is There a Need for a Restatement of Baptist Doctrine and Polity," he captured the problem by posing two answers to the title's implied question and noting that "either horn of which may get us into trouble." "If we answer yes," he explained, "we fly into the faces of those orthodox fundamentalists, who stand guard over the traditions of the church and dare to jealously defend the 'doctrines once for all delivered to the saints' and to see that no one word used by the pioneers of the church in that original document shall be changed." But, if the answer were no, he continued, the response would "bring upon us the condemnation and censure of modern scholarship, reactionaries, and progressives, and be styled as back numbers, behind the times and out of line with the march and progress of modern religious thoughts and recent Biblical interpretation." Taylor sought a middle ground, using the US Constitution as his model, and argued that "the doctrines of our church are sufficiently flexible and elastic enough, if properly understood and properly stated, to touch every phase of human welfare."[1] Well into the 1930s, Taylor, like many other black (and white) ministers, worked to reconcile what he saw as the conflicting theologies of fundamentalists and modernists with the goal of making them useful for his pastoral work.

Although African American ministers were excluded from full fellowship with their white brethren in the 1920s and 1930s, they spent a great deal of time writing about many of the same topics that concerned the fundamentalists as they sought to respond to the gauntlet the fundamentalist movement had thrown. Editorials and articles decrying the changes in biblical interpretation, intellectualism, and social customs were a common staple in the pages of the *National Baptist Union-Review*, the *Star of Zion*, the *Christian Recorder*, and, to a lesser extent, the *National Baptist Voice*. Overwhelmingly, editors, authors, and readers denounced the growing tide of modernism while at the same time extolling that "old time religion." Even those denominational papers that tended to view the white fundamentalist movement with less sympathy, such as the *National Baptist Voice*, worried that modernism had gone too far.

As the black Baptists and Methodists labeled modernism a white phenomenon, they wrestled with other tenets of the fundamentalist challenge. Historians have debated how to define fundamentalism, and, indeed, when examined too closely, any list of doctrines that purports to define fully the term usually falls short.[2] To say that fundamentalists believed such ideas as the Virgin Birth or the divine inspiration and inerrancy of the Bible is to be too imprecise. Large numbers of evangelical Protestants who would never have called themselves fundamentalists subscribed to those notions. Indeed, the idea that the church is the community of believers only has deep roots in Christianity, both Protestant and Catholic. When one tries to measure how sympathetic African American denominational papers were to fundamentalism, one quickly realizes the shortcomings of the term fundamentalism. For the purposes of this study, it will mean an anti-modern evangelical movement that stressed notions such as biblical inerrancy, the Virgin Birth and deity of Christ, the need for holy living, and an emphasis on the literal return of Jesus. Black Methodists and Baptists tended not to call themselves fundamentalist, even though they agreed with white fundamentalists on many topics. And in the 1920s and 1930s, as the debates in white seminaries and denominations raged, African Americans used their denominational publications to underscore their adherence to what they understood as traditional evangelical Christianity, even as they declined to self-identify as fundamentalists. Instead, black Baptist and Methodist writers used their understanding of evangelical Christianity to delineate an understanding of belief that would embrace traditionalist notions without siding definitively with either white modernists or white fundamentalists.

In this respect, the African American Baptists and Methodists were re-molding and reshaping what fundamentalist movements offered them: a chance to declare their allegiance to traditional evangelical Christianity as they understood it and to use that same Christianity to chart a course for their members to navigate the treacherous seas of modernity and post–World War I American society. Their attachment to the basic tenets of evangelicalism placed them squarely in the traditionalist camp. This "traditionalism" included a heavy emphasis on reading the Gospels and seeking a conversion experience that would produce life-altering behavior. Its anti-modernism was an interpretation of the biblical directive to "live in the world but not of the world." Outright endorsement of the "fundamentals," as expressed by white fundamentalist leaders, was rare but did occur. More common was the discussion of "old time religion" or "conservative religion," both of which entailed hewing to the traditional evangelical notions of the Virgin Birth, the inerrancy of the Bible, and the need to evangelize a fallen world. They saw no need to be progressive in their theological outlook. As will become apparent in Chapter 5, they argued that Christianity already had what it needed to change the world—the world of segregation and hate. When people had the correct understanding of Christianity, the political and social world would change. In this respect, black Baptist and Methodist writers more closely resembled Social Gospelers, whose abiding faith that they could change the world was frustrated by the harsh realities of American society.

Although they espoused a theological traditionalism that accorded well with what many white fundamentalists believed, black denominational papers shied away from outright acceptance of all fundamentalist tenets. Among their reservations was premillennialism, the reading of biblical apocalyptic texts as a guide to an imminent cosmological war between the forces of good and evil and the second coming of Christ. As historian Timothy Weber has noted, the dispensational premillennialist program was a post–Civil War development in Protestant Christianity, begun by John Nelson Darby and spread through books, pamphlets, and preachers.[3] Indeed, not all white fundamentalists aligned themselves with the movement, but for many it was key both to their view of cultural developments and to their understanding that the inerrant Bible provided them with an eschatological forecast. For non-Pentecostal African American Protestants, this reading was relatively uncommon. It did speak to a few, but the majority of the writers in Baptist and Methodist denominations either rejected the focus on biblical prophecies outright or were silent on it. They did use apocalyptic imagery, but not always to predict the future. Like the white southerners in historian William R. Glass's research, black Protestants resisted being caught up in a tide of innovative Bible reading.[4] Unlike Glass's whites, their resistance stemmed as much from their understanding of the Bible as more straightforward in its message as from their place as a marginalized and segregated group. African American Methodists and Baptists, as self-appointed arbiters of theological orthodoxy in the black community, could not afford to appear to be reading their Bibles incorrectly.

Moreover, just as they had differed in their views of white fundamentalism, the denominational papers varied in their expressions of support for traditional evangelical theology. Traditionalist voices appeared more frequently in the National Baptist Convention, Unincorporated's *National Baptist Union-Review* and the AME Zion's *Star of Zion*. These two denominational papers accounted for most of the concern over progressive religious ideas, again lending tantalizing evidence but not proof of a theological divide between the two large Baptist denominations (National Baptist Convention, Unincorporated and the National Baptist Convention USA) and two of the black Methodist denominations (AME and AME Zion). None of the four papers, however, nor their attendant annual meeting minutes, was decidedly progressive, although the National Baptist Convention, U.S.A.'s *National Baptist Voice* did entertain more progressive language and ideas than the publications of the other three bodies. Suffice it to say that the overwhelming majority of black Protestant voices lent their support to religious traditionalism, and two denominations were more vocal than the others.

A part of that religious traditionalism was a healthy skepticism of evolutionary theory. Black Methodists and Baptists engaged in a lengthy debate over Charles Darwin's theory of evolution, its relationship to creation accounts in the Bible, and its effects on religion in general. In this respect, black Protestants were adding their voices to a raging battle that has both rightly and wrongly been tied to white fundamentalists. Evolution was indeed a considerable topic of discussion in *The Fundamentals*—historian Ronald L. Numbers has estimated that one-fifth of the essays dealt with evolution—but it was not the fundamentalists' cause célèbre, even if it was with that brush that they were tarred by white secular media.[5] For writers and editors of black denominational papers, though, evolution was linked to modernism, and modernism could not be tolerated.

Throughout their reflection on their denominations' doctrinal positions, these writers were not willing to concur with the fundamentalist proposition that they had to select one side or the other. Instead, black Baptist and Methodist authors sought an alternative way, one that would lead them further in their quest for theological independence and would embrace that which they knew to be the traditional positions of evangelical Christianity (biblicism, revivalism, adherence to the tenets of the Virgin Birth and the atonement, for example) without forcing them to cast their lot with the fundamentalists. They would not side with modernism, but they could not live with fundamentalism either.

The *National Baptist Union-Review*, which had led the charge against white modernism, made sure to remind its readers of its evangelical orthodoxy, often using fundamentalist-leaning terms and ideas. Editor Jonathan H. Frank ridiculed the "liberal, convictionless type of Baptists," accusing them of being willing to welcome "any ism that comes down the road; they see no difference between Calvinism and Arminianism . . . they not only swallow any old teaching that irreligious cranks bring down the road, but become the willing tool of others to the destruction of the interests of their own denomination." These Baptists, he contended, were a "wishy-washy, milk-and-cider, flim-flammy (whatever that may mean) type of Baptists without whom any church will be better off."[6] Frank's use of "any ism" calls to mind the original *Fundamentals*, which labeled a section "ISMS." and argued against them. Included in this section of the treatises that gave rise to the fundamentalist movement are Mormonism, "Eddyism" (Christian Science), and Spiritualism.[7] Indeed, in response to a letter from a reader, Frank argued that Christian Scientists and their founder, Mary Baker Eddy, had corrupted the message of Christianity and used their new invention for monetary profit. "Mrs. Eddy's God," he explained, "is not Jehovah of the Bible. Neither does Mrs. Eddy rank Jesus in his true position. Mrs. Eddy knows nothing of the Holy Ghost, and her teaching of sin, sicknesses, and the realities are—we are about to say—laughable."[8] That Frank wrote against Christian Science and that he had used the term "ism" are not proofs that he had read *The Fundamentals*, but they do speak to his sympathy with the underlying evangelical Christianity that informed the fundamentalist movement. Like white fundamentalists, he was also wary of the Pentecostal movement. In an observation of a recent trip to Chicago, Frank noted that "I have seen more cults, sects and denominations in this city." Among them he listed "the 'Church of the New Jerusalem,' the 'Gateway to Holiness,' the 'Holy Ghost Band,' the 'Church of Strange Tongues,' the 'Holy Rollers,' the 'Do Rights,' 'Christian Science,' 'Feet Washers,' and a dozen more," and lamented that some of them had managed to convert blacks. "Ignorance is the mother of much of the devotion one witnesses in Chicago," he sighed.[9] Frank did not, however, make Pentecostals a regular target of his attacks, perhaps because he was aware of the new movement's growing appeal among African Americans.

Like fundamentalists and their evangelical predecessors, the *Union-Review* stood on the side of the divine inspiration of the Bible and its use as the sole source of knowledge and understanding of the divine. "Yes, we believe the very words of the Bible, as originally spoke or recorded, are the result of inspiration," a 1928 editorial began. After assuring readers that the "Holy Spirit so revealed himself to the minds of the writers," Frank pressed the point further. "Not only were the writers inspired," he argued, "but the words they spoke were God inbreathed, inspired words." As proof Frank offered the text itself: "Hundreds of times we read in the Bible, the 'God said,' 'the Lord spake,' 'Thus saith the Lord,' and Jesus said heaven and earth will pass before his word shall fail. In the last book we read of a warning to any man who dares to add to the things written in the book."[10] A few years later, the *Union-Review* proudly declared on the front page that "our Baptist churches are always proud of saying that our churches are principally built on the Bible, the Word of God."[11] Frank would not stand for biblical criticism of the German or liberal variety. Against the movements that would read the Bible as a product of the society and times it was written, he sided squarely with the traditionalist camp and defended the divine inspiration of the text.

That traditionalist view could also be called "conservative," at least according to Frank. He announced to readers the upcoming 1929 meeting of the National Baptist Convention, Unincorporated in Norfolk, and described the delegates as "going to Norfolk, steeped in the fundamentals of our Baptist genius touching both polity and government and loyalty to the doctrines taught in the New Testament." Those fundamentals were not necessarily what white fundamentalists embraced; rather, they embodied "conservative religion." Frank continued, "we are Baptists of the year A.D. 1929—in doctrines so conservative that we hold not one new teaching, abandon not one essential, yet so new that we aim to welcome everybody into our spirit fellowship of good will and prosperity."[12] His position in 1929 was similar to his position in 1927, when he told his audience that "Colored Baptists . . . know nothing and care little for 'the new' in theology."[13]

Frank's rejection of the "new" in theology can be read simply as a rejection of modernism, but his cautionary words against applying biblical prophecies to current events make his definition of "new" that much more complicated. Clearly, the liberal Protestantism espoused by men like Harry Emerson Fosdick was a new development in the history of Christianity. But so too was John Nelson Darby's dispensational premillennialism. While Frank did not name the type of biblical prophecies he opposed, he did disparage the practice in general. Writing during the First World War, he warned his fellow Baptists not to read apocalyptic ideals into the world events. "Union-Review readers," he noted, "should not be carried off their feet by modern prophets who are predicting things of which in the very nature of the case they have no certain knowledge." Borrowing biblical language itself, he added, "Beware of the dealer in Bible prophecies, 'of that time knoweth no man,' said Jesus." Instead, Frank called for a renewed emphasis on evangelism.[14] In another editorial, he specifically addressed the biblical books of Daniel and Revelation, noting that his readers should not "be too dogmatic, too assertive in their interpretation of the book of Daniel and the Revelation." His complaint was not that these books had prophecies in them—"future world history may be there," he conceded—but he cautioned against reading too much into current events. "Beware of the teachers," he reminded his audience, "who see plainly the divine course of events illustrated by the present war outlined in those books." Rather, "we think there are more cryptic exhortations tending to encourage the people burdened and tired than there are references to the Eternal Plan of the Ages." Not only did Frank use a traditional understanding of these biblical texts, he attacked "the modern prophets who juggle with figures, words, and phrases to make them teach what they were not apparently written to reveal."[15] He rejected some type of prophetic reading of world events, likely premillennialism, as too new, too innovative. His understanding of "conservative," of traditional evangelical ideas, was an understanding that predated all developments of the late nineteenth and early twentieth centuries, as well as those previous (or even ancient) attempts to claim complete understanding of God's ultimate plans.

The National Baptist Convention, Unincorporated's paper was not the only periodical to stress adherence to traditional evangelical ideals. The African Methodist Episcopal Zion Church's publications, the weekly *Star of Zion* and the *A.M.E. Zion Quarterly*, also signaled their allegiance to traditional evangelical views. The AME Zion church, like its sister denomination, the AME church, was founded in the early nineteenth century by free blacks who wanted autonomy from white Methodists. While the AME's publication, the *Christian Recorder*, did occasionally discuss traditional evangelical tenets, it did not spend as much time on them as did the *Star of Zion*. And while neither denomination's publications managed the emotion that Jonathan Frank had given to his anti-modernism diatribes, both placed themselves squarely in alignment with Frank's perception of traditional evangelicalism.

The topics black Methodists addressed ranged from the notion of truth to the divine inspiration of the Bible to the Virgin Birth. On each topic, they sided with evangelicalism as they had long known it. From time to time, the term "fundamentals" did appear in AME and AME Zion publications. But it tended to refer to the basic building blocks of evangelical tradition, rather than a new movement to turn back the clock on the religious landscape. In an editorial on the topic of "truth," *Star of Zion* editor W. H. Davenport declared firmly that "truth is not broad and liberal—it is narrow. It will not admit of modification, amendment, or emendation. It is firm. It will not accommodate itself to popular applause, to whim or passing fancy. It is stern, irrevocable, changeless." The subtext of Davenport's argument was that truth, or biblical interpretation, was not something open to change or debate. Indeed, he said, "truth runs on a narrow gauge and whistles, clear the way. . . . And 'If the truth (Son) therefore shall make you free, ye shall be free indeed."[16] The editor of the *A.M.E. Christian Recorder*, Richard Wright Jr., who had trained at the liberal University of Chicago, could also espouse traditionalist interpretations. He charged that "falsehood in religion stalked abroad in Jesus' day as it does today. But as man approaches unto Truth he is freed. Intellectual Falsehood has had its sway." He rallied his readers to "fight under truth's banner, and that alone."[17] The same year, the *Recorder* also published the "Report of the Committee on the State of the Country," delivered at the AME's 1925 Annual Conference in Danville, Kentucky. The Conference Report put itself squarely in the camp of divine biblical inspiration. "As for us," it declared, "we accept the Bible as the inspired word of God, written by men of different stations and in different periods, with its every page bristling with vital and eternal truths. Teeming as it does with history, law, prophecy, biography, poetry, and philosophy,—pointing the way to a life of endless bliss beyond the grave, we accept it as the greatest book the world has ever known, and as one which will survive 'the war of elements, the wreck of the matter, and the crash of worlds.'"[18] For the *Star* and for its parent denomination, the notion of divine inspiration of the Bible was crucial to Christianity. A complement to that divine inspiration was the idea that the Bible was inerrant and eternal.

When they did label themselves as fundamentalist or list "fundamental" tenets for Protestant Christian faith, African American denominational newspapers defined the terms very much like their white fundamentalist counterparts. Elder E. George Biddle, writing on "The Fundamentals" for the *Star of Zion* in 1921, listed them as "'The Inspiration of the Scriptures,' 'The Virgin Birth,' 'The Vicarious Sacrifice of Christ,' 'The Divinity of Christ.'" "No one," he declared, "can be a Bible Christian or a Zion Methodist unless they hold to these 'Fundamentals.'"[19] In 1930, Biddle again used the term "fundamentals" when discussing the divine inspiration of the Bible. "No one ever has found," he argued, "any contradictions in the Bible in reference to the great fundamentals of our Holy Religion."[20] In 1931, Biddle numbered the Virgin Birth among his "Mysteries of the Kingdom," and said it "baffles the scientists, disconcerts the logician, and frightens the weak-kneed theologians so much that they are willing to deny 'The Virgin Birth,' though angels from heaven and God Himself bear witness to the fact."[21] Biddle was still emphasizing the need for belief in the Virgin Birth as late as 1937 (he died in 1940), calling it "as firmly established as is the being of God."[22]

Biddle was not the only AME Zion minister calling for support for the fundamentals. His colleague, Dr. E. D. W. Jones, announced that in the upcoming 1926 AME Zion general conference, he would "call and vigorously call for a restatement of our articles of religion, our Zion Methodist doctrine, our fundamentals." He continued, "I fear that in our attempts to accommodate ourselves to the whims of a Christless society and to meet the demands of a liberal rising generation that we are forgetting that we are Methodists." Jones despaired that "our old hymns are being substituted by transpositions of catchy secular ditties." He concluded, stating, "we need no new doctrine for this new day; for the old doctrine meets the requirements for all days and can stand all clash of arms and changes of revolutions."[23] Likewise, Zion Methodist Richard Alexander Carroll of Spartanburg, South Carolina, told *Star* readers that "the safety of the Church is predicated upon the fundamentals of the Christian principles instilled in the fathers, enough to have us reflect it into the generations which are to follow." Setting the argument as a series of rhetorical questions, Carroll asked, "Is the Church safe when it will tell the unsaved, 'I was told not to do certain things, but my parents were fogey and did not know, and besides, this is another day?'" He answered that question with the assertion that "it was as much as our parents could do to save us with restraint, and certainly we cannot save ourselves without it; and if the young people are not saved, the Church cannot be." His next question, "Is the Church safe when the world has crept into her pales, and silently stolen the hearts of the worshippers [and] dethroned righteousness," he followed not with an answer but with another question, "Is the Church safe without Christianity which is the sole purpose of the Church in the world?" His questions and the gist of his argument all led to the obvious conclusion that Carroll, like many of his AME Zion brethren, saw the world the way white fundamentalists did: as an anti-church, modern terror, lurking in the shadows and appearing in the open to steer the people away from salvation.

But largely, African American religious papers (and their governing denominations) tended to avoid including themselves in the formal category of fundamentalist. In his Quadrennial Address of the Bishops, AME Zion bishop G. C. Clement told his audience that the "Fundamentalists and Modernists have contended in bitter strife to the confusion of the unchurched and to the amusement of the believing, and to the disruption and retardation of the Kingdom." "Happily," he contended, "our Communion has felt little of this eruption . . . the Bible remains the only standard of faith and doctrine required from membership in our fold and much latitude is allowed in its interpretation."[24] Implicit here was the conclusion that, once again, black denominations were safe from the modernist problem and remained instead stalwart defenders of the faith.

For these writers, the best way to lead their communities was to stay on the narrow path of truth, as they understood it. If black preachers ventured away from the traditional, into modernism for instance, they risked both individual damnation and community censure by whites. Fundamentalism was not necessary in their congregations because they were already traditionalists. They understood the message of the Gospels—the divine, revealed word, the required individual conversion experience, and the rejection of all worldly interests. In their eyes, white fundamentalists were right to combat the modernist heresy, but the fundamentalists' efforts had led them to stray from the old-time religion, not preserve it. The white fundamentalists had veered beyond the traditional lines of evangelicalism and into new, uncharted, and at times theologically suspect territory. Fundamentalist interest in dispensational premillennialism, for example, appeared too innovative and untested.

While African American Protestants lined up with white fundamentalists on many common tenets, they did not voice dispensationalist notions with nearly the same frequency. In fact, these Baptist and Methodist writers, with a few notable exceptions, tended to read the eschatological texts of the Bible with both an interpretation that relied on past explanations of apocalyptic passages and a reluctance to embrace John Nelson Darby's complex and often innovative system of reading for clues about the end of time. In this way, they closely resembled the reluctance evinced by white southern Protestants who heard about dispensational premillennialism from itinerant fundamentalist preachers in the 1920s and 1930s. Both groups—white southerners and black Protestants in general—shared a common heritage, one that the white Protestants calling themselves fundamentalists were also privy to. That heritage demanded a common sense, straightforward understanding of biblical texts, not necessarily a convoluted system that appeared to border on heterodoxy. Their reluctance, however, did not mean that African American Protestants found no common ground with dispensationalists. They did, but their use of apocalyptic and eschatological texts demonstrates that they appropriated that which fit their biblical reading and their worldview, not what white dispensationalists may have wanted them to accept.

Those apocalyptic texts and themes popped up in their denominational writings in unexpected and inconsistent places. The *National Baptist Voice*, for example, which often voiced theological modernism, occasionally ran articles that espoused premillennialist notions, if not outright doctrines. In a church dedication message in Chicago, reprinted by the *Voice*, Convention president Dr. Elias Camp Morris declared African American Christians' solid belief in "the divinity of Jesus Christ," but then cautioned of "troublous times which have the whole world in its grip at this time." These times, he warned, were "only a fulfillment of the words of Jesus Christ and an indication that His Kingdom is soon to come." But the coupling of world events with the warnings of imminent judgment were not followed by additional and more troubling predictions. Instead, Morris lapsed back into fairly traditional preaching on the need for salvation, the absolute power of God, and a hopeful discussion of Jesus leading the way "towards the pearly gates of a new Jerusalem."[25] In the same issue, Dr. R. B. Roberts of Memphis, Tennessee, wrote on the text of II Chronicles 9:17 ("Moreover the king made a great throne of ivory and overlaid it with pure gold.'"). His reading of the text discussed the "throne of Solomon" and the "six steps" as typological foreshadowing for the incarnation, baptism, temptation, crucifixion, resurrection, and "triumphant ascension to glory" of Jesus. After demonstrating the "type and antitype," Roberts tied the text to final judgment scenes in the Book of Revelation, specifically Rev. 5:13 and 1:5–8. But while the method of linking Hebrew Bible texts to New Testament texts to demonstrate fulfillment of prophecies in a less than obvious way (the six steps to the throne as stages in the life of Jesus) might seem apocalyptic, his choice of texts in Revelation was not so. Revelation 5:13 tells of every creature on earth praising God, while 1:5–8 contains a description of Jesus as the "faithful witness," whose death redeems humanity and proves the power of God. Rather than turn to a historicist millennial viewpoint or continue on into a futurist dispensationalist argument, Roberts used the six steps to lay out a plan for salvation to his congregation. The six steps of the throne were analogous to the six actions people could take to "sit with Him upon His throne," Roberts explained, enumerating the steps as:

   I. Conviction of sin.
   II. Repentance of sin.
   III. Faith resulting in pardon or justification;
   IV. Sanctification or entire submission to God.
   V. Perseverance to the end, unyielding steadfastness.
   VI. Death and glorification.[26]

For Roberts, the verses in question were not so much a guidebook to future events (or even an explanation of past human events) but instead were part of a comprehensive plan for salvation contained in scripture and plainly understood by those who read it. Reading with guidance was still a part of his mission, as likening the six steps to Solomon's throne to the stages of the life of Christ was not an obvious connection. But the temptation to use the method which dispensationalists so often used and to link it to world affairs, tribulation, and future apocalyptic battles was not present in his exegesis. Instead, the exercise served as a means for the believer to understand the actions required of him or her in order to gain eternal life and avoid eternal punishment.[27]

Other pastors, both in the pages of the *National Baptist Voice* and in other publications, flirted with apocalyptic imagery but without any real ardor. In 1921, Dr. A. J. Stokes, in what appears to have been a sermon submitted for publication in the *Voice*, told of "John's Wonderful Figurative Vision." His choice of the term "figurative" raises questions about his interpretation of the contents of Revelation. This vision, according to Stokes, was indeed revelation: "Brother John was permitted to see all these glorious things recorded in the Book of Revelation without which, what would the Christians do?" But Stokes returned to the more traditional interpretation of the "woman clothed with the sun, and the moon under her feet, and upon her head a crown of twelve stars" (Rev. 12:1). For Stokes, the woman was plainly a symbol of the church, "the coming wife, the bride of Jesus Christ," and the light from the sun was "light to every soul that will have it without receiving any from any source but its own Creator." Although he did engage in a bit of numerology, interpreting the twelve stars in her crown as "intended to represent in her crown the twelve tribes of the Children of Israel, and then to represent the twelve apostles of the Lamb," Stokes did not press the analogy and instead turned to two traditional Protestant hymns—John Keith's "How Firm a Foundation" and Edward Perronet's "All Hail the Power of Jesus' Name"—to bring the sermon back to its goal: evangelization.[28] This traditionalism stands in contrast with the dispensational premillennialists, who, as historian Timothy Weber has noted, were concerned with evangelization, but their premises and methods differed from those of Stokes.

Stokes continued his study of the Book of Revelation, writing in the next issue of the *Voice* on Revelation 21:1 ("And I saw a new heaven and a new earth for the first heaven and the first earth were passed away and there was no more sea."). He opened by saying, "this text may have been metaphorical; John might have been metaphorically speaking, but what he says is as true as the existence of God; true as the angels live and as true as Christ died; he tells us in this mighty vision he saw a new heaven and a new earth. A new heaven?" Stokes interpreted the new "heaven" as "heaven" and the current "heaven" as referring to the sky, stars, sun, and moon. This "present heaven" could be "fearful," as when "in Texas some years ago . . . a blaze of lightning shot from our present heaven and struck the dry prairie and burned up hundreds of cattle, millions of birds and other animals good for man." Stokes then proceeded to describe the "new heaven" of Revelation 21 as what his audience would probably have thought of as "heaven," without any qualifying terms as old or new.[29] He demonstrated that a preacher could use the apocalyptic and eschatological texts in a traditional manner, rather than resorting to Darby's newfangled invention.

Occasionally, writers would embrace notions of imminent world catastrophe, although these themes were employed in ways that were quite different from those of white fundamentalists. For African Americans, the world as they knew it always contained distinct and present dangers, whether they lived in the North, South, East, or West. Racism was rampant in the United States, and African American denominational newspapers had been pointing this out since their very beginnings. Lynching, "race" riots, discrimination, segregation, rape, and other threats manifested themselves in all parts of the country to one degree or another. While Chapter 5 will further examine African Americans' larger interpretations of race relations and the duty of Christians to address racism, the use of current events sometimes appeared in vaguely eschatological ways in black denominational publications. These appearances, however, rarely crossed the line into full-blown dispensational premillennialism. Instead, the writers used them to great effect to illustrate the plight of African Americans.

Star of Zion editor W. H. Davenport began one editorial skeptical of calls for imminent judgment. "One hot summer night in Florida," he began, "we heard a preacher thundering from his pulpit that the world was growing worse day by day, and that the judgment was imminent." Davenport indicated that the preacher cited "the Bible in support of his affirmation," but then discounted the preacher's position, arguing that "sporadic texts can be quoted to bolster any wild and erratic statement." In this way, Davenport echoed historic Protestant readings of the Bible and warned against rushes to judgment and error. But he conceded, "there is much, however, to give color to the views of the pessimist." He went on to list a few examples: "The crimes—robberies, murders, banditry, burglaries, boot-legging, child stealing, infanticide, the killing of parents, thievery, and graft all conspire to undermine confidence in the permanence of our civilization and the affectiveness [*sic*] of the Church." These factors made him think of the ancient civilizations of Greece, Babylonia, Egypt, and Rome, which "failed because they became impervious to the voices of their higher sensibilities and pursued the dismal march of death." Davenport cautioned, however, that Christians of the twentieth century had a distinct advantage in their Christian faith: "our faith in God rejects the idea of the ultimate conquest of evil." He assured his readers that "justice and righteousness will win. Crimes will cease. Truth will prevail. Right will triumph." All of these things would occur because the church was evangelizing and calling attention to the words of Jesus, stating "'therefore all things whatsoever ye would that men should do to you, do ye even so to them: for this is the law and the prophets.'" He also employed and slightly changed the words of Frederick Faber's hymn, "Oh, It is Hard to Work for God," saying "'Right is right since God is God/ And right the day will win/To doubt would be disloyalty/To falter would be sin.'"[30] For Davenport, eschatology was a way of promising a just accounting of human deeds at the end of time.

Eschatological imagery was useful as a means of exciting the base. In concluding his remarks to the 46th Annual Session of the National Baptist Convention, Unincorporated, President J. E. Wood called upon the attendees to spread the word of God and exhorted them, "When for the last time the King of Day mounts up the Celestial Highway, drawn by prancing steed, whose feet are shod with fire, and Milky Way shall fade, and stars shall tremble and planets burn up, and kingdoms and throne shall crumble, and all the works of men pass away, then I want you and me and the faithful soldiers in Christ everywhere who come to appear before our great Commander, laden with trophies won on many a battlefield, to hear our great Redeemer say, 'Well done, good and faithful servant.' Let us labor together here and rejoice together before His beatific throne in heaven."[31] What started out as a rousing description of the end of time became, by the time Wood finished, a call to evangelize. He did not dwell on the exact timing or nature of the end of time; for him, it was as portrayed in the Book of Revelation and as interpreted throughout Protestant history: a warning of the need to convert now and not later. *Star of Zion* editor Davenport displayed this tendency clearly in a 1927 editorial snippet in which he noted that the Reverend J. D. Cauthen of Gethsemane Church in Charlotte, North Carolina, had recently used the text, "I saw the dead, great and small, stand before God, and the book was opened." Revelation 20:12 provided this preacher with the chance to remind his congregation of the real consequences of sin and the truth of eternal punishment. "It was," Davenport summarized, "a profitable and helpful service."[32] Once again, the Book of Revelation was a tool for conversion, not a distinct roadmap for the future.

To be sure, African American religious editors occasionally included distinctly premillennial articles in their publications. For example, the *National Baptist Union-Review* in 1933 ran a reprint of a *Tabernacle Voice* article by white Baptist A. Reilly Copeland, in which Copeland used Revelation 6 and 16, Matthew 25, Genesis 18 and 19, Amos 3, I John 3, and Isaiah 26 to prove that the League of Nations and the collapse of the Ottoman Empire (which he called Turkey) were evidence that the Antichrist was indeed coming and coming soon.[33] In 1934, the *Union-Review* ran a reprint of a *Western Recorder* article, "Evangelism, Hastening the Second Coming of Christ," by T. W. Callaway of Chattanooga, Tennessee. Pastor Callaway argued that the Second Coming "should not be a divisive issue, regardless of what particular theory is held. Surely those who know and believe the Word expect the coming of the Lord at any moment." What Christians needed, he continued, was to employ "evangelism as a method of hastening that glorious event," adding that "such should be the chief endeavor of the church."[34] Articles such as these, however, were not regular features. Moreover, they illustrate the tendency to include a wide variety of viewpoints in the pages of denominational papers. The editors and their readers were very well read in current events of the day, as well as theological developments, whether they concurred with them or not.

Premillennialism's efforts to parse world events with a prophetic aim received scorn from these editors. Indeed, the *Star*'s W. H. Davenport poked fun at the date-setting tendencies of premillennialists in 1925, noting that "the world did not come to an end on the 6th of February, 1925. . . . What the angels in heaven do not know, the ultra-religionists might well leave alone." "But," he added as a last jab, "if they keep on guessing they may hit it someday, although they have made some very bad guesses in the last fifty years."[35] Like J. H. Frank had observed years earlier, the date setters and prophecy readers had not yet been right, and Davenport reminded his Methodist readers of this fact.

Of course, not every African American minister maintained his distance from premillennialist thought. The Reverend Eli George Biddle, AME Zion minister and veteran of the Civil War's Massachusetts 54th regiment, gave premillennialism in general and Darby's system in particular attention in his columns for the *Star of Zion*. But a closer inspection of Biddle's use of premillennialism, as well as his embrace of other strains of Protestant thought, reveals a man who was extraordinarily wide-reaching in his knowledge and who used a variety of interpretations to read his Bible and understand the world around him.[36] In 1922, Biddle published a series of articles in the *Star of Zion*, "Pre-Millennialism: Or the Doctrine that the Second Coming of Christ Precedes the Millennium." The series, which spanned at least three issues of the paper, presented Biddle's understanding of premillennialist thought, hewed largely to Darby's dispensationalism with a few exceptions, championed the notion that he was living in the final dispensation, and made the case for a pre-Tribulation Rapture. In so doing, he managed to cite some of the texts that historian Timothy Weber lists as favorites of dispensationalists: Matthew 24 and 1 Thessalonians 4.[37]

But Biddle did not continue his ardent support of premillennialism beyond this series. He wavered between the more traditional interpretation and a vaguely premillennialist interpretation in his columns over the next several years. In February 1927, he rejected corporate salvation, "by what they call a 'social gospel'—saving a community while ignoring the individual sinner," calling it "un-Biblical, utopian, fallacious, and doomed to failure, because it is not God's method."[38] But rejection of Social Gospel thought or modernist thought alone does not a fundamentalist or dispensational premillennialist make. By 1927, many Protestants had rejected the Social Gospel; Biddle joined with them. While he did believe that "satan will yet make a preeminently desperate attempt to retain his sovereignty of this world," and that the "'World Courts,' 'Leagues of Nations,' and great commercial combinations are simply 'hood-winks' and deceptions of satan," the real issue facing humanity was the tendency to believe that they could end injustice in the world themselves. Instead, Biddle argued, "the pure reign of Christ is to be restored to this sin-cursed world. All iniquity, injustice, unrighteousness, and impiety will be overthrown." Biddle predicted that "with no racial prejudice, no intolerance, or unkindness, all peoples, without regard to race, color or creed, will live harmoniously together as children of God, brothers and sisters of one Father and mother." That last word Biddle felt compelled to explain, noting "we say 'mother,' for God is a mother as He is a Father."[39] Biddle repeated this mother argument in another article in 1932. After he assured *Star of Zion* readers that the Bible was "infallible," that "both the written and The Living Word are imperishable . . . absolutely reliable . . . pure and chaste . . . eternal," he tucked into the end of this solidly traditionalist description of the Bible an astounding assurance: that the Bible "Manifest[ed] not only the fatherhood, but also the motherhood of God."[40] God as mother was never a part of fundamentalist theology, nor premillennialist, and in this one word, along with his focus on racial equality in the millennial kingdom, Biddle demonstrates again the tendency of African American writers to interpret theological messages in their own way. William Bell Riley, John Roach Straton, Rueben Torrey—none were interested in including racial equality as part of the better world to come. Such promises would likely have repelled their white audience members. But for African Americans, the future hope of racial justice was a powerful draw. Moreover, given the continued persistent racism, violence, and segregation, divine intervention may have seemed the only way that African Americans would see equality in the United States. But that was not the focus of premillennialists writing in the 1920s.

Moreover, the combination of a new gendered term for God—as mother as well as Father (Biddle capitalized the traditional masculine noun but not the feminine)—reveals Biddle's willingness to use new ideas and modes of thought without respect to categories drawn by white commentators. For white fundamentalists, and indeed most contemporary Protestants, the use of a feminine noun to describe God was simply wrong. The history of Christian interpretation of the Bible had long included references to the

church as the "bride of Christ," but God had remained a masculine enti-
ty, male gendered and powerful. Biddle's term mother anticipated feminist
theologians like Mary Daly and Rosemary Radford Reuther—women who
had not yet been born in 1927.

Even as he occasionally employed premillennial-leaning terms, Biddle
also diverged from dispensationalist readings, and even the Bible translation he made use of was one to which premillennial fundamentalists would
have objected. In the 1928 occurrence, he mentioned his Weymouth and
Moffatt translations of the Bible. His use of Moffat, over the traditional King
James Bible, also demonstrates that Biddle was willing to explore new av-
enues of biblical scholarship. At least one commentator complained about
the text in Moffatt, which he claimed "robs the verse of the sonorous quality
of the King James rendering." For T. C. Dunham, the Moffatt translation
represented a threat to the "youth of the present generation," who could
"lose touch with an important part of our cultural heritage."[41] These issues
did not seem to bother Biddle, however, as he continued to use his Moffat
Bible, while also referring at times to his Scofield Reference Bible, the edition compiled by premillennialist Cyrus Scofield with helpful cross-refer-
ences for the devout dispensationalist.[42]

Some of Biddle's interest in fundamentalism and its various tenets may
stem from his familiarity with individual leaders. Writing in 1929 on "Our
Invisible Defenders," E. George Biddle quoted "the sainted Dr. A. J. Gordon" as arguing that asking in Christ's name meant that Christians became
connected with the Holy Spirit "'so that to ask what we desire of Him is
to ask what He desires for us.'"[43] His invocation of Adoniram J. Gordon,
who, according to Joel Carpenter, was one of the "early leaders" of the "interdenominational revivalist network that formed around the era's greatest
evangelist, Dwight L. Moody," illustrates yet again Biddle's ability to tran-
scend white-drawn boundaries.[44] Although he died in 1895, before the formal inception of the fundamentalist movement, Gordon was involved in
what Ernest Sandeen calls the "millenarian movement."[45] Gordon, though,
was a local figure for Biddle. He spent his final twenty-six years as pastor of
Boston's Clarendon Street Baptist Church, and, as historian Margaret Lamberts Bendroth has chronicled, Gordon made headlines with his pastorate
there and his activism.[46] Little wonder that Biddle, who was originally from
Boston and who was serving as an AME Zion minister in Connecticut and
Massachusetts, was familiar with him. Beyond Gordon and a mention of
Charles Spurgeon, Biddle made no specific reference to any other premi-
llennialist figure or fundamentalist leader.

Moreover, Biddle was comfortable with a wide range of theological traditions. He was a consummate reader of many types of Protestant theol-

ogy and frequently employed them in his prose. From Marcus Garvey to "Christian Manhood" to "The Deity of Jesus Christ" to "Our Marvelously Constituted Body," Biddle's pieces in the *Star of Zion* covered an astounding array of topics, texts, and points of view.[47] He was not afraid to voice his opinion on so many issues that his articles and letters to the editor constitute a comprehensive overview of the questions facing many Protestant ministers of his day. Biddle, for example, was an early reader of Reinhold Niebuhr, the American minister who helped form the Christian Realist movement and would later become an outspoken opponent of Nazism in Germany. From time to time, Biddle returned to Niebuhr's *Does Civilization Need Religion?* In 1928, Biddle referred to it as "Niebuhr's great book," and noted that it was "highly recommended by the Religious Book Club and unqualifiedly endorsed by such eminent scholars as S. Parkes Cadman, Henry [*sic*] Emerson Fosdick, Francis J. McConnell, and Charles H. Brent." After quoting the book at length, Biddle wrote, "I have quoted so copiously from this excellent book because I want all my brethren to read and ponder it as I have."[48] Biddle was not the only AME Zion reader of *Does Civilization Need Religion? Star of Zion* editor W. H. Davenport spoke highly of it in 1928 as well. And while Davenport did not indicate whether he had received his copy of the book from the Religious Book Club, the mentions of it in the *Star of Zion* lend support to historian Matthew S. Hedstrom's work on liberal religion in the early twentieth century.[49] In 1930, Biddle returned to quote from Niebuhr's book to prove that "'Jesus is valuable to the modern Christian because He offers an escape from the theological absurdities.'"[50]

Biddle's forays into various strands of Protestant theology are illustrative of the practice of many African American ministers from the 1910s to the 1930s. Protestantism, by its very emphasis on reading, helped propel these men into the study of religious trends. Their place in American society, by virtue of their race, demanded a thorough knowledge of the world around them. These two factors combined to produce Baptist and Methodist ministers who were not only cognizant of theological trends but also acute critics of them. They took that which agreed with their worldview and theology and rejected that which did not. But because they were outside the debate being held by white Protestants—both the fundamentalist/modernist debates and the debates among the fundamentalists themselves—African Americans were free to interpret the Bible and current events without the restrictions of the debates that raged around them. They grappled with the issues fundamentalism and modernism had raised even if the white proponents of those camps had no idea African Americans were doing so. Eli George Biddle could employ eschatological rhetoric and Scofield's Reference Bible while also reading Reinhold Niebuhr and the Moffatt translation. To Biddle and the editors of these denominational newspapers, the central question was not which side supports this position; it was does this position have support in scripture? When it did, they agreed with it and advanced it; when it did not, they rejected it as "new" or even "infidel."

Premillennialism fell into the second category because it ran counter to traditional Bible reading as they understood it, and it smacked of theological quackery. Too many times in Christian history, events had made fools of the date setters and prognosticators. Moreover, the racially oppressive climate in the United States had been present for generations, thus removing for African American Protestants the urgency of dispensational premillennialism's message of spiraling world crisis. Moreover, African Americans occupied an already marginalized position in American society; they could not afford to embrace what appeared to be a new heresy.

The theological discussions in these periodicals do make clear that, if these ministers had received copies of *The Fundamentals*, they were not quoting them in their public writings. An argument from silence is difficult to sustain, but the lack of mention of *The Fundamentals* again begs the question of whether the booklets really were sent to every minister in the United States and Canada, or whether they were sent to every white minister in the United States and Canada. National Baptists, AME, and AME Zion ministers were free to read the fundamentalist debates in the secular and religious press, but if they had access to the writings that had initially fueled that debate, they were not using them. And since these men tended to employ and cite every publication at their disposal, it would seem that they did not possess Lyman Stewart's books.

While they may not have had direct access to *The Fundamentals*, black Baptists and Methodists did discuss one of its foci, the topic of evolution—both its use in school curricula and its relationship with biblical inerrancy—frequently in their denominational papers. The debate entered with a flourish in the mid-1920s, unsurprisingly, given the Scopes trial, but it continued to engage the various parties in a vigorous discussion for another decade. As historian Eric D. Anderson has noted, "the story of black responses to Darwinism is complex and marked by unexpected turns." For the most part, the ministers and laypeople in this study fell outside Anderson's theory that "black Christian intellectuals had a vision of progress that made them open to theological change."[51] For these writers, evolution was a thorny problem. On the one hand, they were influenced by the notion of uplift and education, both of which demanded that they accede to or at least acknowledge the role of scientific advances as part of what the modern society demanded of its informed citizens. It would also lend ammunition to black sociological critiques of African Americans' perceived hyper-religiosity and their charges that "the black church" was an obstacle to black racial progress.[52] To merely oppose evolution would be to align themselves with those people who rejected much of scientific discovery of the previous seventy-five years. Moreover, it could potentially confirm white stereotypes of African Americans as intellectually deficient. But neither could the ministers embrace the teaching of evolution wholeheartedly. Their firm understanding of the role of God in creation meant that these commentators could not and would not endorse the theory fully. It served as an example of the dangers of modernism in American culture. To admit that the Bible was deficient in its explanation of human origins would be to grant modernists a critical victory, and that victory could leave the door open to further attacks on religious truths. Instead, these writers would have to seek a middle way. That middle way quickly became for them an affirmation of scientific progress combined with a cautionary note that theology would always trump human knowledge and that what mattered most was not the pursuit of scientific inquiry but the pursuit of salvation. In the process, however, they managed to accommodate modernism more than they would have liked to admit.

The debate within African American religious communities over evolution and the Scopes trial has drawn attention from at least one other scholar. Historian Jeffrey Moran has rightly argued that our understanding of Scopes needs to include a reading of race. Race was omnipresent in American society in the 1920s, and it appeared frequently in the discussions of the implications of evolutionary theory on such diverse topics as eugenics, race-based intelligence, and race-based physical appearances. But while Moran sees the exchange as one between "secular black intellectuals" and black ministers, the majority of whom he classifies as antievolution, it was even more complicated. Within the ranks of the clergy, a debate raged about how best to reconcile religious belief with the currents of modern science, how to conform to the standards of uplift while avoiding a confirmation of white racial stereotyping, and how to present African American religion as both up-to-date and traditional.[53]

With few exceptions, black Baptist and Methodist writers did not tie the antievolution effort to the fundamentalists in their discourse. African Americans either did not see the notions as linked or were unwilling to tar the antievolutionists with the fundamentalists' brush or tar the fundamentalists with the antievolutionists' brush. The latter could stem from general sympathy toward fundamentalist causes, but it could also likely come from a more critical reading of news reports. The major players in fundamentalism were not in Dayton, and many of them were not necessarily publishing opinions about the trial. One notable exception to the absence of linking the antievolution movement with the fundamentalist movement was a *Star of Zion* editorial, "'Dishonest Scoundrels,'" in which W. H. Davenport very correctly and succinctly observed that William Jennings Bryan was "aroused in the interest of the fundamentals of the Christian religion," had "no patience with modernists," and along with the "fundamentalists want[ed] the scientists to 'keep hands off our theology and Bible.'"[54] But even this exception illustrates that Davenport was aware that Bryan sided with the fundamentalists and that fundamentalists in general wanted to preserve theology and scripture from what they perceived as marauding attacks by secular scientists and biblical scholars. Indeed, while the white fundamentalists were not flocking to Dayton, they were no friends of evolutionary theory, Charles Darwin, or John Scopes. They were galvanized to attack evolution initially because of the modernism associated with it.[55] As already demonstrated, African American religious papers were strongly opposed to modernism in all of its myriad forms, even as they allowed it to creep into their discourse.

The presence of modernism could take the shape of endorsement of evolution for some papers at some times. The AME Zion's *Star of Zion* led the publications in outright support for the teaching of evolutionary theory in public schools. A July 1925 column mocked the state of Tennessee for its antievolution law, noting that "Tennessee might as well go on record as opposing the teaching that the world is round since it is so well written that there are four corners to the world."[56] The following week, editor Davenport wrote with prose reminiscent of H. L. Mencken, the Baltimore *Sun* columnist and acerbic commentator. "An obscure village slumbering between the hills of Tennessee," he began, "where darkness oozes out between the trees has suddenly become the cynosure of the Nation's eyes. A modest retiring, unknown school teacher has been shot into public notice because some ultra-enthusiastic moss-back indicted him for teaching evolution." Caricaturing the residents of Dayton as "the one gallused inhabitants of the wilds, with inseparable corn cob pipes, mountain dew and convenient guns," he also mocked the journalists, scientists, "free thinkers, nincompoops, and psycho-analysts, agnostics, lawyers, preachers and teachers, realtors and other humbugs [who] have relegated young Scopes to the limbo of forgetfulness while they crucify our Lord afresh and make a football and plaything of the Christian religion."[57] Davenport's sardonic wit here was directed at the white people of Tennessee and, in particular, the residents of Dayton, whom he characterized as hillbillies, but he also attacked the intellectuals who supported Scopes in their efforts to challenge religion. In the eyes of Davenport, both Tennessee whites and their detractors failed to understand their role in history and the role of religion in society. Science could make advances, but science without religion was morally bereft.

Far more prevalent than support for evolution were statements of compromise or of faith that religion would withstand whatever potential cultural conflicts science could throw at it. Such statements reflected a broad consensus among the various Baptists and Methodists, and they began well before the Scopes trial and continued on into the 1930s. In them, writers and editors alike signaled their strongly held view that Christianity held the truth and that science could not provide an alternative to religion. This stance was firmly rooted in American evangelicalism and its insistence on Scottish realism, the notion that the Bible was divinely revealed but could be understood through the use of God-given reason. But Scottish realism and its heirs in American religious thought had contended that science was valid only when it confirmed religion. For many of the ministers in these black denominations, however, the acceptance of religion and science together was at once a distancing themselves from modernism while also embracing it. They began to argue that the Bible had limits on what it could prove scientifically, a first step on the road to modernism.

The middle path was a hard one to find, let alone follow. A *Star of Zion* editorial in 1922 lauded antievolution efforts as a way of protecting the young minds of schoolchildren. The paper affirmed its belief in "freedom in the pursuit of knowledge," adding that "we believe in the sane application of evolution to our methods of thinking and governing, but we believe that teachers of unqualified, runaway atheism and agnosticism as taught by Darwin whose own soul was ruined cankered with the rust of conceit and eaten the worms of doubt and death should be legislated out." Having thus passed judgment on Darwin's immortal soul while also supporting the freedom of inquiry, the editorial concluded that a panel of scientists and "moral leaders" should be formed to provide expert guidance on the matter. Churches had two goals: "We must keep ourselves from the religious bigotry of the middle ages when popes and priests attempted to throttle thought and dam up science and liberty, and we must also save our people from the peril of agnostic metaphysics and from the loss of the props of faith." Editor W. J. Walls aligned his paper with notions of educational and scientific progress, while firmly remaining adamantly Protestant and anti-Catholic. In so doing, he allied himself with contemporary secular commentators who saw antievolutionism as a return to the medieval inquisition.[58]

The *Star*'s denominational sibling, the AME Zion *Quarterly Review*, cautioned ministers to refrain from entering into debates over evolution and to instead argued that "we would do better business and make greater progress in the direction indicated, by sticking to 'the glorious gospel of the happy God.'" The unnamed writer added that "the question of how we came here is of minor importance; of major significance is why we are here. The Bible practically passes over the first and concerns itself almost exclusively with the second."[59] To argue that the question of how life arose was "minor" demonstrates that individuals within the denomination placed less emphasis on notions of biblical inerrancy and more on evangelism, but white fundamentalists, and indeed many traditionalist Protestants, would have argued against this notion, claiming that inerrancy, the Bible as scientific and historical text, and evangelism were inseparable.

For the *A.M.E. Christian Recorder*, the Scopes trial would "prove nothing, except the silly ignorance of the Tennessee legislators who in the twentieth century would put such a statute on the law books of their state." Editor Richard Wright Jr. reasoned that "whether evolution is right or wrong is not a question of human law, but of divine law." But he went further, adding, that it "is a question of science. Men consecrated to science are endeavoring to solve the problem of man's origin. If human intelligence can solve it, they will succeed." Having voiced his support for the scientific inquiry, he hastened to add that religion and science were not antithetical. "Science is not religion's enemy," he contended, but that science "is the enemy of superstition and charlatanism, science is the enemy of that religious leadership that persists on the ignorance of the people that sort which did not want public schools and colleges. But Jesus said 'know the truth'" (John 8:32). Like the *Star of Zion*, the *Christian Recorder* associated such laws with a distant and uncivilized period in human history. "Christianity does not need," the editorial concluded, "the Tennessee legislature with laws savoring of the dark ages to bolster it up."[60]

Just months later, the *Christian Recorder* repeated its stand, voicing its confidence in the permanence of religion, arguing that "God has made the world and man, and his laws are immutable." The law being challenged and the trial itself were the results of "misguided souls [who believe] that science and religion are at odds. There never was a greater mistake. True Science is the greatest handmaiden of true religion." Editor Wright also took aim at Tennessee's racial segregation laws, noting that the "Tennessee legislature is not able to stop evolution by its anti-evolution laws, any more than it stops miscegenation by its intermarriage laws. The laws of God are immutable and the puny efforts of ignorant legislators will never change them."[61] Religion, not science or human laws, was the constant.

For good measure, the paper followed up one week later with another editorial, opening with an affirmation of the eternal nature of Christianity.

"We believe," it began, "in God. We believe in Truth. We believe in the Bible. We believe in Jesus Christ. Our belief is unshaken after years of study of science, after years of study of evolution, after years of study of higher criticism." As proof of the supremacy of faith over science, Richard Wright related the story of an "ignorant young college graduate" who had challenged him to prove that Jesus was the son of God. When the editor said he could not, the young man crowed in triumph, but the editor then challenged him to prove that he was his father's son. "And we both concluded," Wright recounted, "that 'there are lots of things we believe which can't prove, and many of them are dearest to us.'"[62] While the testimony of the young man's mother was apparently not considered in this exchange, the *Christian Recorder* had, to its own standard, sufficiently proved its point: science posed no real challenge for the true believer. The corollary, that religion need not be subjected to scientific scrutiny, also held true.

The AME Zion's *Star of Zion* shared the *Christian Recorder*'s suspicion of people who claimed evolution had all the answers and religion none, as the paper attacked Clarence Darrow for his insults to William Jennings Bryan. Darrow's comment to Bryan about "your fool religion" drew particular umbrage from the *Star*'s editor, William Davenport, who countered that "religion is the strongest and most vital influence in the human breast and the legitimate cause of evolution was not advanced" by Darrow's slurs. Davenport contrasted the power of "ancient systems" of religion with the transformative power of Christianity to "change the most vicious and abandoned to law-abiding, home-loving, and God-fearing creatures." But while he was outraged by Darrow's comments, Davenport still defended the general theory of evolution. "The trouble," he wrote, "is not with evolution per se but with the men and women of insufficient breadth and depth who haven't sense enough to teach it without undermining the basal principles of our holy religion."[63] For Davenport, as for Wright, evolution's challenge was not that science threatened religion. Instead it was the attitudes of certain scientists and their advocates, attitudes that placed science above religion and made the teaching of evolution a threat to the religious development of students. In a February 1925 editorial, Davenport argued that classroom science teachers needed to be more experienced, observing that they "have not lived long enough to learn much of the subject they attempt to teach."[64] The insistence on expertise and experience reflects a preference for education and status. For Davenport, himself a seminary-trained minister, the importance of higher education and training was key to the proper understanding and transmission of knowledge. Yet education itself could be a Trojan Horse, as the rigors of higher education often led to a questioning of religious beliefs. By his advocacy of further training, Davenport left his door open to more challenges to religion and possibly more modernism. His middle way was not as moderate as he might have concluded.

In the immediate aftermath of the Scopes trial, the voices for compromise continued. The moderator of the National Baptist Laymen's Movement of the National Baptist Convention, Incorporated argued that evolution was no real threat to Christianity. In a lengthy message to an assembly in Baltimore, the moderator—unnamed by the *National Baptist Voice*, but who was John L. Webb—first indicated his clear preference for the Bible's creation account.[65] He also listed a set of tenets that would make a fundamentalist's heart sing: "the Virgin Birth, Deity of Christ, as well as the humanity, the baptism of our Lord, the death, the burial, the resurrection—indeed, the bodily resurrection, the ascension and the second coming of our Lord which the Church has always looked for and which has been an encouragement and will always be an encouragement to the followers of Christ." There was, he argued, "no real war between the Bible and theistic science," and "Christianity is safe, at least a good many people seem to think so." For Webb, the bottom line was not that evolution contradicted the creation accounts in the book of Genesis. Instead, the reason why evolution would not pose an imminent threat to religion was that "as long as the present debate in the religious and theological world has no bearing on the real soul of Jesus' teachings, there is as little danger of hurting Christianity as there would be of hurting an oak tree by writing an essay about one of its acorns, or by damaging the Washington Monument by hitting it with a toy balloon."[66] The debate over the creation accounts in Genesis did not necessarily mean for him an attack on the salvific message of Jesus. Instead, the gospel remained intact and powerful, despite attempts by misguided people to link doubts regarding the validity of one part of the Bible to the part Webb considered of tantamount importance. Yet again, though, the reasoning Webb employed contained modernism. To say that some portions of the Bible could be inerrant but not others, or that some accounts were literal while others could be discounted, was to concede important ground to the very intellectual trend against which black Baptists and Methodists had so vigorously argued—modernism. Webb had unwittingly made the case for an opening of the Bible to a type of hierarchical importance, the notion that the New Testament was sacrosanct, while the Hebrew Bible could be read less strictly. To be sure, Christians since the beginnings of the religion have struggled with how to reconcile these two sections of scripture. Yet what Webb was doing went far beyond the Apostle Paul's argument that the New Testament fulfilled the Old.

Not everyone was comfortable with such an interpretation. The Reverend

F. C. Van Buren of Belmont Street AME Zion Church in Worcester, Massachusetts, for example, typified the argument against Webb's comfort with evolution. In a sermon entitled, "Why I am Not an Evolutionist," excerpts of which were reprinted in the *Star of Zion*, Van Buren repeated the now standard claim that the "Bible does not only have no fear of science but welcomes all it has verified and has ever antedated man in all of the knowledge he possesses by many creatures." But Van Buren, after proclaiming his support for the Genesis creation account, was not willing to say that Christianity and evolution could coexist. Indeed, he held that the two were at war and that the "doctrine of Evolution is simply another definition of infidelity for its adherents have said in their heart, 'there is no God.'" For Van Buren, to grant that science had disproved the creation story was to abandon all of the truths of the Bible. "I may as well," he argued, "concede that the entire Book is but fiction, uninspired and useless as far as it relates to the fundamentals of the Christian faith." To believe evolution, he concluded, was to "destroy faith in the Bible."[67] Van Buren's notion of biblical totality, that every part of the Bible must be true, stood more closely to the fundamentalists' and the traditionalists' notion of scripture. *Union-Review* editor Frank also refused to give ground to the evolutionists. "Under the guise of 'Evolution,'" he railed, "infidels are seeking to advance their Unitarianism, an ism that is a stranger to things spiritual and supernatural. The so-called 'inherent forces' proclaimed by that sorry lot of intellectuals negates the fundamentals of true religion, the religious essential to our substantial [African American racial] advance."[68] For Frank, uplift of African Americans included a rejection of modernism in any form, even if that meant, in this case, rejecting evolution and scientific progress.

But commonly, African American denominational publications urged ministers to avoid entanglement in the evolution debate. An editorial in the *Christian Recorder* admonished preachers not to worry about preaching for or against evolution. Instead, Richard Wright contended, "a preacher must preach Jesus Christ. Evolution has nothing to do with Jesus Christ, any more than any other scientific principle." "Besides," he added, "if a man does not understand evolution, he should not parade his ignorance."[69] Common in the *Recorder*'s argument and in Webb's address was the notion that evolution did not pose any challenges to the Christian's understanding of Jesus. Indeed, both sources could have further argued that evolution and Genesis did not agree, but the gospel of Jesus, safely ensconced in the New Testament and far removed from the creation accounts, needed no scientific proof or quarrel. Most black Baptist and Methodist editors and contributors tended to focus on the New Testament, likely for the twin reasons of soteriology (the saving message of Jesus was harder to link to Genesis) and of evangelism (the saving message of Jesus was more important to their worldview than having to parse the difference between creation accounts and evolutionary science). Rather than attack the science, they wanted to preach the gospel. But that position was a step along the road to the modernism they despised.

Even the most ardent anti-modernists could take the position of cautioning pastors to avoid the evolution debate in their weekly sermons. Asked by a reader in early 1926 to "'inform the young preachers about science,'" the *National Baptist Union-Review*'s editor Frank advised that they "will make themselves ridiculous by denouncing science or in attacks upon scientists without cause." But he also carefully explained that there were scientists "who make the wild assertions . . . who make science a god." These scientists "belong to the crowd of infidels and atheists who are doing so much loud talk, showing how little they know of some other facts of the universe." Instead, Frank advised, science was limited in what it could know, "to time present, limited to facts present, limited to matter, to demonstrable processes, and certified knowledge, limited to experience," and thus scientists were limited to being "interpreters of natures." "Preachers," on the other hand, "are the interpreters of spirit, of grace, of the super-natural, that is above nature." Having dispensed scientists to a lower level of knowledge than pastors, he concluded by stating, "There is only one true religion. There are many true sciences. Let's try to keep our thinking clear and right."[70] But Frank had let the proverbial camel's nose under the tent by giving ground to the argument against the pulpit discussion of evolution and science.

Likewise, the *A.M.E. Christian Recorder* carefully told its readers that the book of Genesis was both divinely inspired and greatly misinterpreted by modern readers. "Genesis is not a book of science," the paper explained, "not a book of geology, astronomy or anthropology as we moderns know it." The book's author "was no scientist. He wrote from inspiration." And that inspired author, according to the editorial, had sufficiently answered the question of the origins of the universe: "the answer was 'From God'. . . . Nobody has been able to add a single idea to this."[71] Both the *Union-Review* and the *Christian Recorder* were constructing the terms of the science versus religion debate. To claim the moral high ground of religion and inspiration meant ceding the moral low ground of science. Both editors were willing to do so because it allowed them to preserve their evangelical heritage while also ensuring that they did not run counter to the prevailing intellectual forces. But in so doing, they fell prey to the advancing modernism around them.

Modernism, however, offered African American Protestants an avenue to cultural advancement through uplift. "'There is no conflict between religion and science," the *Christian Recorder*'s Richard Wright reported over-hearing at "an office in the *Amsterdam News*." The speaker was one of a group of laymen in the building, and the editor mentioned it to "show that with the enlarging intellectual horizon of the colored man, these questions which during the centuries been discussed by our white friends are being discussed by our people." Wright added that religion would "never be in danger of losing its hold or its interest. Only the church must keep pace, and must be able to answer the questions of each age as they arise."[72] The animated and spontaneous discussion of the relationship between religion and science was further proof for the AME paper that African Americans were gaining ground intellectually in the United States and that they could do so without sacrificing their religious beliefs.

Indeed, for AME Zion bishop E. D. W. Jones, African American lead-ers' embrace of evolution placed them squarely among the best citizens of the country. Speaking to the Twenty-second Annual Conference of the Na-tional Association for the Advancement of Colored People in Pittsburgh in 1931, Jones noted that the "Negro race in this country was 'as far removed from the Scopes trial in Tennessee and the religious and educational enact-ments of legislatures against evolution and discoveries of science as the en-lightened Englishman is far removed from the cave man.'"[73] For Jones and for many other African American Methodists and Baptists, the demands of a segregated society meant that they needed to work constantly to improve their knowledge, behaviors, and status. By embracing scientific progress, Jones argued, blacks could claim their proper place in America. Here evolu-tion meant a social evolution from ignorance to knowledge, from segrega-tion to integration. But it came with a steep price, as the proponents of tra-ditionalist evangelicalism called for an affirmation of religion, not science.

That conflict meant that editors of black denominational papers had to continue to argue the superiority of religion over science and often ran ar-ticles that "proved" religious claims. "The fear that science will or can be overthrown," an unnamed author wrote in a front-page *National Baptist Union-Review* article, "is found upon investigation to be groundless. Sci-ence aims only to throw more light upon religion by applying to religion its method—investigation." Here the author was advancing a view of science in the tradition of Francis Bacon—science was factually and empirically sound. The subject of the article, a Dr. N. A. Peyton, claimed that "science and religion are not 'necessarily incompatible.' They can be good play-mates—each respecting the other's claims."[74] Indeed, *Union-Review* editor Jonathan Frank turned to multiple articles in a two-year period, including "Science Supporting Religion" and "Asserts Bible is History of Facts."[75] He also ran reprints, including one from the Bible Institute of Los Angeles's

(BIOLA's) paper, *The King's Business*, a white fundamentalist publication, positing that there was no conflict between "True Science" and the Bible.[76] In 1929, Frank ran another reprint, this one from white creationist George McCready Price, which argued that new discoveries in radioactivity confirmed the Bible.[77]

The *Star of Zion* also made the case for the supremacy of religion, often appearing to verge on being antievolution without explicitly embracing that position. In "Science: The False Messiah," editor W. H. Davenport argued that science could not fulfill a human yearning. "Mankind hungers for what science cannot give," he maintained, "Men want peace, love, joy. . . . He who worships the inventions and evolutions of science as the hope of the world worships a false deity who will lead him into a chaos of confusion, and a mirage of hopeless pessimism."[78] Davenport continued to sound the call for religion, observing that people were "fundamentally religious, and that cannot be subtracted from [them] by biology or anything else."[79] Continuing in the same vein, the Reverend E. George Biddle noted that it "is unfortunate that so many of our Twentieth Century scholars deny God, repudiate Christ, renounce Paul and the Apostles; while they utterly fail to give us any responsible plan or purpose for the origin of the things they claim to be wiser than angels, patriarchs, seers, or prophets, they belittle the schools and teachers of former ages." Biddle went a step further, though, and condemned the same "scholars" who "deny the Bible account of the creation, but they give us absolutely nothing in its place that has the least semblance of reason about it; nothing they present has any enlightenment or inspiration."[80] While Biddle bordered on antievolutionism, his real issue here was with those who would ignore religion or replace it. A few years later, he called into question the science of eugenics, not because it had moral and racial complications—indeed, few contemporary commentators would have argued those complications—but because it appeared to wrest from God the power to create good in the world, a position Biddle could not support. Instead, the "Blessed Master" was "far ahead of the twentieth century scientists" and "knew all the sciences." While the scientists could ponder the breeding of a better type of livestock or a better human, it was God who had created both in the beginning, Biddle argued. "There is no conflict between science and religion," he declared, "when each keeps its proper place."[81] And so Biddle added his voice to the chorus of separation of church and science, an accommodation, conscious or not, of the arguments more progressive advocates had been advancing in secular venues for some time. By the 1930s, the question of science and religion had become, for African American Protestants, a matter of both/and, rather than either/or.

They could no longer stand uniformly against evolutionary theory, but they could make it conform to their notion of religion.

Throughout the 1920s and 1930s, African American Baptists and Methodists wrestled with how to preach the old-time religion without also becoming relics of the past. Their position on the margins of American society complicated their participation in the discussions over religious doctrine and modernity. As Protestant ministers, they believed they could not reject the theological traditions of their denominations, but they could also not risk further marginalization by rejecting progress, in the form of science, outright, or by embracing millennialism, which would open them to ridicule. Instead, they tried to embrace the past while making accommodations with the future, a position that came with its own perils. Even as they sought to prevent modernism from creeping into their denominations, assuming that it was not there already, they became modernist in their understanding of the relationship between religion and science, often noting that there were limits to what scripture could tell about history and science. That they could comfortably occupy this middle position does raise the question of why historians have tended to bifurcate the two positions (fundamentalist and modernist), rather than entertaining the notion that there existed a continuum between the two extremes, a continuum on which there were many points to occupy. On the topic of accommodations to modernity in society, black Baptists and Methodists could agree with fundamentalists that drinking and dancing were evils, as the next chapter will demonstrate. But while they could agree on social expectations and disagree on science, African American Protestants were unified in their belief that religion spoke to the racial conditions in the United States, as Chapter 5 will explore.

4

"Only the Gilded Staircase to Destruction"

*African American Protestants Confront
the Social Challenges of Modernity*

"Brethren," National Baptist Convention, Incorporated president L. K. Williams addressed his annual meeting in 1929, "we are living in a gay, swift, giddy age, and it is placing its definite impact upon all found in its wake. Giddy, pleasure loving and pleasure seeking people are a standing challenge and a menace to our churches." Specific among the threats was the "reckless divorce craze," which Williams credited with ruining the home life of Christians and allowing them to engage in gambling, going to the movies, and reading "cheap vulgar publications." While such distractions had a deleterious effect on men, Williams was more concerned about women. According to him, the social changes—from courtship rituals to movies to novels—made women "relinquish the ancient, feminine reserve which has safely guarded them in the past and caused them to be feared, honored and revered by men." "Smoking, half-dressed, pleasure-mad idle women," he warned, "can do untold damage."[1]

For Williams and for many other African American church leaders and denominational publications, American society seemed at odds with the mores and standards of their past. As these writers grappled with the changes modern culture presented, they often took to their editorial pages to express their concern with the direction American society had taken. Those concerns, at first blush, very closely resemble the concerns white fundamentalists expressed about the world around them, but black denominational papers had different motives. Keeping African Americans on the straight and narrow was part of the tradition of uplift in black society, and when black denominational papers expressed their reservations about social changes, they did so using the lenses of race, class, and biblical adherence.

Discussions of fundamentalism have usually included a focus on the early movement's militant anti-modernism, both its adamant opposition to theological modernism and to the changing society fundamentalists saw around them. Indeed, white fundamentalists in the 1910s to 1930s did wish to return American society to a pre–World War I understanding of social mores. The fundamentalists received much of their early national media attention from their concerns over drinking, dancing, gambling, and baseball games on Sundays.[2] Their theological anti-modernism and their social anti-modernism coexisted within the movement, with both strains seeking to preserve that which they saw progress threatening—the Bible and social customs.

In this regard, African American Protestants very often, intentionally and unintentionally, mirrored white fundamentalists in their concerns over the effects of modernity on American society. Black denominational newspapers and quarterly journals included articles excoriating patrons of dance clubs and speakeasies, attacking those who would gamble, especially on the Sabbath, and decrying the way women dressed and acted in this strange new world. As they encountered each of these challenges, black ministers, editors, and leaders demonstrated a clear sympathy for the anti-modernism of the fundamentalists. So often did they side with them that it would be easy to conclude that in this facet of fundamentalism's definition, black Protestants were fundamentalist. But that conclusion needs to be tempered with an eye toward black politics and the location of African Americans in a largely segregated society. As African American commentators wrestled with these issues, they outlined a different critique of modernity—a critique that both sided with white fundamentalists and opposed their status quo mentality at the same time. African American evangelicals sided with fundamentalists' stands on social issues not because they adhered to fundamentalism but because they saw these stands as biblically grounded. But simultaneously, black Protestants were bound to defend large portions of social customs because of their emphasis on uplift. Uplift for them meant a way to demonstrate black society's ability to conform to white expectations in dress, sobriety, and aspirations. Historian Evelyn Brooks Higginbotham has described this discourse as the "politics of respectability," and noted that it was a "deliberate and highly self-conscious concession to hegemonic values."[3] Higginbotham's subjects were the black Baptist women affiliated with the Baptist denominations of this study, and their arguments very often match those of the men who wrote for denominational papers, showing that the men were not *sui generis* but instead engaged in conversation with the same topics of importance to their Baptist sisters. Because they occupied positions of relative privilege, the Baptist men, and their African Methodist counterparts, were able to disseminate their views more widely. But the overall discourse on behavior was also an adherence to biblical guidance, as historian Anthea Butler has observed.[4] White power demanded it, but, more importantly, so did the Bible. The allegiance to biblical teachings and the desire to improve African Americans' lot in life, however, could run counter to each other, especially as Baptist and Methodist preachers sought to reconcile their support for Prohibition with their suspicions of white southerners' interest in Republican presidential candidate Herbert Hoover in 1928.

Black Protestant writers were very much aware that any transgression by any African American would have far reaching consequences, both for the black community itself and in the eyes of white observers. As they encountered a shifting social world, the editors of denominational papers mourned the changes they saw and hearkened back to a time of what they perceived as traditional dress, behavior, and interactions. Yet even as they were trying to preserve the past, a past one scholar has referred to as having a "conservative, near-Victorian code,"[5] they recognized that they did not want to preserve the discriminatory nature of the society that had invented and embraced that code. At the same time as they yearned for improvement in social position, these writers found that the change they wanted was not the change they were seeing. Rather than integration and equality, all around them they saw loose moral standards.

Those loose morals had many causes, including dances, movies, and gambling, all of which shared a common denominator—they were usually performed outside of churches and thus away from the moral guidance of pastors, elders, and other God-fearing people. As historian Lerone A. Martin has demonstrated, black pastors were very concerned with how worldly amusements detracted from church attendance and morals.[6] "What is the danger of these [non-church activities]?" Baptist J. C. Austin asked the assembled National Sunday School and Baptist Young Peoples Union Congress in Dayton, Ohio, in 1935. His response was simple: "It is cheating, lying, gambling, a loss of temper, a waste of time, being eaten up with a zeal for [worldly pastimes], and the disposition to fight and murder about them."[7] While Austin listed a variety of dangers, his fellow Baptists and Methodists tended to focus on one in particular—dancing. African American denominational periodicals were filled with examples of outrage against dancing in general, new forms of dance in particular, and the consequences of dancing for the participants. Dances, like movies and gambling, presented a competitive alternative to church activities, and they allowed young people to spend more time in the secular world. While gambling appeared occasionally, with the AME Zion's *Star of Zion* lamenting its nature as "immoral, dishonest, unchristian," and labeling it an "unseen peril," dancing and dance halls were a far more contentious problem and one which united black Protestant leaders in their denunciation.[8] Playing to the stereotypes of Baptist and Methodist opposition to dancing, the writers in the *National Baptist Union-Review*, the *Star of Zion*, the *Christian Recorder*, and other publications portrayed dancing as the path to perdition. The establishment and maintenance of dance halls threatened society, they argued, because they provided an easy place for young people to associate without the watchful eyes of their parents. Moreover, close proximity and suggestive moves led to lust and unacceptable contact between the sexes. The dance halls themselves were bad enough, but when some churches held dances, the writers/editors saw it as an endorsement of and capitulation to the further deterioration of society. As historian Susan K. Cahn has demonstrated, these black leaders had reason to be concerned about the behavior of black young people in dance halls: by the 1950s, white southerners would link rock 'n' roll music and dancing to racial stereotypes of African American immorality.[9] That characterization would serve to further ostracize and hyper-sexualize the image white people had of African Americans. Cahn places the origin of white Baptist leaders' concern over dancing at 1945, but black Baptist and Methodist ministers had been troubled by it for decades before the end of World War II.

Dancing was dangerous, and black religious writers expected their "better class" to abstain from it. Commenting on a 1918 dance held in Salisbury, North Carolina, and organized by a meeting of the "colored Doctors and Dental Association," the AME Zion's *Star of Zion* argued that the merits of the dance depended on what type of dancing was engaged in by the attendees, with "black" dance styles on the list to be avoided. "If the vulgarities common to Negro dances," editor Harvey Anderson explained, "were allowed by such a high order of race representatives as our Doctors and Dentists, then the ministers were right in condemning it." Among the dances with "vulgarities," the editor counted "the 'Bunny hug,' 'turkey trot,' 'fox trot,' 'Walkin' the dog,' 'the wriggle,' 'the muscle dance,' and especially the 'Shim me-Shi Wabble.'"[10] To single out "Negro dances" begs the question of whether the editor believed that "white dances" would be socially acceptable and provides evidence that these ministers were troubled not only by the behaviors they saw but also by how those behaviors fit into a white-constructed ethos. The notion that the "better class" of African Americans—doctors and dentists—would engage in such demeaning activities troubled the *Star of Zion* and presumably its readers. Those individuals of the race who had risen above their less-educated brethren were supposed to set a good example.

Concern over dancing spanned African Methodist Episcopal denominations, with the AME *Christian Recorder*'s W. E. Watson drawing a distinction between dances for the glory of God and the "Modern Dance." The latter, according to Watson, was "a serious hindrance to a person who is desirous to form a noble Christ-like character." Among its other dangers, the modern dance was held late at night, a time "which should be utilized for the rest of the mind and body." Because the person who had danced late into the night fell prey to "mental dissipation," a euphemism for wasting one's time, he or she was not fit to "give any attention to acts of devotion to religious exercises," such as Bible reading or prayer. Moreover, Watson continued, the dance "appeals to the baser passions of man, and is therefore dangerous to social purity." Because of the dance's "mingling of sexes," "study of undress usually adopted at the ball," and "sensation," Watson concluded, "it is better never to dance at all than to run risk of dancing the dance of death in the ball room."[11] For Watson, the modern dance was merely a prelude to or substitution for sexual activity, just performed fully clothed and in public spaces. Such conduct was unbecoming to the Christian and the black Christian in particular.

Other denominational papers also opposed dancing. The Unincorporated Baptists' *National Baptist Union-Review* reprinted "Ten Reasons vs. Dancing," which employed a combination of biblical citations to explain why dancing should be avoided. Among the reasons dancing was wrong, the uncredited author included that it "destroys our influence. We are commanded to 'abstain from all appearance of evil'" (1 Thess 5:27). It was also physically hazardous to women, and "as to its effects on males, read Matt. 5:28." ("But I say unto you, that whosoever looketh on a woman to lust after her hath committed adultery with her already in his heart"). Dancing also led to drinking and sex, and the article contended that "a majority of the abandoned women are ruined by the dance." It concluded, "Our duty is found in Eph. 5:11."[12] ("And have no fellowship with the unfruitful works of darkness, but rather reprove them"). The *Union-Review* also reprinted a white Baptist *Western Recorder* article on "The Evils of Modern Dance," by Pastor R. C. Campbell. According to Campbell, dancing contributed to the decline of armies, virginal maidens, "happiness and good homes," because "there are fiends hanging around dancing schools and ballrooms and hotels for the sole purpose of luring and ruining girls and young women." Dance halls were "scenes of sexual stimulation," from which "the virgin often goes to the loss of virtue, and the young man hitherto clean, to the den of infamy." The dance, he concluded, was a danger to the very fabric of society, including the "pillars of home, church, society, and state."[13] A "Borrowed Editorial" in the *Star of Zion* opined that the dance was "the queen of evils. It is the invention of the Devil and he is the operator thereof. It is maintained solely for evil purposes." Warning again of the risk of committing adultery in one's heart, the writer continued, the only reason people danced was to gain sexual arousal.[14] Common among the concerns of these editorials was the effect dancing would have on young women and, to a lesser extent, young men. The women were impressionable, much like the white fundamentalists' portrait of African Americans, and had to be protected from the evils of society. Men were victims of the dance in that it could excite their passions and inhibit their ability to discern right from wrong. While these "borrowed" columns were written by white authors, their appearance in black denominational papers indicates the esteem in which the editors held their views.

But editors could also look to their own denominations for opponents of dancing, and they often gave them the column space to make their case. The perceived threat of dances and dancing led the president of the Alabama State Baptist Convention and pastor of the Tabernacle Baptist Church in Selma, Alabama, Dr. J. V. Jemison, to write to J. D. Crenshaw, editor of the *National Baptist Voice*. Jemison expressed his view that "the dance evil" had led young people to ignore both church teachings and church services and had contributed to the younger generation's "utter disregard for their parents and their God." He exhorted his fellow ministers to "lift up your voices against this evil, of dancing, because it is the open door for immorality, whiskey drinking, the card evil, and almost all other evils." Nor was Jemison done, vowing that "you will hear from us again on this matter, for I am not through."[15]

Neither were many of his fellow clergy. That inevitable tie dance had to sex invited dangers in the home, they warned. Dancing led to the break-up of marriages, as the Reverend S. T. Hawkins told *Star of Zion* readers. In dance halls, a husband and wife might dance with other partners, which meant their "affection" for each other would never be the same again. "Just look at this picture," Hawkins explained, "there is a man's wife locked in the arms of some other man, lying on his bosom, head leaning upon the man's shoulder in close hug, twisting over the floor, and who knows but these two what is being whispered in the ears of that man's wife." While we might not know what was "being whispered," Hawkins provided a foretaste of what would happen: "And after a few days, trouble begins, homes destroyed, divorce given, and he or she is then turned out to live an unholy life." Just one dance in the arms of a man not her husband would lead a married woman to a life of prostitution. Of course, Hawkins did not elaborate on what might happen to a married man who danced with another woman. His concern was only for the "weaker" sex and women's susceptibility to immorality. Clearly, he concluded, "Christians should not dance."[16] A *World*

Evangel reprint in the *Star of Zion* agreed: "The dance hall and the church will not mix."[17]

Dancing was not only a threat to society; it was also a threat to the religious fiber of Christians and a racial threat to black Christians. As W. J. Walls explained in a 1924 *Star of Zion* editorial, the church writ large needed to oppose any support for dances and indeed to eliminate them altogether. Seeking to distance himself from the stereotype of a minister who warned of damnation if individuals engaged in certain behaviors, Walls instead carefully noted that "we do not hold that dancing itself sends anybody's soul to hell, but we do know from all observation (for we have never danced), that it is one of the contributing causes to the weakness of the race, the dissipation of religious influence, and therefore the downfall of character." Dancing was a slippery slope, a perilous first step on a journey that harmed the individual and the race as a whole. When African Americans engaged in dances, Walls intimated, whites were watching and using their observations to continue the subjugation of all blacks, not just the dancers. The answer for Walls was clear: "We must preach a whole gospel for the salvation of the individual:—body, mind, and soul. There is no perfect character that is not built upon this basis."[18] Walls continued his war on dancing over the next few months with a series of editorials that discussed the growing consensus among religious organizations, both in the United States and abroad, that dancing and piety did not mix. "We may have a membership that dances," he warned, "and we may have a membership that is active in piety, but we cannot have both at the same time." Even the Roman Catholic Church had spoken out about the moral dangers of dancing, which led Walls to conclude that it was time to take action, as "we make ourselves the laughing stock of the Devil and his agents by our timidity to handle fearlessly" those church members who continued to defy church discipline and dance.[19] Walls, like his fellow Protestants, held the Roman Catholic Church in disdain, so to have the "Romanists" jump ahead of Protestants on a social issue was a clarion call to arms. Black evangelicals needed to act to rid themselves of this social problem immediately.

The overwhelming consensus among black evangelicals in the interwar period was that dances and dancing harmed the individual and the group. Dances and dancing led to sexual activity outside of marriage, they lured young people away from church, and they further exemplified the errant course of American society. Dancing led to damnation, both of the individual soul and the black race in general. To combat white prejudice, African Americans had to hold themselves to a higher standard, but dancing would inhibit that objective. Instead, dancing—biblically condemned and socially awkward for race leaders—needed to be abolished if African Americans were to advance as a group. Black Baptists and Methodists sought to distance themselves from condoning dances, and they worked to make anti-dance positions a mark of their race.

Dance halls, with their inherent physical intimacy, raised concerns about the sexual desires of young people and the changing courtship rituals in modern society. Freed from the watchful eyes of their parents, young people in the United States, regardless of race, found new sexual freedom. This new freedom, combined with new roles for women, led black Protestants to decry the changing morals around them. Much like their commentary on dancing, their indictment of sexual behavior and the more liberated role of women closely resembled the concerns white fundamentalists held on the same topics. But once again, for the African American commentators, the stakes were higher. Their race was being watched both by God and white society. The repercussions of transgressions against either were both eternally and temporally dangerous. Changes in courtship and the spread of sexually transmitted diseases threatened society and wrecked families. Whether these concerns were demonstrably more prevalent in the 1920s and 1930s than they had been in the past did not matter to the clergy. Anecdotal evidence and the perceived lack of shame involved in these transgressions were enough to send them back to their typewriters.

As the US Army struggled with the spread of sexually transmitted diseases among its troops during the First World War, black evangelicals rushed in to offer religious reasons for maintaining Victorian mores and argued for them both among soldiers and the civilian population. "It is to be a war," a *National Baptist Union-Review* editorial announced, "not a campaign or a battle—the present movement against sexual immorality." Compounded by gambling and alcohol, sexual immorality here meant prostitution, from which husbands contracted sexually transmitted diseases and then brought them "to their own homes, poisoning wives and fathering blind children [which] is an alarming situation." Taking its cue from the nation's current status as a belligerent in the Great War, the answer the *Union-Review* advanced was "no truce declared, no armistice allowed, no deflection of the onslaught"—the church had to ensure its members were pure both in heart and in behavior, as well.[20] Continuing the martial theme and perhaps reacting to the US Public Health Service's efforts to combat sexually transmitted diseases, the *Union-Review* followed up with an editorial, provocatively entitled "Fleshly Lust!" The continued threat of "vices, venereal diseases, and drunkenness" meant that not only did governments need to work against them, but more importantly so did the clergy. "War time reforms," the editor proudly proclaimed, "are not a new thought in Baptist churches." But "young ministers" should ensure that they held themselves to the same standards they preached, lest "ignorance, low ideas, lack of ambition, godlessness breed contempt for all things noble and true." With a quick reference to the Sermon on the Mount, "'Blessed are the pure in heart; they shall see God,'" the editorial closed.[21] The message was plain—the bodily temptations threatened both soldier and minister alike, and the minister who strayed risked his own soul and the reputation of his entire race. The spotlight on black behavior was intense, but it was even more intense on that of the black clergy.

Denominational writers also discussed the topic of sex education, sometimes referred to as "sex hygiene," in an effort to drive it from public school curriculum. As historian Christina Simmons has observed, African Americans of the era tended to support a Victorian understanding of sexual relations, placing a premium on "'continence,'" sexual relations only for reproductive purposes, and "limiting public speech about sexual matters." But while the subjects of Simmons's study—the secular black reformers—sought to subvert the racial order and marginalize whites to highlight white "hypocrisy," the Baptist and Methodist clergy instead reinforced the Victorian mores.[22] Even their willingness to discuss the topic was a means to combat the evils of the day and ultimately banish them. The *National Baptist Union-Review* framed the issue of teaching sex education in schools as one that needed proper instructors, and those instructors had to display the proper moral fiber—they had to be married and "preferably a physician." The *Union-Review* explained that marriage "is a divine institution, the way toward fatherhood and motherhood, the fondly cherished goal of every normal human." To have unmarried teachers handle the delicate subject of sex education would upset the traditional gender roles. "Thinking girls laugh when the bachelor maid proceeds to tell them of the relation of sex," the editorial continued, "and boys miss masculine qualities when all about them is feminine." To allow an unmarried, and presumably virgin, woman to teach about human sexuality both permitted the woman to take part in a discussion that by all rights she should have no knowledge of nor standing to discuss, and also emasculated her male students. Indeed, the editorial questioned the ability of female teachers to foster masculinity in male students in any way whatsoever. "Women teachers may by precept, they cannot by example or by the influences of personality," it continued, "inspire our boys toward the manly qualities." While the topic of sexual hygiene was important "for the youths of the race" the editorial concluded, "we shall regret very much to learn that the study of matters of sex has been assigned to people who are not versed in the branches we have enumerated, and in pathology, to teach sex education."[23] Women's inability to broach delicate subjects in the classroom revealed their inability to foster proper gender roles among their students altogether. The editor's subtext was one of concern over unmarried women in the classroom at all, and one of reservation about married women teachers.

The topic of who would teach "sexology" continued to vex the *Union-Review*. The need for education was clear, it argued in a 1919 editorial, because children were being born to parents infected with sexually transmitted diseases. "'Tis a pity millions of children must begin existence carrying the sins of their fathers and mothers," the piece lamented. Adults should restrain their sexual appetites outside of marriage so that they could eventually welcome healthy children to their post-marriage families, then "in due time children and youths ought to be wisely taught by safe teachers the sacred subject of sexology." Again, the newspaper stressed the necessity of "safe teachers," admonishing that only "well qualified physicians" could provide "a wise adjunct to education."[24] Of course, given the almost complete absence of public education for African Americans in the South and the presumable shortage of doctors willing to come to a class to teach about sex anywhere in the country, the editor's arguments were really a means of preventing the subject from being taught in schools at all. Ironically, in the same issue of the *Union-Review*, an advertisement ran, promising "Sex Knowledge." A person need only send 75 cents to the Modern Book Co. in Union Square, New York City, to receive "in plain wrapper a 276-page illustrated book which gives all the sex information you should have—in a wholesome and clean way."[25] While the editor had his concerns over sex education, his publication clearly did not believe that those concerns equated to denying an advertisement space or denying the paper revenue.

Black evangelicals also wrote about marriage, with denominational papers uniformly supportive of the institution of marriage, and of marriage as the only proper venue for sexual relations. Reprinting an article in 1927 from the California *Advocate*, the *Star of Zion* labeled adultery "America's Greatest Peril." The unnamed author had "assumed that all decent citizens took the Seventh Commandment [prohibiting adultery] seriously and that those who violated it were degenerates or rebels," but recent developments seemed to show that chastity was under attack nationwide, as ministers did nothing to stop the assault.[26] The *National Baptist Union-Review* reprinted Bishop W. T. Manning's address before the Triennial Synod of the Church of England in Canada, in which the bishop warned of an attack "against the sacredness of marriage and the family, the standards of sexual purity and those holy ideals of the relation between man and woman which Christ has given us."[27] The *Union-Review*'s Baptist rival, the *National Baptist Voice*, agreed on the need for the preservation of marriage and reprinted President L. K. Williams's remarks on the topic. Williams, in the same speech noted at the start of this chapter, placed the blame for the derailing of society squarely on divorce. "The church must check the reckless divorce craze now sweeping through this country," he argued, "it can do this by holding up the Christian ideals of marriage and urging its members to re-inforce the home with the Christian religion."[28]

Other preachers agreed with Williams about the need to preserve the institution of marriage. AME Zion bishop Cameron C. Alleyne described the effects of divorce on children, effects that were very much gendered. According to his 1937 address to the Watertown (NY) Ministerial Association, divorces "rob so many children of complete parent bond. Something must be balanced in this parenthood. The mother is given to pampering. It is hers to comfort the child with tender words. The father is given to the sterner qualities of discipline now." Divorce upset this delicate balance and presumably meant that children would be cared for only by women with their "tender words" and "pampering," further weakening them and robbing young boys of their future manhood. As Alleyne saw it, divorce meant "substituting calories for character and vitamins for virtue," with women supplying the calories and vitamins and men the character and virtue.[29] A 1932 sermon by Houston pastor Dr. T. J. Goodall, reported by Miss Mary L. Jones in the *National Baptist Voice*, stressed the need for women to "supplement [their] husband's efforts." "If more thought was given," he continued, "to the questions of the duties of wifehood and husbandry there would be fewer cases on the divorce dockets." According to Jones, "Pastor Goodall denounced companionate marriage as one of the greatest social evils of the day."[30] Clearly the preacher believed that marriage was not an institution of shared responsibilities with either partner possessing the ability to terminate the relationship. Instead, marriage was a divine institution that no human should break apart and one in which the wife deferred to her husband, a fairly traditionalist interpretation of marriage in America.

A lengthy and unattributed 1937 article in the *Star of Zion* made the case that marriage was a divine institution, created by God, and that the preservation of the "sanctity of the marriage vow" was critical to the success of the United States of America. The article took a hard line on biblical understanding of marriage and divorce, insisting that Jesus had "evidently regarded as out of harmony with the institution" the modifications Moses made that permitted divorce. Indeed, of the many civil law reasons for divorce ("Adultery, Abandonment, Desertion for a period of years, Cruel and Abusive treatment, Habitual Drunkardness, Imprisonment, etc."), the writer noted that adultery was the only cause Jesus recognized as "sufficient reason to break the marriage bond." The existence of legal divorce laws was one of the "three major crimes" the United States was "being condemned [for] in the thought of the world," the other two being "the crime of lynching [and] the crime of Race segregation." The author suggested that the answer to the divorce problem lay in a rethinking of marriage as divine, an increased effort by the clergy to stress the sanctity of marriage, an increase in the age of consent, a more uniform set of marriage laws, the dissolution of "our double standards of morality," and an end to women working outside the home. "Give the American home a fair field," the article concluded, "and put the God fearing mother at its head; give her a chance to raise her children in the fear of God instead of the fear of starvation, and the next generation will see a people whose God is the Lord and who will regard the marriage covenant as sacred."[31] For the unnamed author, divorce upset traditional gender roles, handicapped children's potential, and ranked with lynching and racism as a threat to American society. The Reverend W. F. Lovelace concurred that Jesus only permitted divorce for "the cause of fornication" and used a more colorful image to describe the dangers of divorce, telling *National Baptist Voice* readers that it was "the gory ox whose horns are full of innocent blood."[32]

Commentators occasionally ventured beyond just discussing hetero-sexual relationships within marriage, condemning any possible instance of same-sex intercourse. A 1929 *Star of Zion* editorial warned ominously that "new forms of lustful gratification have been invented—a form which is lower than the beasts of the field." While editor W. H. Davenport did not de-scribe the act in question, he did note that "young men holding responsible positions are said to be so taken up with this new form of vice that they seek gratification in the vilest and most loathsome fashion," concluding that "it makes one vomit to think of it."[33] The lack of description, other than to say that young men were engaged in the act, leads to a presumption of homo-sexuality. Two years later, the *Star* ran another editorial, "Vile Affections," in which Davenport named homosexuality as the "vile affections." Moving from euphemism—the "unnatural use of the body is a subject which must be dealt with with much delicacy in public discussion"—to the actual term "homosexual proclivities," Davenport fretted that Americans were hearing more about the "unpleasant subject" in a variety of ways, including popular novels. Thus emboldened, he cited Paul's "great indignation" on the topic in Romans 1 (in which Paul lists several actions humans have taken in spite of God's offer of righteousness, stating explicitly, "And likewise also the men, leaving the natural use of the woman, burned in their lust one toward an-other." [Romans 1:27]). The editor raised the issue because he had heard rumors that the "loathsome practice" was growing "among young men." Addressing the various reasons offered for homosexual behavior, the edi-torial offered opinions on each: "If it is a disease, as some claim, the patient should be quarantined. If it is 'a sort of cult of abnormal vice,' the degenerate should be divorced from society and should have no contact whatever with youth. The very thought is abhorrent to decent people, and all who indulge the vile habit should be anathema. Certainly no church, no school could use such a person in any capacity and expect the support and cooperation of the community, not even of the vulgar elements."[34] While Davenport did not cite him as a catalyst for the editorial, the Reverend Adam Clayton Powell's outspoken concern over homosexuality in Harlem coincided with initial 1929 *Star* editorial. Historian George Chauncey has noted that Powell, pastor of the influential Abyssinian Baptist Church in Harlem, led an effort to expose and "attack . . . homosexuality in the African-American community—and particularly in the rectory."[35] Once primed to critique same-sex relations, *Star* editor Davenport returned to the theme when the matter presented itself, which was infrequently. Of far more concern to him, and to most African American evangelicals, were marital relations, extramarital affairs, and premarital sex.

Concomitant with their views on sexual relations, ministers discussed birth control, with most condemning it. A 1931 *Star of Zion* editorial linked the topic of birth control with modernism, which it said was "setting a fast and furious pace. So fast and furious that it often makes one dizzy and nauseous." In this case, the editor was concerned about a recent committee of the Federal Council of Churches of Christ in America (FCC), an ecumenical organization that had formed in 1908 and that white fundamentalists saw as an example of the ills of modernism. The committee's report had urged "'careful and restrained' use of contraceptives in controlling human birth and determining the size of families.'" Editor Davenport's response to the report was one of clear Protestant interpretation: "nowhere in Holy Writ is there a hint or suggestion about birth control, or regulating the size of families." For him, the doctrine of *sola scriptura* had primacy. In a foretaste of later twentieth-century debates over contraception and abortion, Davenport argued that to "put the imprimatur of the Church upon the immoral practice of arresting the orderly process of nature is hostile to Christian doctrine, and subversive of the welfare of society." Implicit in his use of the phrase "imprimatur of the Church" was an attack on the FCC's apparent abandonment of Protestant norms, as his fellow Protestants would have read the phrase as a reference to the Roman Catholicism's imprimatur. The committee's report, he concluded, was "unscriptural and unethical," and he urged more deliberation and less haste.[36]

Not everyone shared Davenport's opposition to birth control. A few months later in the *Star of Zion*, the Reverend H. C. McDonald lamented that in "these days of spiritual weakness we hear and read more about birth control than we hear and read about Christianity." He called on preachers to preach "the gospel and take up the fight for birth control." He reasoned that contraception was already being practiced by married couples and that by fighting against the distribution of information about safe contraceptive practices, the clergy was "doing their best to blindly lead healthy women into a trap of a lot of damnable quacks." If ministers would "preach the old time gospel and follow the lead of the Holy Spirit and let Jesus be the preacher," he concluded, they would "learn to preach and not to abuse."[37] But McDonald was an exception rather than the rule. More typical was the opinion of Deets Pickett, writing to Davenport to explain why many people "throughout the world" had an "unfavorable opinion of the American girl." "No one," he sweepingly declared, "who knows his way around will dispute that the war, the new freedom of women and other modern influences, not to omit increased knowledge of contraceptive methods, have caused many young women to abandon the standards of their mothers."[38]

The very mention of sexual relations and birth control in denomination-al publications raises the question of how these periodicals navigated the anti-obscenity laws of their time, particularly the Comstock Act of 1873, which forbade the interstate distribution and advertisement of material deemed obscene. As historian Andrea Tone has observed, the Comstock Act was not merely one to "control women by banning contraception and abortion," but a larger attempt to enforce Victorian morality in an age of rapid transformation.[39] Most likely, the material escaped the notice of post-al inspectors because it was included in religious publications, which were likely presumed "safe," and because, if noticed, the writers upheld the status quo of Victorian culture rather than attempting to flout it. Even the title of McDonald's pro-contraceptive piece appeared to be against the practice: "Birth Control Versus Christianity." Black ministers and editors of Baptist and Methodist publications stood shoulder to shoulder against the chang-ing interpretations of dating, sexual relationships, and, when they men-tioned it, birth control. These topics brought the various parties together in their attempt to protect a vital portion of the life they had known: the proper relationships between men and women. In the white imagination, African Americans "engaged in sexual behavior that whites saw as immor-al,"[40] so the ministers closed ranks to defend their fellow blacks and warn against the worldly and otherworldly penalties of such transgressions.

The transgressions of birth control were further example for these writ-ers that women were abandoning their traditional roles as mothers and wives. The writers' response to this change reveals another way in which African American evangelicals sided with white fundamentalists and other traditionalists on social issues. Dancing, divorce, sex education, dress and hair styles, and drinking lured women away from the family and consequently weakened the African American race as a whole, the denominational papers argued. For black Baptists and Methodists concerned with uplift and evangelism, the basic building blocks of their society were the family, with the sober and disciplinarian husband, the loving and submissive wife, and the dutiful children. Should African Americans as a group reject this model of domestic relations, they feared, both the individuals and the race would suffer. The injunctions to live as a gendered family were biblical, the consequences of violations both temporal and eternal, as white detractors could easily and already did paint a picture of amoral blacks as threats to civilization. In order to preserve the race and to improve its lot in American society, women had to do their feminine duty.

Women who did not conform to traditional expectations were dangerous, and the Bible had already provided examples of the consequences, black denominational papers warned. For example, the *A.M.E. Zion Quarterly* notified its readers of a "sermon series by Rev. S. G. Spottswood" of New Haven, Connecticut, entitled "Red Women of the Bible." The preacher had delivered a set of homilies devoted to those women in the Bible who did not conform to expectations, thus rendering them dangerous examples for today's impressionable women. Among these sultry biblical figures Spottswood discussed were "Potiphar's Wife, the Perfect Vampire" (Genesis 39, in which Potiphar's unnamed wife attempted to seduce Joseph and, when he refused, accused him of rape); "Delilah, Mistress of Intrigue" (Judges 16, the account of how Delilah managed to discover the secret of Samson's strength and then deprive him of it); "Jezebel, the Woman Who Wore the Pants" (I Kings, Ahab's wife who managed to turn him away from monotheism); "Herodias, the Adultress" (Mark 6:14–24, a woman who had married her own uncle and then abandoned him for Herod, then conspired with Salome to have John the Baptist executed); and "The Scarlet Harlot" (presumably from the Book of Revelation 17). Common among these "wanton" women was their ability to deceive and subvert male hegemony. "These sermons, we are told," the *Quarterly* reported, "were undertaken to bring excessive crowds in the church and they did."[41] Clearly the good Christians of Spottswood's New Haven congregation wanted to hear sermons about the "fallen" women of the Bible, as these characters were all horrible role models as wives and mothers and used sex as a weapon against men. Potiphar's wife acts upon the sexual impulses she feels, then exacts revenge when Joseph spurns her. Delilah subverts Samson's strength through sexual innuendo, while Herodias seeks to silence a prophet for speaking out against her relationship, and Jezebel turns King Ahab against Yahweh. The Reverend Spottswood had added a modern twist, casting Potiphar's wife as a vampire and Jezebel as the "Woman Who Wore the Pants," clearly a reference to the inappropriate modifications to traditional dress codes. His choice of these women during a period of increased discussion of women's roles and rights was no accident. He was warning his parishioners of the perils of modern social expectations, and the *A.M.E. Zion Quarterly* reinforced his message by spreading it to a wider audience. Presumably other ministers were inspired to pen their own "Red Women of the Bible" sermon series.

Just as much as they sought to marginalize women who did not follow traditional gender roles, African American ministers sought to provide examples of and praise to women who followed the traditional path. Contrast Spottswood's sermon series with a sermon given by the Reverend W. S. Ellington, DD, the pastor of the First Baptist Church of East Nashville, and reprinted in the *National Baptist Union-Review*. "The Model Woman," he told the "Large Audience Present," was one who lived like Eve, "who was always present with her husband when God visited the Garden of Eden." Rather than dwell on Eve's interactions with the serpent, Ellington stressed her role as Adam's companion, constantly at his side. Or the model woman was like Sarah, the wife of Abraham and mother of Isaac, or Hannah, the mother of Samuel, both of whom prayed for children to honor God. After disparaging modern women's propensity for fancy clothes ("Right here I would like to say that it is necessary that our mothers teach their daughters that it is far more honorable to work hard for an honest living than to become the plaything for some dressed up dude") and modern courtship rituals ("The modern method of courtship is wretched, when on the night the young man calls the curtains must be lowered, the mother must go to prayer meeting while the daughter sits in the parlor with a fellow, both of them occupying a seat not big enough for one"), Ellington named the "'Model Young Woman'" as Mary, mother of Jesus, "because she loved good company."[42] In Ellington's estimation, women should dress modestly, stand by their men, and make a home for their children.

The *National Baptist Voice* joined the growing conversation about women's dress and behavior when it printed the Reverend M. D. Dickson's address to the Union District Sunday School and BYPU Convention in July 1927. "Bobbed hair," according to Dickson, "is a relic of antiquity and was always a mark of shame and disgrace," so women should not wear their hair short. He added a condemnation of modern dress, tobacco, and "strong drink," and ended with an explanation of why he could not stay silent. "Because," he answered his unseen questioners, "every bobbed hair and short dress woman, every dancing Salome, every drunkard, every one who defiles his body with tobacco, must stand before the Judge of all the earth, who will do right."[43] Women's modesty was a real concern for Dickson and other

black preachers, both for religious and social reasons. Their souls were imperiled by immodesty and the sexuality it implied, and their race would be
judged harshly by whites.

Concerns about women and their behavior could move from the ab-
stract landscape to the anecdotal portrait of one of these women. R. A.
Adams derided contemporary women's behavior, wondering in one case
why such a woman laughed when a man insulted her. Adams recounted the
story of a "young woman who stood on a street corner in St. Louis, waiting
for a bus," around seven in the evening. A young man waiting nearby struck
up a conversation and within "ten minutes he had invited her to make a trip
to Chicago with him, spend the night there, and return the next day, at his
expense." The woman declined the invitation, laughing and saying "'Why,
I am on my way to Kansas City.'" Adams was clearly concerned about her
mirth and evidently asked her "why she did not angrily resent the insult
[of being invited to accompany a stranger to a new city]" and why she had
laughed at what Adams obviously saw as a slight against her character. "She
was amused," he continued, "to have a man—a perfect stranger—regard her
as a woman of the world, or to seek to degrade her with no possible encouragement." Adams concluded that women as a group had lost "respect for
womanhood" and now believed that all women were "easy marks."[44] Adams
saw a diminution of women's dignity in this Kansas City–bound traveler.

A woman traveling alone and not being insulted by a stranger's inappropriate actions was just the tip of the iceberg. "Ashamed of Her," the editor
of the *National Baptist Union-Review* wrote, reflecting upon an encounter
with a woman of questionable dress and make-up on the street: "When
we saw her a-gadding down the street, dress cut off, both the top and the
bottom, and sleeveless, lips painted red, eye brows painted black, cheeks
covered with some kind of white stuff, hair straightened (not any special
objection to that, however) hat entirely unbecoming and skirt too narrow
to allow full, natural step, we said to ourselves, 'What man is fool enough
to walk by her side? And who would marry a thing like that?'" The editor's
assessment of the young woman in question condemned her appearance as
too fashionable and too made up—save her straightened hair—and he used
traditional gender notions to frame his critique. She had clearly not met his
standards for what a proper "lady" would wear in public. But his indictment
of her had racial implications, as well. "People," he continued, "especially
white, looked at each other and laughed." Her appearance was shameful to
him, he argued, and comical to white observers, which reflected poorly on
other people of her race. Rather than castigating the woman in person, he
turned away, "ashamed to be in sight when one of our race in appearance

more fitted for a lunatic asylum was walking a public thoroughfare." Her demeanor and dress meant that she "well should keep off the street till night time."[45] For African American women, the challenge was daunting. They were representatives of their race, the pastors argued, and thus had to pre- serve the traditional modes of dress and comportment in order to maintain their and their race's dignity.

The critique of women's changing roles came not just from African American ministers but also from African American women writing in denominational publications. They echoed the call for women to serve as good wives and mothers and linked the roles to the essence of Christianity. Jeannette M. Freeman provided an extensive litany of social dangers fac- ing the "Modern Generation," as she referred to young people in the early 1930s. As a mother herself, she "wonder[ed] whether the youth of today will stand with patience by the crib of the next generation and transmit the value of Godliness into the minds of the infant, through their lives." Free- man faulted her own generation's maternal skill, and she saw their failures reflected in the worldview of her children. While the view was "beautiful" to them, it was "only the gilded staircase to destruction." Parties (the "laughter at the party"), music ("the race and fury of jazz"), alcohol ("the tiny glasses at the whoopee spree"), sexual relations ("the stumble and fall climbing to bed"), and billiards ("the knocking of balls in yonder pool-room") were "all evidences of the blinking eye of the last Generation and the blind-folded eye of the present." Inherent in her indictment of modernity was a condem- nation of how women had handled the Jazz Age and how they had neglect- ed their duties when so many worldly pleasures were available.[46] Drusilla Dunjee Houston, writing for the Associated Negro Press and reprinted in the *National Baptist Union-Review*, agreed with Freeman that parents were at fault. Who was to blame for the problems manifesting themselves in the younger generation? Her answer was clear: "the parents of America, who got off the path of righteousness and are too cowardly to fight the things that are ruining their children." Among the laundry list of issues, Houston included the "'flapper,'" "the moving picture [that] has glorified the 'scarlet woman,'" "painted women," jazz, and "vulgar vaudeville."[47] As both Free- man and Houston demonstrate, the perils of the modern era placed women in far greater danger than men, as women were thought to be both more impressionable and at the same time guardians of home and hearth. With such temptations omnipresent in their world, women would leave their roles as wives and mothers and abandon their senses in order to achieve transient pleasures. The goal of uplift may have inspired some black women to achieve success outside the home, but for the more traditionalist writers in denominational papers, just as for Evelyn Brooks Higginbotham's Baptist laywomen, women had a proper place, and African Americans as a whole needed to protect their families and their reputations.

As if dancing and changing gender roles were not enough to trouble the writers in black Baptist and Methodist publications, the debate over Prohibition's efficacy and its future in America added more grist to the mill. The dangers of drink were many, and black religious commentary on social issues often linked alcohol's propensity for loosening inhibitions and impeding judgment with black participation in dances, gambling, and other vices. For black preachers and writers, alcohol served as the gateway drug to a life of iniquity and a future of damnation. The Bible warned of the excesses of wine, and, as good Christians, these men read that warning into their own lives and those of their parishioners. But they were also very aware of the ways in which white Americans, especially white southerners, had used the dangers of alcohol to demonize African Americans and disenfranchise them. Historians have correctly observed that the temperance and Prohibition movement gained momentum in the South as a further means of aiding the efforts to disenfranchise black voters.[48] When popular sentiment in the United States began to question the wisdom of total, national Prohibition, African American preachers were faced with difficult choices. Siding with the prohibitionists meant that they would remain true to their traditional understanding of their roles as moral advisers to society. They could uplift the race through clean living and thus prove wrong the segregationists' stereotype that blacks could not remain sober. But when the 1928 presidential election cast the debate in terms of a dry, Protestant Republican and a wet, Roman Catholic Democrat, the racially indifferent record of the Republican Party, combined with the shifting allegiances of white southern Democrats, made the seemingly simple question of legislatively enforced abstinence a much more difficult proposition. Just as it was for many fundamentalists and other evangelicals, Prohibition was very important to black Baptists and Methodists, but the politics of the late 1920s and early 1930s— as well as the Roman Catholicism of Al Smith—forced them to consider how much they would do to retain a ban on alcoholic beverages.

Previous scholarship on Prohibition and on the 1928 presidential election's effects on black voting patterns has tended to isolate, rather than combine, the two. Scholars have portrayed Prohibition as a moment of temporary hyper-morality, a reaction to industrialization, or a rural/urban reaction to immigration.[49] Regardless of its origins, it found fertile ground in the American South, as lawmakers who were already in the process of rewriting state constitutions to keep blacks from voting used the specter of drunk, hypersexual black men as a threat to the region's white women and way of life. Interestingly enough, these southerners abandoned their practice of statewide efforts and joined the bandwagon of an amendment to the US Constitution, embracing federalism even as they sought to preserve their states' rights to regulate voting and promote Jim Crow legislation. Black voters nationally saw what was happening and at first remained steadfastly loyal to the Republican Party—the party of Lincoln. But Republicans took what black votes there were (historian Nancy J. Weiss has pointed out that roughly two-thirds of African Americans lived in Jim Crow states in the early 1930s, where they had no real voting power) for granted and ignored or angered African Americans with a long list of slights in the 1910s and 1920s.[50] While these two trends—the country away from alcohol and black voters away from the Republican Party—may seem to be unrelated, for black religious leaders, they were inextricably linked. Much like the black clubwomen of historian Lisa G. Materson's Chicago in the 1920s, black Baptist and Methodist writers saw a connection, but unlike the clubwomen, the Methodists and Baptists wove religion into their interpretation.[51]

In terms of support for Prohibition, the National Baptist Conventions (both Incorporated and Unincorporated), the AME Church, and the AME Zion Church all voiced praise for the elimination of alcohol from America. Articles such as "Temperance" and "Alcohol and the Body" informed of the dangers of drinking, while others kept readers current on the latest discussions and their advocates.[52] For these papers, the threats posed by alcohol were both immediate and eternal, and those concerns led some writers to overlook racist stereotypes of blacks and to side with white temperance arguments that alcohol made blacks violent. The editors printed pieces tying the effects of Prohibition to a "better class of Negroes" emerging from their drunken stupor. For example, the *National Baptist Voice* ran an article by J. H. Larimore, entitled "The Negro and Prohibition," which admitted that the "race question" was "one of the impelling reasons for prohibition in the southern states," and included "a series of letters addressed to both white and colored leaders" to prove that "prohibition accomplished its purpose."[53] A similarly titled item, "The Negro and Prohibition," ran a few months later in the *Star of Zion*, and reported on the experiences of Dr. James A. Bond, director of the Kentucky Interracial Commission, in riding in the "colored compartment" of a train on two separate occasions, once before the ratification of the Eighteenth Amendment and once after ratification. The pre-Prohibition account included "poorly dressed men and women, loud and boisterous, many in various stages of intoxication" following a "Saturday afternoon holiday." Bond related how there were fistfights, "knives and guns flashed," and the conductor was almost thrown from the moving train. A journey on the same train after Prohibition allowed Bond to encounter "a well-dressed, happy, jolly, good natured" crowd. The conductor now could treat them in a "good-natured, gentlemanly" manner, and Bond passed his time asking his fellow passengers what difference Prohibition had made. Their answers included increased black homeownership, black home cleanliness, "school children were better fed, better clothed and better prepared with books," and that "jails and jailers had been put out of commission." Bond whispered to himself, "'Thank God for prohibition,'" as he left the train.[54] *National Baptist Union-Review* editor J. H. Frank concurred, noting that "colored people have attained their largest material prosperity under prohibition."[55]These sentiments were generally shared by many black Baptists and Methodists and should come as no surprise, given the prevalence of Victorian morals among these writers, as well as the long-standing tradition among black clergy of campaigns for racial uplift, which included an ardent support of temperance and prohibition efforts.

Once discussion in the United States turned to the success or failure of Prohibition and its attendant federal enforcement, however, African American denominational papers began to waiver in their solidarity for the Eighteenth Amendment. Their concerns were multi-fold and were compounded by the candidates in the 1928 presidential election. In that contest, black Protestants faced a difficult choice: vote for a wet Roman Catholic Democrat, Al Smith, whose party included a pro-Prohibition plank in its platform, or for a dry Quaker Republican, Herbert Hoover, whose party also supported Prohibition but had done little to endear itself to a constituency that still remembered its promise as the "party of Lincoln" and its inability to deliver political and social equality. The presidential contest in 1928 was a transitional moment in American party politics for many reasons. Not only did Smith run as the first major party Catholic presidential candidate, but also his Catholicism and his support for repeal of Prohibition caused a number of southern states to break with their traditional voting habits and back Republican Hoover. Both candidates had their shortcomings in the eyes of black Methodists and Baptists. The varied reactions of the denominational newspapers help illustrate how black voters at large weighed these issues and began their shift away from Republican Party loyalty. They also highlight how African American evangelicals could deviate from enthusiastic embrace of traditionalist religious beliefs and instead adopt more progressive stances when they fit their understanding of racial aspirations.

Some black evangelicals were concerned that Governor Smith was Roman Catholic and feared that he would be subservient to the Vatican and the Pope. Such anti-Catholic claims were not unique to these writers; indeed, anti-Catholic nativism has a long and virulent history in the United States and among evangelicals and fundamentalists.[56] For the *National Baptist*

Union-Review, Roman Catholicism was a real and present danger to American democracy. In 1918, Jonathan Frank had warned of Roman Catholics' divided loyalties. In an editorial entitled, "Beware," he wrote that "millions of Roman Catholic people, mostly of foreign birth, give their first allegiance to the Pope. They not only get their religion from Rome, but their politics, also."[57] Almost a decade later, when Al Smith's aspirations for higher office began to gain momentum, Frank stepped up his attack, both on Smith and on Catholicism in general. "What is the Matter with White People?" he asked in an eponymously titled editorial in 1927, claiming, "They crowd about a casket, women fainting, men trampling each other, to see the face of a foreigner, Roman Catholic, Italian, theatre actor, a man who married and divorced women, who spends thousands of dollars, but not for religion, moral reforms or for charity, or any other utilitarian purpose." In his list of "very strange things" white people did, Frank stated that when a "representative of the Pope of Rome comes to America and the governor of New York and the mayors of New York City and Chicago, respectively kneel in public places and kiss the foreigner's finger ring!"[58] For Frank, Catholicism was at once a danger to American democracy and a peculiar idiosyncrasy of white people, much like theological modernism. After ridiculing Catholic veneration of relics (writing that "to us it is laughable to see grown men and women bowing to a bone said to be the leg-bone of St. So and So . . . why is it intelligent people believe such stories?") he predicted that should the upcoming Democratic National Convention in Houston nominate Smith, "the south 'solid south' will break."[59] More troubling to Frank, however, was the threat to the American way of life. Should Smith become president, he warned, and should "Romanism" win, the pope's rulings would trump the US Constitution. "Freedom of speech, religious liberty, the Little Red school house, newspapers, the Bible and the ministry," he railed, "all will be under the ban when Romanism wins."[60] Frank's virulent anti-Catholic views parallel his strong stance against theological modernism. Indeed, of all the publications, the *Union-Review* was the most consistently opposed to Smith purely on the grounds of his religion.

The *Union-Review* also raised concerns about Smith's political affiliation and his stand on Prohibition. On the eve of the Democratic National Convention, Frank asserted that, although Hoover and the Republicans were not working to assist African Americans, neither were they "on record for doing any thing directly against us." Contrasting that with the idea that Democrats were no friends of blacks, Frank concluded that in a Hoover administration "the interests of Colored Americans will be more safe than they will be in the hands of any Democrat available for the presidency."[61] By the end of September, Frank was even more solidly in favor of Hoover because of his stated position of supporting the Eighteenth Amendment. That position, Frank believed, would gain Hoover the support of a list of political bedfellows, perhaps strange from our perspective: "all mothers anxious about the futures of their sons and daughters," Anti-Saloon League members, Masons, "ten million members of the Ku Klux Klan," "all 'dry' Democrats," "Colored Americans," and even bootleggers, whose support Frank attributed to their fears that Smith's repeal of Prohibition would mean the legal sale of alcohol and "that means the end of bootlegging."[62] In his electoral forecast, Frank imagined a coalition of backers so broad it boggles the contemporary mind, but he was willing to work with people he hated, even white racists, in order to defeat what he saw as a greater evil—the presidency of a wet Roman Catholic Democrat.

For W. H. Davenport and the *Star of Zion*, the election was less a discussion about Roman Catholicism than a referendum on the preservation of Prohibition and a commentary on the sad state of racial affairs in the country. Davenport ran much more moderate editorials than his *Union-Review* counterpart, and he published a pair of endorsements, one for Smith and the other for Hoover, in the weeks leading up to the general election. Even Davenport, however, could not resist hyperbole in the final days of the campaign, arguing for the need to protect Prohibition.

As the Democrats gathered in Houston, Davenport charged that southern Democrats were being disingenuous about their concerns over Smith's stand on alcohol. Instead, he alleged, their opposition to the governor was a "palpable subterfuge" to hide their real fear—his religion. The editor inferred that he would expect no less from a bigoted group led by "Senator [Tom] Heflin [a vicious segregationist from Alabama] and his ilk," and offered it as further proof that white southerners were using "virtue" to mask "vice." Davenport did not explicitly link this "hypocrisy" to the way the same people treated African Americans, but he did imply a connection.[63] Other *Star* editorials about Smith and Hoover noted the need for both parties to abstain from race-baiting and observed that Hoover and the Republicans could be considered allies of African Americans more than the party that had nominated Smith.[64]

The real issue for Davenport was the safety of the Eighteenth Amendment. When Hoover accepted the Republican nomination, Davenport wondered how sincere was Hoover's support for the Volstead Act, the congressional legislation to enforce the amendment, since Hoover had endorsed an appointed committee to investigate the law's violations. Davenport mocked this position, saying "everybody knows" the extent to which Prohibition was being violated. He also mourned the lack of appeal to African Americans in Hoover's acceptance speech.[65] The preservation of Prohibition topped Davenport's list of priorities, and he warned his readers that a Smith election could allow him to appoint Supreme Court justices who would "declare the 18th Amendment unconstitutional."[66] By late September, Davenport was sufficiently worried to portray drinking as an evil of epic proportions. "Alcoholism, the saloon," he warned somewhat hysterically, "has been a great curse to the nation, greater than slavery, and we recoil at the contemplation of its return in any form." Yet even as he gave such a vital reason to vote for Hoover and against the return of a curse he deemed greater than the enslavement of millions of African Americans, Davenport lauded the racial progressivism of Smith. But that progressivism in the face of the Klan's racial antipathy was not enough to sway Davenport to the Democratic Party. Instead, he urged his audience to vote for Hoover. "A vote for Hoover," he concluded, "will be a vote for the preservation of the home, society, and the continued prosperity of the country. What we need most is bread, not beer."[67] Davenport's positioning of drinking as an evil greater than slavery is hard to justify, but perhaps he truly believed that alcohol's curse would afflict all humans, rather than just one race, and destroy all of society, and thus the comparison, for him, was valid.

His fellow AME Zion bishop, George C. Clement, did not agree and wrote a front-page article in the *Star* in early October 1928, entitled "Why Support Governor Smith." According to Clement, the future of African Americans in the United States depended on a careful reading of the racial realignment of the two parties. True, he argued, southern Democrats were biased against African Americans. Senator Tom Heflin "hates the Negro with an unreasoning and vicious hatred," he observed, "the more to be feared because it finds its basis in race antagonism." And true, the Republican Party had traditionally been "considered the 'Ark of Safety' for the Negro." But the two parties were in the process of a massive shift on race questions. The Republican Party, Clement argued, "has taken over the Klan bag and baggage in the North, while in the South, a glad welcome is extended to the anti-Catholic Democracy—so-called dry wing, by the 'lilly white' Republicans." Because the Democratic Party had nominated Smith and thus endorsed "toleration," Clement reasoned, black voters should put aside their historic voting patterns and opt for Smith. "Of all the voters," he wrote, "the Negro should espouse the side of toleration in this campaign. He cannot afford to embrace the side of bigotry and prejudice." His logic ran both as an appeal to toleration and as an endorsement of the proposition that the enemy of my enemy is my friend. Only by the very end of the piece did he mention Prohibition, which he believed would "prevail by the will of the nation's awakened conscience, as well as by act of legislation."[68] Clement optimistically thought that a retreat from racial and religious prejudice would usher in an age of greater awareness of the dangers of alcohol and a consensus not to break the law.

The Reverend James T. Gaskill did not share Clement's optimism or his support for Smith. Gaskill answered the bishop with his own front-page article, "Why Support Hoover." The North Carolina pastor instead framed the election in a simple binary: "the 'Wet' and the 'Dry.'" To vote on the side of the "Wet" meant to side with "saloons," the "liquor traffic," and "sin and wickedness." To vote dry meant to count yourself on the side of the church and "righteousness," which by the transitive property "represents God." Gaskill dismissed what he saw as a false dichotomy of white segregationist support for Smith, noting that "it is not a question as to whether Tom Heflin, the Ku Klux Klan, Senator [Furnifold M.] Simmons [Democrat of North Carolina] or any other race-haters support Hoover or Smith." Instead the central issue was "which of these vital issues will I and other lovers of God and righteousness in this Christian nation support?" Gaskill was so upset by Clement's support for Smith that he questioned the bishop's religious sincerity and integrity, in an election in which the central issue was "world against the church, the devil against God." The position for all good Christians, regardless of their denomination or race, was plain: "all Christians ought to vote for Hoover."[69] For Gaskill, the campaign offered a set of stark contrasts. Those stark contrasts, in turn, meant that African American evangelicals and all others who called themselves Christian needed to get out the vote to preserve Prohibition and defeat those who would weaken it.

Both Gaskill and Clement shared the view that preachers should be involved in politics, and other writers expressed similar opinions. Over at the *National Baptist Union-Review*, the anti-Smith sentiment led editor Frank to print an open letter to the "Negro Ministers of Georgia" from B. J. Davis, editor of the African American newspaper, the Atlanta *Independent*. Davis urged black pastors to ignore efforts by the Smith campaign to keep preachers out of politics, maintaining instead that they should join in the election discussion from their pulpits. Davis praised the white clergy of the South for speaking out against "the foes of clean government and righteousness," and asked black clergy to do the same. He grounded his argument in the contention that the United States was "a Christian nation, and the fundamental principle upon which our Government rests is faith in God." That presupposition meant that ministers had a duty to involve themselves in political debates, especially those as critical as the 1928 election. Davis wanted to "sound the tocsin day in the day out, to tell [the African American pastor] he has a place in the political life of his country." Not only did he have a place, Davis argued, the black preacher "should join his white brother in arousing the public conscience against rum, race hatred, and the devil."[70] The *Union-Review*'s Incorporated counterpart, the *National Baptist Voice*, was silent on the race in the months leading up to Election Day, but once the results were counted, it happily compared the campaign to that of Abraham Lincoln and Stephen A. Douglas. Hoover, like Lincoln, had stood on the side of right. "We cannot but feel," the editor wrote, and claimed to have been making nightly speeches in favor of Hoover, "that we have taken a long step forward."[71]

Hoover's triumph in November 1928 led William H. Davenport to exclaim, "The nation now knows there is a God in Israel." The *Star of Zion* editor expressed his happiness with the preservation of Prohibition, but also voiced hope that the black vote's split was a sign of future empowerment of African Americans in general. The race had proved the God in Israel notion in both the repudiation of "mud-slinging and personalities" and in the fact that "for the first time in sixty years Negroes throughout the country voted the Democratic ticket."[72] Indeed, Davenport was right that black voters would no longer unite under the Republican banner. But while the 1928 presidential contest presented a clear-cut choice for many black evangelicals, that binary began to weaken in the 1932 election cycle. To be sure, the sentiment against alcohol remained, but economic pressures from the Great Depression and concerns over Hoover's lack of attention to black Americans led some African American evangelicals to see the election in a more complex manner. Race and economics could trump biblical concern for these writers.

For example, AME Zion bishop E. D. W. Jones made the front page of the denomination's *Star of Zion* in October 1931, as well as the front page of the Louisville *Leader*, for his denunciation of Prohibition. Speaking to the Kentucky Conference session, Jones took the position that the amendment "fruitlessly attempts to make men moral." Noting that the Apostle Paul had said that Christians lived "'not under the law but under grace,'" Jones argued that Jesus "made no laws" and thus any laws legislated to make people achieve morality were made in vain. He distinguished between human rights and human appetites, and made the case that churches—both black and white—would be better served by concentrating on race relations.[73] Editor Davenport commented that Jones was the first to take such a stand in the denomination and that "this courageous statement of the Bishop will likely provide lively discussion and amazement in some circles."[74] But the *Star*'s pages over the next year did not fulfill his prediction. Instead, the paper printed a few tepid endorsements of Prohibition. By the eve of the election, the *Star*, along with the *National Baptist Union-Review*, did reprint a piece entitled, "Nationally Known Dry Leaders Call for Re-Election of Mr. Hoover," authored by a variety of white supporters of the Eighteenth

Amendment, including William H. Danforth, chair of the Ralston-Purina Company, and Dr. Frank G. Coffin, president of the General Convention of the Christian Church.[75] On the editorial page that week, Davenport urged his readers to reconsider their allegiance to the Republican Party. Arguing for a "more intelligent exercise of the suffrage," he asked his fellow African Americans to "vote for the candidates whose policies they believe will best conserve their interest."[76] The *Union-Review* made no such editorial, but neither did it print an endorsement of Hoover for the continuation of Prohibition. According to the *Star*, African Americans needed to vote for their race, rather than for a particular social issue, no matter how deep the roots of that issue or how dire the rhetoric could be. Far more important for Davenport was how to protect African Americans overall from a variety of threats, not just the danger of demon rum.

The *National Baptist Voice*, so quiet during the 1928 campaign, found its voice with a new editor in 1932 and urged a wider perspective on the issues facing the nation. Disparaging the "prohibition fanatics," editor R. C. Barbour maintained that Christianity was concerned with a variety of "social, economic, and political" issues. The church, he concluded, "sins grievously when it limits its interest to only one sin out of the many afflicting human society."[77] To concentrate only on drinking meant that pastors and their congregations ignored a whole host of other dangers to the human body and soul. Moreover, Barbour chastised both parties for abandoning African Americans and predicted that some black voters would even consider voting for the Communist Party candidate, Earl Browder, because he had named a black man, James W. Ford, as his vice-presidential running mate. Barbour urged his fellow blacks to make a sign to place on "your hat band: SHOULD EITHER THE SOCIAL OR THE COMMUNIST PARTY WIN THE ELECTION, YOU WILL NOT BE ANY WORSE OFF THAN YOU ARE NOW."[78] For Barbour, religious reasons to vote for Hoover, or against a party that openly mocked religion, had evaporated in the face of the pressing needs of black people as a race and the histories of the Democratic and Republican parties' ignoring those needs. Shortly after the election, Barbour penned a rambling editorial that ended with the statement, "we are not going to shed any tears over the election. It was simply a matter of tweedledee and tweedledum, we lost pot Hoover and got kettle Roosevelt."[79] The *Star of Zion*'s Davenport was not as scathing in his election post-mortem, but he did share Barbour's goal of having African Americans vote in their own self-interest. Noting that Hoover had "promised too much" and "ignored too many," Davenport celebrated the electoral shift among black voters. "For the first time in history," he rejoiced, "leading Negroes and Negro papers deserted the Republican party and threw the weight of their influence toward the Democratic party."[80] His elation was so much that, just a month later, he was wondering whether a black candidate for president might be possible.[81] That hope would not be realized for another thirty-six years, but the Republican Party's hold on black voting patterns had indeed ended, and many African American Protestants were pleased with the change. No longer would they counsel their parishioners to vote for a single party or even for a single political issue, save for civil rights.

African American denominational papers would return to the subjects of morality and anti-modernism for many years to come, but the Great Depression and the need for civil rights had forever broken their unity on topics such as drinking, dancing, and divorce. These matters would all be cause for concern over the next several decades, but they never gained the prominence they once held in the pages of National Baptist, AME, and AME Zion publications. There was a limit on how much a Christian should follow the biblical injunctions against certain behaviors when there was a more pressing concern facing the world—the omnipresent specter of racism and segregation. The political shifts in African American voting signaled a different understanding of uplift, as well. The race could be uplifted not only by improving its education levels, its sobriety, and its decorum. Now more than ever, uplift could also encompass the demand that political parties work for black votes and the view that working meant improving lives of African Americans nationwide. The emphasis on race relations and equality had been present in African American denominational life for quite some time, as the next chapter will demonstrate. Rather than define Christianity by adherence to certain behaviors and creeds, African American Baptists and Methodists would define it as how much an individual tried to reconcile differences among the races.

5

"And This Is Where the White Man's Christianity Breaks Down"

Race Relations and Ecclesiology
in the Era of Lynchings and Jim Crow

J. D. Crenshaw, editor of the *National Baptist Voice*, lamented the "Unprecedented Crime Waves" as the year 1921 began. After cataloging the many offenses ("burglary, assassination, robbery, murder, raping, Ku Kluxism, lynching, brutalities and the trampling of all law under the unhallowed feet of blood-thirsty hoodlums"), Crenshaw pointedly observed that "Christian America" was interested in improving such situations abroad, but that it ignored its own problems. "Charity," he wrote, "it is said, and aptly may be applied here, begins at home. This is clearly true, and happily, pointedly, and logically suggests to America—the United States—her own neglected home duty involved the most desperate situation." According to Crenshaw, the world's nations, "even Soviet Russia," were not fooled when the United States made a "pretentious show of altruism when lawlessness runs roughshod over the entire land and the press of the country reeks with daily accounts of crime-waves inundating the whole country." He closed with a stern admonition: "Clean-up here, then go abroad!"[1]

As African American Protestants wrestled with their understandings of modern culture and changes in theology, they were unified on another matter—the true Christian church embraced equality for all races and that equality was not present in the United States. This religious emphasis on the inherent equality of all human beings regardless of race pervaded denominational newspapers from the First World War through the beginnings of the Second World War. Almost every issue of every denominational paper in this study—whether Baptist or Methodist—contained at least one article about the need for either improved race relations or racial equality, and an overwhelming majority of those either mentioned or focused on the dissonance of inequality and Christianity. Against the overwhelmingly present notion in white American society at the time that Jesus was white and Nordic, a situation historians Edward J. Blum and Paul Harvey deftly discuss, African American Baptist and Methodist writers offered their counterproposal—that Christianity was and should be the vehicle by which all races enjoyed equality.[2]

Such an effort and such a view of Christianity should not be surprising. African Americans faced racial hatred on a daily basis, regardless of where they lived in the United States. Those who lived in the South had to contend with Jim Crow laws, lynchings, convict leasing systems, rape as a means of subjugating women, and omnipresent reminders of black inferiority in the white culture. But racism was not confined to the South. African Americans seeking jobs in northern cities found more subtle racism at work, as did those who ventured west.[3]

The universal enemy of racism contrasted sharply with the purpose of Christianity, as understood by black Protestants. In Christianity, they found messages of equality and charity, both of which were lacking in white American society. In Paul's words to the Galatians ("There is neither Jew nor Greek, there is neither bond nor free, there is neither male nor female: for ye are all one in Christ Jesus,") generations of enslaved and free blacks identified the idea that Christianity created one body, not many. Historians have already documented and discussed this interpretation.[4] But it bears investigation during the early twentieth century because it was a part of black Americans' discussion of and response to fundamentalism, while also seeming to be at home in more progressive Protestant thought. For black evangelicals of the early twentieth century, the question was not one of conservative or liberal, fundamentalist or modernist, traditionalist or progressive; instead it was a question of both/and. Strict adherence to biblical texts, for example, could yield clear instructions to aid the poor and embrace all humans as brothers. In fact, African American Protestants used the biblical admonition of Jesus, "verily I say unto you, Inasmuch as ye have done it unto one of the least of these my brethren, ye have done it unto me" (Matthew 25:40), as both a biblical hermeneutic and an ecclesiology. They subjected other teachings in the Bible to the lens of equality and concern for the downtrodden, and they turned this test into a basic understanding of what the Christian church embodied. For them, those individuals who held to equality and charity were Christians; those who did not, were not.[5]

The deeper question for these writers was one of ecclesiology: how could you define the Christian church and include segregationists, lynchers, and racists? The simple answer was that you could not. Any understanding of the Christian message had to include a steadfast belief in the equality of all people before God. Since many white Americans could not meet this simple test, they were not really a part of the church of Jesus. Much as white fundamentalists had labeled liberal Protestants as outside the fold, African American Baptist and Methodist writers defined the church as an organization of like-minded people, alike in that they believed in equality. There were, of course, more layers to the definition of "Christian church" than just equality, but the bottom line for these writers was that social justice had just as much of a role to play in defining the true Christian as did doctrines like the Virgin Birth, the inerrancy of the Bible, and the substitutionary atonement of Jesus. For African American Protestants, doctrinal matters were important, but as the twentieth century progressed, the most important test was one of the examples of Jesus. In this interpretation of "What Would Jesus Do?" they demanded that white Christians observe the basic precepts of equality found in the Bible. As the *Star of Zion* put it, the "Negro would be satisfied if the Nordic would apply the ethics of Jesus, whom we all preach, to this question. If we let Jesus fix it, we believe He would fix it right."[6] The demand for a solution to the problems of discrimination and violence led black evangelicals to combine what might appear to be disparate theological positions into one comprehensive strategy to deal with American racism in its myriad forms. It also marked their differences from white fundamentalists, who reified white supremacist ideas, while providing an opportunity to find common ground with their sometime rivals, white modernists. This ecclesiology was a black evangelical response to the dilemma posed by white fundamentalists: who or what constituted the "true" church? Black Baptists and Methodists answered that true Christians embraced the Bible at all levels and in all its quotidian demands because they read it as God's divine commandments. An inspired reading meant working for race relations and social justice. In this respect, these ministers drew on a long line of prophetic tradition, as scholar Christopher Z. Hobson has demonstrated, to illustrate that both the Hebrew prophets and Christ himself demanded this approach.[7] To ignore it would be to ignore the divine will.

Prominent in the pages of the *National Baptist Union-Review*, the *A.M.E. Christian Recorder*, the AMEZ *Star of Zion*, and the *National Baptist Voice* were articles on lynching—its causes, its events, and its prevention. As they reported on these atrocities against humanity, which were developing into what historian Grace Elizabeth Hale terms "spectacle lynchings," the papers highlighted the evil present and the need for religious intervention.[8] "We Will Continue to Pray," the *National Baptist Union-Review* proclaimed in a July 1917 headline, following the "burning" of a Memphis man and the "outrageous murder of numerous colored people in East St. Louis." The paper compared the suffering of the victims to the atonement of Christ on the cross, stating that "'[w]ithout the shedding of blood there is no remission of sin,' and within the present range of civilization no absolute social progress." The *Union-Review* found hope, however, through "intercessory prayers" and "trusting in God."[9] Following the lynching by burning of three men in Kirwin, Texas, the *A.M.E. Christian Recorder* described the scene for readers and noted that members of the lynch mob "were all known to the sheriff as they vied with each other for the 'honor' of touching off the lights to the human bodies." The paper also observed that the event "occurred directly in front of two churches, and continued until near Sunday morning," but that there was no evidence that the pastors of those churches intervened.[10] The same paper publicized the denomination's "Report of the Committee on the State of the Country," which noted "recent atrocities in Mississippi and Georgia." The atrocities were lynchings, both of which occurred "immediately in the wake of the celebration of 'Constitution Week,' thereby making a mockery of that sacred document, which was framed, as its founders declared 'To establish justice, insure domestic tranquility, provide for the common defense, promote the general welfare, and secure the blessings of liberty.'" Despite the lynch mobs' actions that refuted the words of the preamble of the US Constitution, editor Richard Wright Jr. declared that "we should not despair, but let us not forget that God yet reign, 'Right is right, and God is God / And right the day will win.'"[11] The article did not specify when God would triumph over evil, either in this world or the next, but it did take comfort in knowing that evil could not reign forever.

The notion that lynching was evil allowed African American Protestants to cast the lynch mobs as agents of the devil, and indeed, that conception of them is hard to deny. The *National Baptist Voice* described the South as being "in the deadly and diabolical grip of blood-thirsty delirium of lynching," portraying the lynchers as demons. These "inhuman and bloody night orgies" were part of "an ever-growing horrid condition for the Negro race group in portions of the South." The *Voice* concluded that it was "hellish, and without excuse."[12] Following the Arkansas lynching of Henry Lowry in 1921, the *Voice* questioned the veracity of the Latin saying, "'vox populi, vox Dei,'" the voice of the people is the voice of God, arguing that "if the cremation of Lowery [sic] was vox populi, most assuredly it was not vox Dei." God, according to editor J. D. Crenshaw, had given people the Ten Commandments, which Crenshaw considered the basis for all human law. The lynching of Lowry and all lynchings returned the country to the "barbarism of the cave man . . . and Christianity is confronted with the toughest task of all the centuries since Christ."[13] Crenshaw was not yet done casting out demons and warning about civilization, as he returned to the term "diabolical" to describe the effects of a 1922 lynching, and again when he penned an editorial entitled "Civilization Toppling" after lynchings in Georgia and

Texas, events that led him to claim that the two states "are vying with each other in seeing which can produce the more horrible form of torture."[14] Taking the demonic analogy one step further, the AME Zion's *Star of Zion* reprinted a *Pittsburgh Christian Advocate* article calling for a new federal anti-lynching law under the headline, "The Mark of the Beast." For African American Methodists, lynch mobs were in league with the Antichrist and his minions.[15]

The theological conclusions that these editors drew from lynchings further illustrate the central theme in African American Protestantism, regardless of whether one was a traditionalist or progressive: that God wanted equality, and Christianity should practice and promote it. Reviewing social reformer Kirby Page's book, *Jesus or Christianity—A Study in Contrasts*, the *Star of Zion* lauded the author's thesis that churches had allowed themselves to become entangled with society's "evils." Editor Davenport concluded that the African American would "never be content until he gets a Christian square deal."[16]

Exploring the disconnect between Christian faith in America and the practice of lynching allowed African American intellectual Kelly Miller, a target of some scorn by black ministers for his embrace of theological modernism, to enjoy publication in the *Star of Zion*. Appalled by the recent lynching of "two negroes . . . at the funeral pyre in Northern Texas within the space of a week," Miller raised the specter of evil, describing the "ghoulish process of burning the dead body of the victim for the sheer exhilaration of glutting the passion with hellish delight." "The savage," Miller fumed, "roasts his victim alive in preparation for a cannibalistic feast, but the modern day Christian has no such pretext for inflicting excruciating cruelty. The savage is the better sportsman." One of the cases that outraged Miller was the Sherman Courthouse Riot, in which a mob of white Texans managed to lynch a black man accused of sexually assaulting a white woman, even as Texas Rangers, dispatched by the governor, tried to intervene. In Miller's eyes, particularly damning was the fact that no white religious leaders spoke out against the mob's actions. By Miller's account, the white "Methodist Conference [which] was sitting at Dallas a few miles away," should have noticed the violence and done something. "By means of eye glasses," he argued perhaps a bit too hyperbolically, "they could discern the column of smoke arising from frying human flesh, but not a word escapes their hallowed lips." He continued, "they spend their time excusing the bishops for dabbling in politics or gambling in Wall Street. How can we expect the people to have respect and reverence for the Christian religion, if this be an exemplification of it? There are two colleges and twenty-six Christian churches in Sherman, Texas; but not one man exhibited the courage either of his conscience or of his culture."[17]

For Miller, and for many black ministers, the failure of white pastors to speak out or intervene in such an obviously evil act called into question whites' interpretation of Christianity. That the Christian was called to oppose evil in the world was clear to Miller and his readers, and the white religious leaders of Sherman, Texas, had been weighed in the balance and found wanting.

Hand in hand with the condemnation of lynching went a denunciation of the Ku Klux Klan. The 1915 revival of the Klan and its ascendency during the 1920s was an obvious sign for African Americans—secular and religious—that white Americans had either forsaken Christianity or embraced a very warped interpretation of it.[18] Warning in 1921 of the Klan's spread to the North, *Christian Recorder* editor Richard Wright Jr. noted that the "Ku Klux Klan [was] most busy now" because it suspected African Americans who had fought valiantly in the recent world war would expect equality in repayment for their service, an effort which he said the Klan members were "determined to forestall by fair or foul means." Unfortunately, Wright noted, white Americans were not rising up to counteract the Klan's efforts. "Our white friends," he observed, "are becoming fewer and fewer each year, and if we depend upon them alone we shall be pushed back into serfdom."[19] Indeed, African Americans were often the victims of both white aggression and white inaction to stop that aggression.

For the editor of the AME Zion's *Star of Zion*, W. H. Davenport, the Klan's newfound power exposed white racism's pervasiveness. He contended that both major political parties had Klan members in their ranks and noted that it "is apparent that the only thing that would wrest the South from its Democratic moorings would be the nomination of a Negro for President. Rock-ribbed Southern democracy would support Judas Iscariot if he wore the Democratic label."[20] Davenport kept up his attacks on the religion of the Klan members, noting that "Saint Peter was a Jew. Wonder if the Kluxers have decided not to go to heaven because St. Peter stands at the gate." As further proof that white Americans refused to acknowledge the universality of Christianity, Davenport employed an interpretation of Simon of Cyrene, the man pressed into service by the Romans to carry the cross when Jesus was too weak, as a black man: "The Founder of our Christian religion was a Jew; the bearer of his Cross was a Negro. But since that date the 'Nordics' have been trying to monopolize everything." His depiction of Simon as black anticipated Countee Cullen's poem, "Simon the Cyrenian Speaks," by a few years and fought white "Nordic" interpretations of Christ.[21] In March 1925, Davenport remarked sardonically that white leaders expressed their shame over the Klan yet failed to act to stop it. As he put it, the situation in the United States was one of saying "we are ashamed of the Klan; we are ashamed of our lynching record, and are desperately in earnest about reducing it even though we burn a human being occasionally to throw the fear of God and the distrust of our American Christianity into the natives."[22] For Davenport, white Americans both distanced themselves from the Klan and did nothing to stop it. Indeed, it was for whites a means of racial oppression from which they could benefit without taking an active role.

The Klan's threat to African Americans contributed to the *Star of Zion*'s 1925 choice of front-page placement for a prematurely celebratory article, "Klan's Power on the Decline: Civil Liberties Union Reports: Factional Disputes, Loss of Dues, Political Defeats Fatal to Klan."[23] In 1928, AME Zion bishop G. C. Clement repeated this overly sanguine view in his address to the 28th General Conference. "We have seen," he declared, "the Invisible Empire, so called flourish," only to be "scorched and blasted by its very tap root, by its own nefarious machinations." The Klan was, according to Clement, "weighed and wanting with the whole category of its pious preachments and impious practices, its racial bias, and un-Christian and un-American tolerance, doomed to the infamy it so well deserves."[24] African Americans saw the ties between white Christians and Klan activities, deriding both and calling into question the religious basis of Klan activism. William Davenport noted in the *Star of Zion* that the Klan, with the "weirdness of its ritual, its degradations of the Cross of Calvary to a symbol of hate and bigotry, its appeal to class and racial prejudice," was "far more inimical to the American peace and prosperity than the most rabid Communism, or the most virulent anarchist." But, he believed, Americans had realized its threat and had already begun to "repudiate it and withdraw their support." Yet, in "its last bid for life, like the noisy demagogue, the mediocre and obscure politician, the Klan again returns to its assault upon the Negro. It wants the 15th Amendment [which granted suffrage to African American men] to the Constitution of the United States repealed." Davenport dismissed the effort as "as silly as some of its dupes are," and predicted the security of the Fifteenth Amendment.[25] But although the Klan's overt power may well have been on the decline, violence against black Americans continued for decades to come.

While the rise of the Klan was troubling to African American Protestants, it was but one part of a larger social system that oppressed blacks in the South at every turn and tended to place racial roadblocks in the path of blacks throughout the country. Limiting a discussion of race to lynching or the rebirth of the KKK ignores the myriad ways in which African Americans faced racial oppression in the United States in the early twentieth century, and it fails to consider the nuanced discussions they engaged in as they negotiated the segregated spaces of America. Discrimination against African Americans in the United States in the 1920s and 1930s (and beyond) was a daily occurrence. As a consequence, denominational newspapers wrote frequently about that discrimination, and they interpreted it in light of Christian theology. For black Baptists and Methodists, Christianity demanded equality. But, as the writers often observed, the United States was shot through with racism, even as it claimed to be a beacon for liberty and equality to oppressed peoples around the globe.

Jim Crow laws in the South were a prime example of this hypocrisy. Reacting to claims that black people had not suffered from those laws, Jonathan Frank, the editor of the *National Baptist Union-Review*, angrily countered them and gave a litany of mistreatment: "mob violence, starvation wages, peonage, shameful educational neglect, Jim Crow laws, enforced segregation, miscarriage of justice in courts, brutal police regulations, inadequate housing, non-sanitary localities, disenfranchisements, mistreatment of our women and girls by a vicious element, signs reading 'Niggers and Dogs Not Allowed' and a hundred other insults." Frank then asked rhetorically, "Does anybody think the Jews should have abandoned their new home in Canaan to return to Egypt? The migration of colored people to the North is a great religious movement. God's hand in it is almost visible." For the writer of the original claims, and indeed anyone who would call into question the reasons that African Americans were fleeing the South, Frank concluded "we shall pray his practice be conformed to the Christian standard."[26] By 1928, he had coined a new term for the affliction white Baptists suffered—"colorphobia." As evidence, Frank noted that the white Southern Baptists "persist in drawing race lines where there should be none. That un-Christian practice not only retards their progress but multiplies their problems, a number of which are unsoluable because [they are] anti-Christian." He predicted that God would smile upon white Baptists if they would mend their racist ways, asserting that "after white Baptists everywhere practice their religion in fraternal, Christian conduct toward their neighbors in colors untold, blessing new will be their possession."[27] For Frank and his fellow black Baptists, God could not and would not tolerate such affronts to justice and equality. White segregationists worked counter to the very religion they claimed to follow.

A.M.E. Christian Recorder editor Richard Wright Jr. shared this view and wryly observed that the "white people of the South have passed segregation laws for nearly all the relations of life so far as they dared do so," including "in school, in cars, in residential districts, in theatres, etc." They went too far, however, when the city of Atlanta passed, but the mayor vetoed, an effort to prevent integrated church audiences, "either at such religious services or any preliminary services, mass or Sunday school." The white southern propensity for segregation was so ingrained that Wright predicted: "I suppose there will be an attempt on the part of some Southerners to pass a Jim Crow law in heaven—if they get there."[28] Implicit in Wright's conclusion was his belief that the vast majority of white segregationists would never make it to heaven because they had not followed the teachings of Christianity in their lifetimes.

Wright returned to the topic of a segregated heaven in 1926, when he commented on the white *Richmond Christian Advocate*'s recent editorial about the "race question." The Virginia Methodist's paper, Wright explained, was the "'best Southern white point of view,'" but he could not agree with its position advocating "'separation.'" It was a separation that, Wright argued, "would give [whites] an advantage." Whites had segregated schools and trains, and they would not stop there. "We have never understood," he mused, "how a Christian could advocate such unjust solutions of a question which will never be settled till it is settled right. Do these Christians advocate a separate heaven, and a separate hell? Would they sing in the heavenly choir if perchance a few Negroes were on it?" Wright was particularly concerned that the *Richmond Christian Advocate*'s editor was worried about the subject of amalgamation, or the interracial sexual intercourse of whites and blacks. Black women, Wright observed, were not afforded the same legal protection from such amalgamation. He explained that the "laws of nearly every Southern state promote and encourage [white man with black woman] amalgamation. The safest crime a white young man can commit is to seduce a black girl. He does not get any punishment and does not have to support his offspring." Wright concluded by questioning the racial purity of white southerners: "We would like to know what is a distinct race? Where is the pure race? Do not some of the 'purest' whites of Virginia have the blood of Pocahontas in their veins?"[29] White southerners were not entirely white, he argued, and their attempts at sorting out the races marked them as outside the Christian fold.

This segregation and amalgamation discussion prompted at least one AME minister to ponder the fortunes of a black Jesus coming to America. Writing in the *A.M.E. Christian Recorder*, A. W. Jackson, of Danville, Kentucky, set the scene: "To test and prove whether the Protestantism of to-day is in harmony with Christ's program, just let Christ visit His churches under the garb of an American Negro or just come as a black man." Jackson believed that "He would see American prejudice arm herself and march forth more vociferously than did the Jews when they mobbed Him more than

1,900 years ago." He continued: "It would be a sight to behold to see the black Christ sent away from any white church in all America, were He to apply for membership, and to attempt to worship on terms of equality with them would break up any service in any white church in all America. And some would be ready to mob Him again. What would we do with Him on the trains and the hotels? Jim-Crow Him, of course. He might remonstrate and say at the church, train, hotel or any other place where American prejudice is king: 'I am Christ!' But the answer would be 'Yes, but you are black. You are Negro, and there is no admittance to Negroes, even though Thou be Christ.'" Jackson's black Christ would find no room at any inn or other accommodation. This dire prediction, Jackson argued, was grounded in the pervasive racism present in the United States. "Race Prejudice," he maintained, "is the President of our nation," as well as the Congress, all states' governors, any and every judge, mayor, and law enforcement official. Blacks could not get fair treatment in any secular venue in the country. Indeed, Jackson contended, racism "is the Priest of every church; the President of every School in the land; and the Chief of all the Railroads, Hotels and all else that rest on American soil." Against this omnipresent racial intolerance, Jackson juxtaposed "Jesus of Nazareth, the author of Christianity." It was time for "practical Christianity [to] arm [itself] with truth, justice, love, and righteousness, and go forth against [racism]." He believed that "Christ put into practice is the only force that can sub-due this Giant. . . . let Him go forth at once lest the nation perish."[30] For Jackson, only divine intervention could stop racism in America, and, given the length of time African Americans had been fighting that racism, the conclusion seems a reasonable one. As southern whites continued to lynch, segregate, and hate, and whites in other areas of the country did little to improve the lives of black Americans, a triumphant Jesus—be he black or white—appeared to be the only solution to the situation. *Star of Zion* editor William H. Davenport agreed. The answer to segregation in the South was not in migration, "but in religious education, and the guaranteeing to all of its people of whatever group equal rights before the law."[31] Davenport built on this point in another editorial that discussed the most likely complexion of Jesus. "When the idolaters of pigmentation, and pigmentation only, learn that 'Jesus was not white,'" he observed, "they may sing less lustily, 'All hail the power of Jesus' Name,' and [instead] join the Golgotha chorus, [demanding] 'Crucify Him.'" Quoting his fellow AME Zion minister, E. D. W. Jones, he accused white Christians of creating a "'new kind of religion: the religion of being white.'" The color of Christ did matter for white Christians, but for Davenport and Jones, it was the message Christ brought, not his skin color, that should be the focus of Christian Americans. Neither Davenport nor Jones characterized Jesus as black, instead comparing his skin color to that of the "modern nomad Arab." For them, the color was of importance only as a way of refuting the Nordic appearance of the Jesus white Christians worshipped.[32]

Prayers were also offered as a means of both invoking divine intervention against segregation and demonstrating the error of white churches' ways. The *Star of Zion* called on black southerners to set aside a special time to pray together that "God shall work upon the conscience of this nation, upon the churches operating in His name," that Jim Crow and all segregation laws be abolished and "that the country shall recognize the oneness of our humanity and the oneness of our citizenship."[33] The *National Baptist Voice* reprinted Mornay Williams's prayer to end race prejudice, which discussed the diversity of the life and message of Jesus (born to a "Hebrew Mother," "rejoiced in the faith of a Syro-phoenician woman and a Roman soldier, and suffered his cross to be carried by a man of Africa").[34] The Reverend S. T. Hawkins inquired of the *Star of Zion* in 1931 whether "the religion of Jesus Christ is a religion to disenfranchise people . . . and deprive them of all liberties, just because their skin is dark?" Hawkins found the "remedy" to the problem in the words of Joel 1:13–14, arguing that his fellow ministers should preach "an appeal" to their churches to call a fast and pray and "cry unto the Lord."[35] Inherent in these prayers was a message of the universality of Christianity and the country's willful ignorance of that notion.[36]

The universality of that ignorance made itself manifest in a dispute over an Episcopal church in Brooklyn, New York, in 1929. The Reverend William Blackshear, a white Texas native who was the pastor of St. Matthew's Protestant Episcopal Church in Brooklyn, announced his plan to exclude African Americans from his congregation. The black denominational press (and secular press) immediately seized upon his words as an example of how far astray Christianity was heading in the segregated United States. Kelly Miller argued that Blackshear was not an outlier but representative of white ministerial racism, stating that "what he did in the open, nine hundred and ninety-nine out of a thousand white ministers believe and practice by overt or covert contrivance." Echoing A. W. Jackson's scenario in which a black Christ appeared to white churches in America only to be turned away, Miller observed that if "Christ should appear in Brooklyn or any other city under the guise of a colored man, and should seek membership in the church which He died to create, He would more than likely be met with a polite or blunt refusal." Ever the critic, however, Miller also condemned those African American churches that had failed to "welcome the poor, ignorant, and the humbler to their congregational fellowships." He asked rhetorically, questioning the practice of uplift and its attendant focus on class, "What is the difference between classifying the saints on the color scheme and on the social grade? Which would be the more displeasing to the Christ?" In the end, he concluded, the "Negro should take up the cross where the white man leaves it off."[37] For Miller, both white and black Christians practiced discrimination, but black Christians called it uplift.

The discussion about Blackshear's actions continued, as the *Star of Zion* reprinted a *Pittsburgh Courier* article, "The Color Line and Christianity." Like Miller, the uncredited writer of the article believed that Blackshear deserved recognition for doing openly what many other white ministers did secretly. "Thus the race is indebted to Rev. Blackshear, the Texas clergyman," the *Courier* insisted, "for smoking out those who have been delicately ignoring church jim crowism." The author then pointed out that churches in America already were segregated and that segregation everywhere was an affront to Christianity. He asked, "if it be unchristian to 'refuse any Negro the privilege of enjoying any church privilege,' is it not just as unchristian to refuse any Negro the privilege of enjoying any social privilege? The church is God's house, but so also is the world." He expanded on this line of reasoning to include discrimination in employment, theaters, hotels, railroad accommodations, and restaurants—"Should Christianity be practiced only on Sunday and in the confines of the four walls of a church or should it be practiced seven days a week and everywhere?" For the *Courier's* reporter, white Christians had lost the meaning of religion, and he compared them to residents of "pagan Rome" who "strut blindly and boastfully down the broad road to decay and oblivion."[38]

By the following week, *Star of Zion* editor Davenport was moved to pity for God, "when principles of righteousness, justice, mercy, and peace are being wantonly violated by the 'children' of God, we feel sorry for Him." God had asked the church to be his kingdom on earth, and yet, Davenport argued, its white ministers were "slamming the doors in the faces of those who would serve Him according to the dictates of their consciences." Davenport charged that Ku Klux Klan members were now attending Blackshear's church in an effort to support the pastor and keep blacks from the congregation. Even though God, according to Davenport, had been attempting "for thousands of years" to "bring all men to Him . . . yet His priests join the chorus of hate and would expel black saints, yellow saints, brown saints from His Kingdom!" He concluded that the Klan had never read the Bible, or certainly not Zechariah 4:6, "'Not by might, nor by power, but by my Spirit, saith the Lord,' or they would hesitate to descend upon a service of Divine worship to keep Negroes out."[39] The *Star* also reprinted the *Pittsburgh Advocate's* article, "Pastor Blackshear's Black Sheep," on the next page. It described Blackshear as having claimed that "'St. Matthew's is a white church,'" but also as having called upon his southern upbring-

ing as evidence that he was an expert on blacks and for "'their best interests, having been born and bred in the South.'" As Blackshear retreated to
the position of white spokesman for the black race, an occupation John
Roach Straton, in the neighboring borough of Manhattan, had enjoyed, the
Pittsburgh *Courier* mourned, "if prejudice is to have place in the Church of
Christ, there would seem to be no hope of its eradication from any part of
our life." The paper took solace in the fact that, in response to an angry letter
from James Weldon Johnson, secretary of the National Association for the
Advancement of Colored People, Blackshear's supervising bishop, Ernest
M. Stires, had declared that "such an announcement is indefensible."[40]

Late to the discussion, but just as outraged, the *National Baptist
Union-Review* used the Blackshear matter to make a larger point. In December 1929, it ran an editorial entitled, "Colored Americans Not Wanted."
In the *Union-Review*'s version of the story, Blackshear had placed a sign in
his church, rather than making an announcement, that the church was a
church for white people. Blackshear's actions called into question the ratio-
nale behind white denominations' mission efforts to Africa, the paper contended, while ignoring the racial prejudice at home. "The Blackshear out-
burst," the editor wrote, "calls attention again to the inconsistency of white
church members sending their children, their young men and women, as
missionaries to Africa while right among them are a dark skinned people in
need of the same gospel and to them is exhibited such stuff as the southerner has brought to a sharp angle for acute study. It is but another instance of
the fall down of white Christian professors at the color line."[41] The editorial
asked a question that many other African American religious writers had
also raised: why did white Americans seem to have so much charity and
evangelistic zeal for people of color in other countries and continents when
they could not treat their own neighbors of color with the simple decency
taught by their religion?

The Blackshear case was not an isolated one, as AME, AMEZ, and National Baptists, Incorporated and Unincorporated alike, struggled to contend with racism in churches. In 1930, the *Star of Zion* noted a number
of disturbing instances of racism in Roman Catholic churches, prompting
the editor to remark that it "has long been the belief that Protestants had a
monopoly on this ugly thing, but it appears that our Catholic friends also
have a color bar which they rigidly enforce." Davenport went on to cite
examples from Baltimore and Upper Marlboro in Maryland, as well as St.
Louis, Missouri, and to note that "only two Negro priests hold pastorates
in America." "There is something wrong somewhere," he concluded, "this
continued manifestation of the spirit of anti-Christ has its rootage in Pha-
rasaical [sic] conceit and pride, and unless eradicated will find its fruitage

in the alienation of the darker races of earth from Him whom we invoke as 'Our Father.'"[42] For Davenport, the continued hypocrisy of white Christians in the United States had global and eternal consequences. As long as Christ was presented as white and blacks as inferior, African Americans would turn away from the saving message of Christianity, as would "darker races" throughout the world. White Christians would inflict damage both in this world and the next with their continued insistence on segregation.

Despite the racism, segregation, and hypocrisy they saw in white Christian churches, African American Baptists and Methodists were not willing to abandon Christianity. Indeed, they insisted that the fault lay not with the religion but with its misguided white adherents. Even as they defined Christianity by its focus on equality and condemned the hypocrisy of white racists, religious periodicals exhorted their readers to hold fast to their understanding of the gospel. In so doing, they underscored their definition of Christianity as the church of believers in equality while marginalizing white segregationists. White fundamentalists had raised the allegation that the "church" was the community of believers only insofar as they held to the fundamentalists' interpretations of Christianity. African American Baptists and Methodists qualified the definition of true believers in such a way that it omitted fundamentalists and many other white Christians from inclusion. Once again, black religious writers had employed the language of "otherness" and turned it back on its originators.

Writing in the *Star of Zion*, C. C. Coleman of New Bern, North Carolina, remarked on the "statement made by the mayor of a large southern city over the radio," who called on whites to "'help all whites to get jobs, and let the niggers trust their God.'" Ironically, Coleman believed, the bigot could not "have given better advice." Even though white people had a higher employment rate than blacks, he noted, adapting the words of "Amazing Grace," "it is this sense of our trust in God which has brought us safe thus far."[43] Likewise, renowned African American Presbyterian Francis Grimke admonished blacks not to turn their backs on the religion despite the poor witness of racist white Christians. Writing on "'Jim Crow Christianity'" in an article reprinted by the *National Baptist Union-Review*, Grimke divided the sinners from the religion they professed to practice. He argued that the "shortcomings of some white Christians prove nothing against Christianity. It only shows that they are not true to its ideals and principles. Certain white men treat the Negro as they do, not because they, the men, are Christians, but because they are not." While these white men had claimed the title of Christians, their racial prejudice, for Grimke, had disqualified them from that role. But he also cautioned his fellow African Americans that the "fault is not in Christianity, but in certain white men." The proof was in the words and deeds of Jesus, whose encounter with the "Samaritan woman at Jacob's well and His commendation of the good Samaritan who befriended a man of another race, and a race that hated his own, show how little place prejudice had in His heart and mind."[44] Christ modeled the ideal for the Christian—set aside racial hatred and treat all others as equal. White people had forsaken that central message of Christianity, Grimke and others were arguing. "And this is where the white man's Christianity breaks down," W. H. Davenport told *Star of Zion* readers, "in his relationships with other racial groups. A pound of practice is worth a ton of theological dogmas and Christian theories."[45] The Reverend William E. Guy asked himself rhetorically whether, when judged by the standard of treating one's neighbor well, the "white man was a Christian?" His answer was at first nonsensical, "Apple sauce," but he added "no man who hates another is a Christian."[46] For African American Protestants, the Christian church did not need to choose between conversion and social justice, as they believed many white Protestants, especially in the South, had made a false dichotomy. Instead, the church—the community of all believers in the Christian message—could embody both the evangelism duties and the social justice calling.

Richard Wright stated as much in the *A.M.E. Christian Recorder* in 1925 when he called for "inter-racial cooperation." For Wright, the most important duty of "American Christianity" was "Race Adjustment, on a basis of the teaching of Jesus Christ." Rather than helping their fellow humans, the members of the white churches were divided into "those who honestly believed that the church had to do with the 'spiritual,' and who did not believe that the 'social' should occupy their minds." But African Americans were not blameless. Their "religion was so entirely 'spiritual,' and ethereal, that the white man had no pressure from the outside to stir him to think in terms of social obligation."[47] Wright believed that the time had come to unite the two strains and create a Christian church that converted individuals and changed their living conditions at the same time.

In 1927, Wright expanded and refined his call for equality under the banner of Christianity by employing the Hebrew prophet Amos and likening white Christians to "oppressors." "Moral failure," he declared, "proceeds with treading upon the poor all sorts of economic robbing," including denial of crops, undercharging for labor, segregated and inferior school facilities, and the like. The "oppressors are morally decaying," he continued, "whether they call themselves Israelites, Christians or what not. And God's justice will certain assert itself if there is not a change." The case was simple: white America had become what Amos had warned against—excesses and injustice. Wright chose verses from Amos, including the passage that Martin Luther King Jr. would later make famous in his "I Have a Dream" speech,

"But let justice roll down like waters, and righteousness like an ever-flowing stream" (Amos 5:24). "Amos does not mince words," Wright aptly observed, "God wants Israel to repent, 'to hate evil and love the good'—that is the only thing that will satisfy the justice of God." But the United States was not engaged in such an effort. Instead, he argued that "it is wrong to mistreat your brother and think you can make it all right with God by giving Him a burnt offering. One of these days this American nation will wake up to understand the justice of God is not in the fine churches or great educational institutions, the wonderful choirs and eloquent sermons, it is in hating evil and loving good."

Wright then brought his readers back to the debate over the social mission of the church. It was obvious to him that "any careful study of the prophecy of Amos will convince the student that the so-called 'social gospel' is not new, but a most vital part of the old time religion." Those in the "dominant majority" did not want to acknowledge the truth of this claim, but, he concluded, "Jesus and the prophets are in one accord in the emphasis of this social gospel. It must come. It is the solution of the Negro Problem, the problem of poverty and all the social ills."[48] James W. Eichelberger Jr. echoed this sentiment in his address to the Lake Geneva Student Conference in July 1927. Dr. Eichelberger, an AME Zion minister, told the assembled group, which included Reinhold Niebuhr, Kirby Page, and Sherwood Eddy, that "'there is no room for race in the society which Jesus set apart. Need and capacity were the basis for Jesus' recognition and direction of help toward any individual of whatever race. Mankind is one vast brotherhood of which God is the Father.'" According to the unnamed reporter, Eichelberger also "maintained that a Christian Conception of race would put an end to imperialistic and economic exploitation of weaker races."[49] Wright and Eichelberger gave voice to an interpretation of Christianity that included a heavy emphasis not just on equality but on social justice, echoing ideas found not only in Israel's prophets but also in liberal Protestantism in the United States in the late nineteenth and early twentieth centuries. To combine the two did not appear to them to be a matter of error; it was instead a literal reading of the words of the prophets. As Christopher Hobson has shown, earlier African American ministers had used these texts to indict the United States for its abysmal race relations. Now these men were employing them to define the boundaries of the true Christian church in America.

The prophetic language occurred in other periodicals as denominational papers urged white Americans to return to God's covenant and commit themselves to equality. The biblical story of Jeshurun appeared as a warning to white Christians to return to the fold and forsake their foolish ways. The Reverend R. J. Drummond, DD, told *National Baptist Voice* readers that the central Christian message was "essentially social as it is individual." Linking Christianity to the prophet Jeremiah as well as Jesus, Drummond argued that they both helped the individual "claim his full rights and status" in the face of forces that would have oppressed the individual, but there had been backsliding. That backsliding was occurring in the United States, which Drummond compared to Jeshurun, the name for Israel, in Deuteronomy's Song of Moses (Deut. 32). In the Song, Moses describes Israel as having become passive and content, ignoring the covenant it had with God. In Drummond's retelling, white Christians had become like Jeshurun, ignoring all other callings except their own path to salvation. Drummond wrote, "But, like Jeshurun, since that day the individual 'waxed fat and kicked,' till in evangelistic vision nothing seemed of much importance but the saving of a man's own soul," and individualism led to "grave evils in social and industrial life."[50] For Drummond, self-centeredness prevented Americans from confronting the social ills present in their midst.

The same verse appeared again when the *A.M.E. Christian Recorder* admonished Clarence Darrow for mocking black spirituality. Darrow had defended a group of African Americans, including Dr. Ossian H. Sweet, against a charge of murder in the death of a white man at Sweet's home. The Reverend T. Nelson Baker lauded Darrow for his willingness to defend the men. But Darrow's remarks that the "Negro is 'too blooming pious,'" and "'if the Lord was going to do anything for you, he would have done it long ago'" incensed the minister. After a long defense of Christianity's benefits for blacks, Baker warned his fellow African Americans to beware of false prophets like Darrow. "The Negro cannot afford to turn back on God," he explained, "even from such friends as Mr. Darrow. 'But Jeshurun waxed fat and kicked. Thou art waxed fat, thou art grown thick, thou art become sleek.' Then he forsook God who made him. And lightly esteemed the Rock of his salvation."[51] While the identity of the potential Jeshurun in this case was slightly different—African Americans, rather than whites—the general threat was still the same: if you held to white society's views, and in Darrow's case, white society's lack of religion, you would forsake God and salvation. The danger was present in white society and in the segregationists themselves. Given the situation in the United States, *Union-Review* editor Jonathan Frank put it quite plainly: "God will not, God cannot, with reverence we say it, bless in full measure a people whose selfishness, prejudice substitute Christian affection."[52] The country would not enjoy divine favor as long as it failed to care for the poor and oppressed.

Indeed, while African American Protestants demonstrated that they could embrace fairly traditionalist evangelical positions on matters of doctrine and social customs, they tended to replace their theological conservatism with more progressive notions when it came to race. That they would do so is logical when one considers the language of justice and equality found in Social Gospel and modernist Protestantism. Both groups interpreted the message of Christianity as a temporal one—Christians had a duty to improve society, whether in preparation for the Kingdom of God on earth, as the Social Gospel preachers emphasized, or for the inevitable progress of humanity, as the modernists tended to advocate. African American Baptists and Methodists, already well versed in the theological discussions of their day, saw in these exegeses a message that applied to their current situation. For them, the terms did not necessarily constitute an outright embrace of modernism or its theological baggage. Instead, they were biblically derived and useful notions. Because their origin was biblical, such terms and concepts were necessarily part of the theology all Christians should follow.

For example, in 1917, the *National Baptist Union-Review* ran an *Atlanta Independent* article on Billy Sunday's upcoming visit to the South and the opportunity he had to make a statement for racial equality. "It will not suffice for Mr. Sunday to invade the Southland," the secular black paper wrote and the traditionalist *Union-Review* reprinted, "and denounce adultery, fornication, liars, hypocrites, bums, hobos, rascals, scoundrels, crap shooters, tramps and loafers, and leave untouched the lynchers, the ballot box thief, the segregator, the discriminator, the Negro hater, the promoter of racial strife and the mob leader who burns human beings at the stake because they are black." Instead Sunday needed to confront the fact that his audience in the South would be composed of such people. Rather than be "deathly silent" on the matter, he should speak out. "If Mr. Sunday is sincere and is a lover of God and humanity," the paper continued, "he has a splendid opportunity to preach the Fatherhood of God and the brotherhood of man," and, further:

> That the gospel of the Lord and Saviour Jesus Christ knows no color line and that Jesus Christ died to the saving of all men who would believe on Him; that the black man is a common brother of the white man, and that the white man owes him both Godly and humane treatment; that before the law, the Negro is entitled to every privilege, every benefit accruing to the white man; that the double sessions in the Negro schools are wrong and wicked; that the suppression of the Negro's vote at the ballot box is sin; that the counting him out on election day is stealing; that the unequal division of public school funds is legalized theft; that segregation is born of racial hatred and is sin; that the beating up and shooting down of Negroes on the street is sin; that

the splendidly equipped school facilities for white children and death traps and dilapidated houses for Negroes is a misuse of trust funds and an act of base humanity.[53]

The *Independent*, and by association the *Union-Review*, clearly saw equality and human rights as components of the gospel of Jesus. The Fatherhood of God in this example was an expression of the Social Gospel understanding of the term—a common father created all human beings, and they were interconnected and thus equal before that same father. The notion that all people were brothers was crucial for black Protestants' efforts to end segregation and discrimination. As long as white Christians could evade the acknowledgement of common ancestry and familial ties, African Americans had little to help them convince the segregationists of their error.

The "brotherhood" theme recurred in many places. J. D. Crenshaw, editor of the *National Baptist Voice*, saw 1921 as a year of hope for the future of humanity, despite the previous year's horrible crimes and injustices, or as Crenshaw put it, "despite man's inhumanities to his brother man." "The good of the earth," he wrote, "are hoping for a greater reign this year of the gospel of the Fatherhood of God and the brotherhood of man."[54] While the *Voice*, the publication of the National Baptist Convention, Incorporated, was decidedly more progressive than the *National Baptist Union-Review*, the publication of the National Baptist Convention, Unincorporated, this use of Social Gospel terminology demonstrates the African American emphasis on civil rights, or, as stated here, "the brotherhood of man." Crenshaw's successor, R. C. Barbour, wrote in July 1934 that "American Christianity has never accepted the ideal of the Family of God, with all men as brothers." Indeed, he argued that white Americans had ignored the "four major contributions to the social order, namely: Brotherhood, Self-renunciation, the Golden Rule, and Pacificism."[55] A few weeks later, the *Voice* reprinted a lengthy *Advance* editorial on "Jim Crow Christianity," in which Ronald T. Heacock observed that black Christians had been taught about "the Fatherhood of God, the brotherhood of man," and expected fair treatment from their fellow white Christians. But, Heacock continued, African Americans "learned the difference between our creeds and our deeds."[56] For Crenshaw, Barbour, Heacock, and other African American evangelicals, the message of Christianity was one of both salvation and equality. Salvation occurred when the believer had a conversion experience, but all believers, regardless of race, were supposed to then express that salvation in an external manner. By treating one another with kindness, Christians demonstrated their salvation and improved the world at the same time. Right belief made right living, and right living would make the world a better place. To be sure, traditionalist Protestants, including most white fundamentalists, would have agreed that right living made the world a better place and that evangelism was the best way to achieve that right living. But for African American Baptists and Methodists, the focus on world improvement more closely resembled that of progressive movements, with their attendant focus on justice and the earthly realization of divine goals. Thus the definition of Christianity had to include both doctrinal adherence and concern for social justice.

But black Baptists and Methodists lived in a complicated time and place. The larger cultural ethos demanded that Americans embrace Christianity and patriotism. Against the backdrop of a nation contending with millions of immigrants who were not Protestant, African Americans sought to prove their "Americanness" by distancing themselves from the potential dangers of those immigrants. As white Americans fretted about the religious and political baggage the new arrivals brought with them, black Americans in denominational papers wrote to remind the larger society of their love of country. They were quick to declare that blacks had lost their lives for the United States on foreign battlefields and that they were not likely to join subversive or communist groups. Moreover, they often linked that patriotism with their adherence to Protestant Christianity. Yet the discussion was also a way of shaming white Americans for the tribulations African Americans had suffered at their hands.

Reprinting the Chicago *Herald Examiner*'s 1919 article, "The Black Man Stood Pat," the *National Baptist Union-Review* reminded its readers of how African Americans had remained loyal to the United States during the Great War, noting that a Senate committee heard testimony that showed that "the German propagandists failed miserably in their efforts among" blacks, and that the loyalty was a "splendid tribute to the Americanism of the Negro. . . . Their hearts proved pure gold and they stood by Uncle Sam." Not only had the German efforts failed to sway African Americans, so too had those of radical labor groups, including the International Workers of the World (IWW). "It is that same inborn spirit of loyalty to the government that has prevented the I.W.W. from gaining converts among the blacks of the South, no matter how poor they are or how unjust their position economically," the paper observed.[57] Black Americans were loyal Americans, even though they had to suffer as a people. The *National Baptist Voice* noted that a denominational report had argued that those blacks "'who have served gallantly in the defense of liberty for this nation and all nations cannot be expected to return to a social ostracism which will deny them the privileges of liberty as determined by personal merit." The black soldier's experience in patriotic duty was both a proof of his loyalty and a demand for equality. "'Grave perils portend,'" the report concluded, "'unless the Church of Christ can bring into social institutions the very Spirit of Christ.'"[58] Now that African Americans had had a chance to fight to make the world safe for democracy, as President Woodrow Wilson had cast the country's entry into the Great War, they would demand democracy back home. The National Baptist Convention, Incorporated's paper concurred and stressed the need for a religious effort to achieve that end.

The inherent paradox of black loyalty and white oppression led black denominational writers to critique white adherence to patriotic values. The AME bishop Reverend J. H. Jones, speaking at the Federal Council of Churches (FCC) meeting in Boston, cast the story of African American suffering in terms of an epic battle between "two incompatible doctrines or institutions held sacred by the American whites . . . the institution that makes for Liberty, Freedom, Manhood, Brotherhood, and Christianity . . . and the other . . . of selfishness, domination, slavery, and injustice." The first institution, which included liberty and Christianity, he argued, came ashore at Plymouth Rock, and the second, of slavery and injustice, at Jamestown. White Americans mistreated black Americans despite the tradition of equality, which called into question their Christianity. American Christianity appeared very weak, he admonished, when Christians expressed "our sense of brotherhood to those oppressed in foreign lands and our hatred and malice and discount toward our brethren at home." Despite this situation, however, thousands of American blacks fought to "defend the doctrine of democracy to all the Caucasian races of Europe. These black troops fought for Justice, Fraternity, and Equality," even as President Wilson "sat mum in the White House" while blacks were "burned and lynched within reach of the Capital of Washington." Jones called on the FCC attendees to use their pulpits "in behalf of right and justice and brotherhood, that Christianity prove itself real effective and curative of the ills of our brotherhood."[59] While his audience was predominantly white, Jones did not pull his punches and instead used his opportunity to exhort them to ameliorate the conditions he described. Later that same year, National Baptist Convention, Unincorporated president Edward Perry Jones also linked the patriotism of fallen black soldiers to the religious fate of the United States. "Unless they died in vain," he told the convention at its 1921 annual meeting, "unless the crimsoned soil of France mocks and jeers at the lives given for freedom's cause, America, the chosen home of the oppressed must awaken to her true status." According to Jones, the United States needed to "hold high to the nations of the earth that liberty guaranteed by the constitution for which the fathers died and made glorious a thousand battlefields. And let it here be said that in all the mighty conflicts and achievements the American Negro has been foremost and consistent, and stands today ready as of yore to aid his white brother, but at the same time demands an opportunity to educate his children, live happily with his loved ones, and serve God according to the dictates of his conscience. To ask more would be in vain; to ask less would be unmanly."[60] Jones's counterpart in the National Baptist Convention, Incorporated, Dr. Elias Camp Morris, made a similar argument that same year. Preaching to the assembled congregation at Pilgrim Baptist Church in Chicago, Morris reminded them that the "loyalty of the Negro people has stood unimpeached through all the vicissitudes of the uneven course he has been forced to travel as a free American citizen." Despite the "vinegar and gall" served to African Americans in the form of "disenfranchisement, lynchings, and all kinds of maltreatment," African Americans were not swayed by German propaganda and instead volunteered to serve on the front lines, "both daring and dying for the establishment of Universal Democracy."[61] Black Americans would set aside the injustices done against them, these writers argued, and take up arms for their country. As they did so, however, they demonstrated that they, and not white Americans, were the real proof of American democratic values.

African American denominational writers continued to reiterate that the United States embodied hypocrisy when it espoused human rights abroad but ignored them at home. Given the dire situation, they urged white leaders to keep their attentions on domestic problems, rather than concentrating on evils abroad. As they did so, the writers shaped a damning image of the United States in the world and at home: an image of a country that proudly proclaimed itself as the champion of democracy and equality but that hid a shameful history of mistreatment of blacks. That mistreatment needed to be addressed before the country could claim its place among the champions of civilization. As historian William G. Jordan has already shown, black secular newspapers wrestled with the "two impulses—democratic advocacy and nationalistic loyalty" as they commented on the United States entry into World War I.[62] African American denominational writers added a third factor to the equation: religion. Missionaries and politicians who looked overseas, they argued, neglected their Christian duty by ignoring the plight of African Americans at home.

Some writers questioned the motives of white missionaries who worked to spread Christianity in faraway lands while ignoring the suffering in their own backyards, hinting at without mentioning specifically the biblical injunction to deal with the beam in one's own eye before the mote in someone else's eye. Jonathan Frank of the *National Baptist Union-Review* wondered, "Is it not strange that white Baptists north and south go away over the seas to help dark complexioned people when there are millions of that class right at their doors?"[63] Speaking to the Interdenominational Ministers' Conference at Fisk University in 1928, Bishop L. W. Kyles likened the United States to a character in Charles Dickens's *Bleak House*. America "reminds one of Dickens's picture of Mrs. Jellyby," he noted, "sitting amid domestic chaos and writing letters for the redemption of Africa." Meanwhile, he continued, "Joe, the London Street Arab, sits on the doorsteps of the society for the propagation of the gospel in foreign parts, ragged and hungry, munching a crust of bread." Kyles was clear in his choice of representations here; the United States was the well-meaning but self-absorbed Mrs. Jellyby, while blacks were begging for food and equality. "Going forth to make the world safe for democracy," Kyles closed with a parting jab at Woodrow Wilson's foreign policy, "seems rather a farce when one's home was itself, terribly unsafe for democracy."[64]

The situation at home was dire, black denominational papers tried to explain, and needed both human and divine intervention. In 1921, the *National Baptist Voice* reported that the National Association for the Advancement of Colored People had called on pastors to "preach sermons on 'Justice to the Negro—the Test of Christianity in America,' and to hold a noon hour of service of prayer on Sunday, April 24." Citing the recent climate of lynching, peonage, and racism, as well as "the burning of human beings at the stake," the *Voice* noted that the United States stood "as the archsinner among the nations, and its protestations of democracy are as sounding brass or a tinkling cymbal."[65] Using the same biblical reference (1 Corinthians 13:1–2), the *A.M.E. Christian Recorder* likened the "great moral principles we preach here of Christianity, Democracy, Opportunity, Equality, Feminine Emancipation, etc. all as sounding brass or a tinkling symbol [*sic*]." The lack of racial equality here made the paper wonder, "Are not Americans merely worshippers of themselves? Can they apply these principles to others?" The editor concluded that the "Negro is the test."[66] Indeed, the attention to foreign policy showed just how blind white Americans were to the domestic beams of racism and violence. The editorial page of the *Star of Zion* mocked the *Christian Century* for its March 1925 "remarks that 'The Negro the world round is becoming increasingly self-conspicuous as an exploited human.'" Rather than analyze the problem, or continue to engage in "theorizing about it when the remedy is at hand," the *Star* asserted, it was time to solve the problem, "in quest of the 'Christian answer' to all human relations."[67]

If the missionaries' neglect of their neighbors at home and the United States' interest in development overseas were not strange enough to black ministers, American attention on events in Europe in the early 1930s underscored the country's inability to recognize the board in its own eye. For

Dean Smith of Bishop College in Marshall, Texas, "godless Russia" was really "'the most religious country in all the western world'" because it did not, in his opinion, engage in racism.[68] Kelly Miller, writing in the *National Baptist Union-Review*, noted that people in the United States were concerned about the Nazis, the Turks, and the Japanese, but there were international laws in place which would govern and restrain the perpetrators. He erroneously predicted the "soften[ing]" of Nazi Germany's persecution of the Jews because the world's attention was turned to the situation. He then undercut his own "attention" argument by noting that the world had condemned America's inability to control such atrocities as lynchings, which had "stained the fair name of the land of the free and home of the brave as the 'damned spot' disfigured the lily white hand of Lady MacBeth." In a stunningly optimistic and naïve conclusion, Miller predicted the rise of "moral sense" that would alleviate injustice worldwide. "The Jew in Germany and the Negro in Georgia," he foretold, "along with the despised and rejected of men over the face of the earth will become the beneficiaries of this overruling moral principle."[69]

A few months later, Miller seemed less sanguine about the future of race relations in the United States and prejudice in Germany. After noting Georgia's roots as a "penal colony Anglo-Saxon in blood and Protestant in religion," he drew a distinction between the state and Nazi Germany—the former operated with racial prejudice while the latter's prejudice operated without respect to skin color. The "good white Christians," Miller argued, needed to realize that temporal power was not equivalent with salvation in the world to come. "He that sitteth in the Heaven," Miller admonished, "shall laugh. The justification outdoes the perpetration in compounding outrages against human nature." But when whites in Georgia condemned Nazi Germany, he could not abide their hypocrisy. "The climax of inconsistency has been reached," he railed, "Georgia upbraids Germany for manifestation of race prejudice."[70] For Miller, white Americans' concern over the rise of Nazism revealed their own inability to recognize their similarities with the ascending German party.

The willingness to condemn the United States and extol other countries' virtues, however, could lead to questionable conclusions. R. C. Barbour, editor of the *National Baptist Voice* in the early and mid-1930s, told his readers that Germany would welcome American athletes at the 1936 Berlin Olympics, regardless of their skin color. His experience as a delegate to a Baptist World Alliance meeting in Berlin had convinced him that the athletes would be well treated, and he added that "after living a lifetime in the midst of our Jim Crow churches, segregated cities, and discriminating leaders, Berlin, Germany appeared as a veritable paradise!" Indeed, he conclud-

ed, black athletes would "not find anywhere in the world anything as discouraging, degrading and crushing as American race prejudice."[71] Granted,
the extent of Nazi oppression against Jews had not yet reached its horrific
climax in the Holocaust, but Barbour's assertion that blacks had already
experienced the worst possible racial situation may have been a comparison of apples to oranges. Barbour had two years earlier written an editorial in sympathy with Germany's Jews that simultaneously blamed them for
their situation by failing to speak out against black oppression in the United
States and accused them of neglecting to use their influence to help "other
oppressed minorities in their fight for human rights and a square deal." Indeed, Barbour told his Jewish audience that "in a way, Negroes in America
are glad to see Hitler. He dramatically impersonates Nordic thought" and
showed the world the consequence of its current policies. Barbour closed
by urging black-Jewish cooperation in starting a new colony together, but
in a way that once again employed anti-Semitic stereotypes. "You have the
genius of organization and shrewd business sense," he wrote, "and since we
have made the large contribution in labor in building this civilization, it is
not difficult to see that we could live in a country all our own, free from the
exasperating prejudices of the Nordic civilization."[72] More common than
Barbour's anti-Semitism was the position taken by National Baptist Convention, Incorporated president L. K. Williams that events in Nazi Germany were wrong, but that the United States needed to address its own
problems with lynching and segregation first before condemning abuses
in other countries.[73] But the triumph of Jesse Owens at the 1936 Olympics
was enough to make W. A. Blackwell, editor of the *Star of Zion*, set aside
his concerns over American segregation for at least one editorial. "We are
more or less elated," he wrote, "over the success of Jesse Owens and other
Negroes, especially are we thus affected when the success is made in Nazi
Germany. May our tribe increase and may our representatives overcome."[74]
Barbour's anger at both white segregationists and Jews and Blackwell's patriotic joy over Jesse Owens's triumph over Nazi racial propaganda illustrate
the ways in which African American denominational writers could see other minorities as both allies and rivals. As troubling as Barbour's words appear in the light of current knowledge, he expressed a sentiment held by
some African Americans—that their plight was unique and their friends
few and far between. White racism and segregation marginalized and hurt
Jews and other minorities, but it also managed to prevent them from forming a cohesive opposition.

For the most part, however, black denominational writers could see the
larger picture of injustices against a wide variety of people. Commenting

on the 1937 meeting of the Young People's Society for Christian Endeavor, the AME Zion's *Church School Herald-Journal* commended the meeting's theme, "'Christ For the Crisis,'" but urged the participants to recognize that their own communities could be home to various crises. "Shall it be 'Christ For the Crisis,'" the paper asked, with each individual determining the crisis, "avoiding conflicts with their customs, their self-determined ways?" Or would it be the more favorable alternative, "shall we go back and let Christ help in every crisis?" The latter would allow the young people who attended to address a variety of issues, from racism to war in Spain and beyond. Christ was not to be applied selectively, the article concluded: "He is either for every Crisis or no Crisis at all. Give Him a chance."[75] National Baptist Convention, Incorporated president W. H. Jernagin agreed. "The primary duty of the Christian Church is to deal with the problems of this world here and now," he told an assembly of Sunday school delegates in Dayton, Ohio. "Two thousand years ago a man with a clear and far vision stood in the crowded market place of the city of Jerusalem," he continued, where many people from many walks of life gathered. After witnessing injustices in the market, Jernagin contended, Jesus "enunciated the doctrine of human brotherhood, social justice, spiritual regeneration, and human transformation."[76] Jernagin's implication was clear: the United States stood as the twentieth century's equivalent of the Jerusalem market, and the gospel of Christ demanded action in this world, not the next.

For African American Baptists and Methodists, the United States of their day presented a set of paradoxes that only a progressive interpretation of Christianity would solve. Their everyday experiences of racism and discrimination, combined with their witness of lynchings and assaults, stood in stark contrast to the assertions of white Americans that the United States loved liberty, freedom, and democracy. Disenfranchisement and Jim Crow alone disproved those assertions, yet black Protestants still had to prove themselves as loyal Americans in order to get their arguments heard. Challenged by the fundamentalist/modernist controversy to defend evangelical Christianity, they offered their interpretation of the gospel. Feared and marginalized by whites, they took the message of Christ and turned it into a weapon against their oppressors—a divine call for social justice in their time. To work for the Kingdom of God on earth was not for these writers a question of being liberal or progressive or modernist. It was, instead, a duty. The Hebrew prophet Micah had asked what God required of people, and the answer had been to do justice, to love mercy, and walk humbly with God (Micah 6:8). For black evangelicals, using the message of Christ to achieve equality was to do justice and love mercy, so that they could walk humbly with God. The command was thousands of years old, not new, and its interpretation was not an innovative understanding of the gospel for them. It was, for them, the plain truth.

Conclusion

The improbably named editor of the *National Baptist Union-Review*, Benjamin Jefferson Davis, was in no mood to be charitable as he wrote his editorials in 1941. With the country's focus on the war in Europe and President Franklin Delano Roosevelt stressing the Four Freedoms, Davis had had enough. "Our position," he stated plainly, "is that the white man's religion is un-Christian and is not the religion that Christ lived and taught while on earth." White people prevented black suffrage in the South and discriminated against black people nationally. Yet while whites did so, Davis argued, they "charge Hitler with changing words in the Bible, but cannot see their overt acts of changing the religion of Jesus Christ by practice and what they do to other people under the white man's religion." Whites did not understand the message of Christianity, leading African Americans to wonder "how the white man's religion permits him to hate his brother because he is black," when, for a black Christian, "religion teaches him to love his white brother not because he is white, yellow or black, but because Christ has taught him to love his neighbor as he loves himself."[1] The editor's outrage was fueled in part by the continued violence against African Americans—including a courtroom shooting in Conroe, Texas, in June and the lynching of a black man in Florida in May—violence that was ignored by white authorities, including President Roosevelt. "It's all wrong for Germany and Italy to shoot spies in their countries when caught," Davis protested, "but it's no crime for a mob to take the law in its own hands and shoot an American citizen to death because he is a Negro."[2]

Yet even as Davis derided white politicians for their reluctance to help African Americans, he also attacked a black Baptist minister for the transgression of participating in an infant baptism—by sprinkling, no less—at an

Atlanta Methodist Church. The culprit was the Reverend Benjamin Mays, pastor, commentator, sociologist, and president of Morehouse College, a proponent, as historian Barbara Dianne Savage has noted, of educated clergy as leaders of racial uplift.[3] His arc of leadership was still in its early stages, and his influence on a generation of minds at Morehouse College would infuse progressive Christianity into such students as Martin Luther King Jr.[4] His defenders in the Atlanta Baptist Ministers' Union included a man who would become famous for being the father of Martin Luther King Jr. Martin King Sr., head of the Union, whom Davis described as "leading the modernist idea," argued that the matter should be dropped. Against King, "leading fundamentalist" Dr. George W. Jordan argued that the incident violated biblical standards and Baptist teachings. Jordan was joined in his outrage by King's own brother, Joel L. King. Once the matter was made public, the traditionalists seemed content, as did Davis, who noted that "Dr. Mays is all right; he has had a little talk with Jesus, and he and his Master made it all right."[5] The battle was over, presumably won by the traditionalists, who got their public humiliation of the apostate Mays. But generally, African American denominational newspapers were less concerned with theological debates by the time the United States was preparing to enter the Second World War. Even Davis's use of the terms fundamentalist and modernist was not really a reflection on the doctrinal debates that characterized the theological wars of the 1920s and 1930s. Instead, much as his predecessors had done, Davis used modernist as a slur, this time against those in his own denomination who would dare to recognize, let alone engage in, a sacramental interpretation that Baptists had rejected for hundreds of years.

For Davis, and for many other African American Baptists and Methodists, the theological debates of the early twentieth century had faded from memory, represented there only by the monikers once tossed about as insult or compliment. The kaleidoscope of American evangelicalism had rotated once again, and the pieces made a mosaic with the same components in a different pattern. What remained central was the abiding struggle for civil rights. Almost eighty years after Emancipation, African Americans still felt the sting of racial oppression and discrimination. Although Davis could not know it, World War II would not end that pain, but it would give new energy to the effort to end segregation in the South. Buoyed by their distinguished service on the battlefield, African American soldiers would return home and begin to demand fair treatment as a small measure of recognition for their patriotism and valor. Their efforts, and those of countless other blacks, would begin to coalesce in churches and at lunch counters, in classrooms and in bus stations, across the former Confederacy. Daddy King's son would typify this movement—a black Baptist minister who could preach the Bible and use prophetic language to mobilize a groundswell. Indeed, Martin Luther King Jr. would find himself embroiled in debates over how to use his own denomination to combat racism and injustice. As Wallace Best has persuasively argued, King's battle with Olivet Baptist Church pastor and National Baptist Convention president J. H. Jackson stemmed from Jackson's more moderate approach and his emphasis on ecumenism and mission work over the activism and legislation King favored.[6] But before he could battle their successors, Martin Luther King Jr. learned from and stood on the shoulders of his predecessors. As this book has shown, African American clergy in the interwar years navigated a treacherous course for their readers and parishioners as they sought to maintain traditional religious beliefs while also employing that same hermeneutic to advance racial progress. Challenged indirectly by fundamentalists to defend their orthodoxy, they could not call themselves fundamentalists. The white leaders of the fundamentalist movement shunned black religious leaders, demeaned their intellect, and prepared instead for a coming catastrophe. Black Baptists and Methodists, in turn, distanced themselves from the fundamentalist movement's millennialism and its indifference to resolving racial issues. But at the same time, modernism held no real appeal for these commentators, who labeled the movement a white heresy even as they embraced some of its methodologies.

Fundamentalism presented clergy of all races and denominations with a constructed dualism that demanded allegiance to one side or another. You were either with them or against them, and there was no middle ground. For National Baptist and African Methodist Episcopalian church leaders, the choice was complicated by race. African Americans in the early twentieth century, and indeed today, faced the expectation of higher standards, and the consequences of transgressions were that much more painful. In response to the Manichean choice fundamentalism presented, many of these religious writers joined the chorus of voices singing the praises of what they saw as traditional Protestant theology, but not full-fledged endorsement of fundamentalism. They attacked modernism, even as they refused to see that they could at times be modernist. But they did not stop there. Instead they turned the biblical literalism against their oppressors, showing that the message of Christ was meant for all and was meant to eliminate differences, not reinforce them. For these black evangelicals, being a Christian meant right belief and right living, being theologically traditional and socially progressive in terms of racial equality. A Christian did not frequent dance halls and speakeasies, nor did a Christian prevent someone from voting because of skin color. For the ministers in this study, the message was abundantly clear, and Christ demanded it. White fundamentalists had part of the equation right, but they did not have all of the answers, nor did those black leaders who rejected religion or who urged revolt. Truth did indeed run on a narrow gauge. The track of these writers' discussions should lead historians away from the legacy forced on us by the fundamentalists and modernists themselves—that a Christian had to choose only one side. African American Protestants show us the myriad ways contemporaries of the debate could interpret and respond to it.

A close reading of these writers helps us to see a more complex picture, and it casts light on religious influences in politics in our own time. African American evangelicals wanted to live in a world free from both individual and corporate sin. They wanted their fellow African Americans to embrace sobriety, hard work, and proper dress not just as a means of racial advancement but also as a way of carrying out biblical injunctions. Men like Jonathan Frank and William Davenport fought for racial equality, but they were troubled by women's equality; they did not see those two movements as related. Instead, they wanted black women to defer to black men, and white men and women to treat black men and women fairly. Both of those goals derived from their religious faith.

On the topic of faith today, commentators have often failed to see how religious beliefs can influence actions and goals. In 2014, voters in Utah's 4th Congressional District elected the first black Republican woman to the United States House of Representatives. Mia Love, a member of the Church of Jesus Christ of Latter-Day Saints (the Mormons), confounds political pundits, who wonder why a black woman would want to be either a Mormon or a Republican, let alone both. If the Mormons have been historically unfriendly to African Americans, why would she join their church? If Republicans are indeed declaring a war on women, and more so on black women, why would she seek membership in the GOP? Love's religious faith and her political inclinations demonstrate the limits of overly broad sociological approaches to religion and politics, just as the subjects of this book should force us to be more careful in our study of African American religions and of the civil rights movement, as well as our commentary on race, minorities, and discrimination today. Racial minorities do not necessarily see common ground with each other, nor do those same minorities liken their struggles to those endured by the LGBTQIA community. When pundits lump disparate groups together—all those who suffer discrimination, for example—they minimize the experiences and views of the various groups and create artificial affinities. The end effect is a form of marginalization imposed by outsiders without regard to beliefs, motives, or experiences.

The sociological focus on race also prevents us from seeing the complexities of religious belief. Martin Luther King Jr., for example, has become for

American schoolchildren the public face of the civil rights movement. His message of equality and love clearly deserve a prominent place in our curriculum and our aspirations. But King's legacy has been whitewashed, his religion minimized, and his willingness to speak truth to power confined only to a group of select "bad guys" in the American South, men like Bull Connor, the cruel commissioner of public safety in Birmingham, Alabama. The religious language in King's famous "I Have a Dream" speech during the March on Washington has been forced to the side. Indeed, King's occupation as a pastor seems to be in many accounts the only mention of his religious beliefs. King was not the only black Baptist preacher who made it to the mountaintop but did not see the promised land. His father's and grandfather's contemporaries had glimpsed it as well. Informed by their Protestant tradition of reading, inspired by the Bible's message of justice, they sought the beloved community, and they did so in the face of a hostile culture. They combined seemingly contradictory notions and texts in an attempt to fix a fallen world. But their descendants still wait for a lasting solution.

Notes

Introduction

1. See, for example, "Gay Marriage and a Moral Minority," *New York Times*, November 29, 2008. For a contemporary explanation of the apparent disconnect, see Caitlin Flanagan and Benjamin Schwarz, "Showdown in the Big Tent," *New York Times*, December 7, 2008.

2. Matthew Bowman's recent book challenges historians to reconsider whether fundamentalism or modernism posed this challenge. The voices in this study do respond to both camps' interrogations of Christianity, although African American evangelicals tended to frame the discourse more in the mold of a fundamentalist war on heresy. For them, modernists did not have the right to ask which side a Christian was on because the modernists were to them not Christians. See Matthew Bowman, *The Urban Pulpit: New York City and the Fate of Liberal Evangelicalism* (New York: Oxford University Press, 2014).

3. Ernest Sandeen, George Marsden, and Joel Carpenter, the most cited authors in the historiography of fundamentalism, all decline to discuss race, either as a factor in shaping fundamentalism, as a topic of interest for fundamentalists, or how African Americans may have participated in the movement. See Ernest Sandeen, *The Roots of Fundamentalism: British and American Millenarianism, 1800–1930* (Chicago: University of Chicago Press, 1970); George M. Marsden, *Fundamentalism and American Culture: The Shaping of Twentieth-Century Evangelicalism, 1870–1925* (New York: Oxford University Press, 1980); and Joel Carpenter, *Revive Us Again: the Reawakening of American Fundamentalism* (New York: Oxford University Press, 1999). More recent scholars, including Matthew Avery Sutton and Darren Dochuk, are beginning to correct that oversight. See Sutton, *American Apocalypse: A History of Modern Evangelicalism*, (Cambridge: The Belknap Press of Harvard University Press, 2014);

and Dochuk, *From Bible Belt to Sunbelt: Plain-Folk Religion, Grassroots Politics, and the Rise of Evangelical Conservatism* (New York: W. W. Norton, 2011).

4. One notable exception to the lack of scholarship on African Americans and fundamentalism is Albert G. Miller's "The Construction of a Black Fundamentalist Worldview: The Role of Bible Schools," in *African Americans and the Bible: Sacred Texts and Social Textures*, ed. Vincent L. Wimbush (New York: Continuum Press, 2000), 712–27. For examples of some of the very fine work done in the general area of African American religions after the Civil War, see Evelyn Brooks Higginbotham, *Righteous Discontent: The Women's Movement in the Black Baptist Church, 1880–1920* (Cambridge: Harvard University Press, 1993); William E. Montgomery, *Under Their Own Vine and Fig Tree: The African American Church in the South* (Baton Rouge: Louisiana State University Press, 1993); Wallace Best, *Passionately Human, No Less Divine: Religion and Culture in Black Chicago, 1915–1952* (Princeton: Princeton University Press, 2007); Paul Harvey, *Redeeming the South: Religious Cultures and Racial Identities Among Southern Baptists, 1865–1925* (Chapel Hill: University of North Carolina Press, 1997); Robert Gregg, *Sparks from the Anvil of Oppression: Philadelphia's African Methodists and Southern Migrants, 1890–1940* (Philadelphia: Temple University Press, 1993); and Anthea Butler, *Women in the Church of God in Christ: Making Sanctified World* (Chapel Hill: University of North Carolina Press, 2007), to name a few.

5. Ernest Sandeen led the scholarship that defined fundamentalism doctrinally, and Matthew Avery Sutton has given his argument new life. See Sandeen, *The Roots of Fundamentalism*; and Sutton, *American Apocalypse*. George Marsden shifted the focus to the fundamentalists' interaction with American culture. See Marsden, *Fundamentalism and American Culture*.

6. Timothy L. Smith, "The Evangelical Kaleidoscope and the Call to Christian Unity," *Christian Scholar's Review* 15, no. 2 (1986): 125–40. I thank David Harrington Watt for drawing my attention to Dr. Smith's analogy.

7. See Christopher Z. Hobson, *The Mount of Vision: African American Prophetic Tradition, 1800–1950* (New York: Oxford University Press, 2012).

8. See Edward J. Blum, *W. E. B. DuBois: American Prophet* (Philadelphia: University of Pennsylvania Press, 2007). For an extensive look at how one progressive evangelical leader battled others within his own denomination, see Randall Maurice Jelks, *Benjamin Elijah Mays: Schoolmaster of the Movement, a Biography* (Chapel Hill: University of North Carolina Press, 2012).

9. See Barbara Dianne Savage, *Your Spirits Walk Beside Us: The Politics of Black Religion* (Cambridge: The Belknap Press of Harvard University Press, 2008); and Moses Nathaniel Moore, "Orishatauken Faduma and the New Theology," *Church History* 63, no. 1 (March 1994): 60–80.

10. See Dennis C. Dickerson, "African American Religious Intellectuals and the Theological Foundations of the Civil Rights Movement, 1930–1955," *Church History* 74, no. 2 (June 2005): 217–35; Dickerson, *African American*

Preachers and Politics: The Careys of Chicago (Jackson: University Press of Mississippi, 2010); and Jelks, *Benjamin Elijah Mays*.

11. For an example of the standard account of the distribution, see Marsden, *Fundamentalism and American Culture*, 119.

12. Savage, *Your Spirits Walk Beside Us*, 20–30.

13. For an examination of how fundamentalism was characterized as backward, see Mary Beth Swetnam Mathews, *Rethinking Zion: How the Print Media Placed Fundamentalism in the South* (Knoxville: University of Tennessee Press, 2006), 67–89.

14. Mary R. Sawyer, "Black Protestantism as Expressed in Ecumenical Activity," in *Re-forming the Center: American Protestantism, 1900 to the Present*, eds. Douglas Jacobsen and William Vance Trollinger (Grand Rapids, MI: William B. Eerdmans Publishing Company, 1998), 284–85.

15. See Butler, *Women in the Church of God in Christ*. Butler's analysis augments and refines that of Evelyn Brooks Higginbotham. See also Higginbotham, *Righteous Discontent*, especially 185–229.

16. See Lerone A. Martin, *Preaching on Wax: The Phonograph and the Shaping of Modern African American Religion* (New York: New York University Press, 2014).

17. David Henry Bradley, *A History of the A.M.E. Zion Church*, vol. 2 (Nashville, TN: The Parthenon Press, 1970), 201–2.

18. Butler, *Women in the Church of God in Christ*, 8.

Chapter 1

1. "'Cuff': The True Story of a Negro Slave," *The Pilot*, December 1929, 79, 82. Cuff was not alone as a black evangelical in fundamentalist journals. In September 1929, the Reverend H. L. Lundquist published an article, "A Negro Scrub Woman at the Death Bed of a Jew," in which the unnamed woman, who "spends her evenings in the Evening School of the Moody Bible Institute," converts a dying Jew to Christ. See Lundquist, "A Negro Scrub Woman at the Death Bed of a Jew," *Moody Bible Institute Monthly*, September 1929, 19.

2. Carpenter, *Revive Us Again*, 9.

3. For discussions of the emergence of fundamentalism, see Marsden, *Fundamentalism and American Culture*; Sandeen, *The Roots of Fundamentalism*; Virginia Brereton, *Training God's Army: The American Bible School, 1880–1940* (Bloomington: Indiana University Press, 1990); and William R. Glass, *Strangers in Zion: Fundamentalists in the South, 1900–1950* (Macon, GA: Mercer University Press, 2001). For an interpretation of the fundamentalist/modernist controversy as a debate over ecclesiology, see J. Michael Utzinger, *Yet Saints Their Watch Are Keeping: Fundamentalists, Modernists, and the Development of Evangelical Ecclesiology, 1887–1937* (Macon, GA: Mercer University Press, 2006).

4. The nature and pervasiveness of racism at the start of the twentieth cen-

tury has been the subject of numerous monographs. See, for example, Grace Elizabeth Hale, *Making Whiteness* (New York: Pantheon Books, 1998); and Joel Williamson, *The Crucible of Race* (New York: Oxford University Press, 1984).

5. Edward J. Blum, *Reforging the White Republic: Race, Religion, and American Nationalism, 1865–1898* (Baton Rouge: Louisiana State University Press, 2005), 15.

6. For an examination of the post-bellum separation of churches and denominations, see, for example, Montgomery, *Under Their Own Vine and Fig Tree*; and Katharine L. Dvorak, *An African-American Exodus: The Segregation of the Southern Churches* (Brooklyn: Carlson Publishing Inc., 1991).

7. C. Allyn Russell, *Voices of American Fundamentalism: Seven Biographical Sketches* (Philadelphia: The Westminster Press, 1976), 107–8. Russell observes that Massee "has been notably neglected" in historical accounts of fundamentalism.

8. J. C. Massee, "How Did the Negro Get His Skin?" Sermon 22, Sermon Book, Box 4, J. C. Massee Papers, American Baptist Historical Society (hereafter cited as J. C. Massee Papers), RG-1054.

9. For an apologetic interpretation of Dixon's views on race, see Donald L. Martin Jr., "A. C. Dixon's Views on Immigration and Race," *Baptist History and Heritage* 26, no. 4 (October 1991): 44–51.

10. J Frank Norris, "Bryan, Norris, Munhall and Others Occupy Front Page with Attacks on Enemies of the Bible," *The Searchlight*, June 29, 1924, clipping in Amzi Clarence Dixon Papers, Southern Baptist Historical Library and Archive (hereafter cited as A. C. Dixon Papers), Box 12, Folder 1, no. 111.

11. "Our Brother in Black," handwritten notes, A. C. Dixon Papers, Box 1, Folder 2, p. 1–2. Dixon was not alone in his admiration for Jasper. W. B. Riley, writing in *The Pilot* on the occasion of Billy Sunday's death, remarked that "the first man to employ kindred speech in sermonizing was John Jasper, the colored orator of Richmond, Va." W. B. Riley, "The Passing of Billy Sunday," *The Pilot*, December 1935, 84.

12. John Jasper, "De Sun Do Move," accessed February 1, 2012, http://www.library.vcu.edu/jbc/speccoll/vbha/6th5.html.

13. "Colored Adult Suffrage," A. C. Dixon Papers, Box 5, Folder 3, p. 2.

14. "Our Brother in Black," pp. 3–4, 9.

15. "The Future of the Educated Negro," undated manuscript, A. C. Dixon Papers, Box 1, Folder 1–5, p. 1.

16. Helen C. A. Dixon, *A. C. Dixon: A Romance of Preaching* (1931; reprint, New York: Garland Publishing Company, 1988), 151.

17. Quoted in Martin, "A. C. Dixon's Views on Immigration and Race," *Baptist History and Heritage*, 49. For an extended investigation into the continuing southern preoccupation with sex and race, and how it played out in churches, see Jane Dailey, "Sex, Segregation, and the Sacred after *Brown*," *The Journal of American History* 91, no. 1 (June 2004): 119–44.

18. A. C. Dixon, "The Future of the Educated Negro," p. 3.

19. For a recent example of how religion and politics intersected in the 1928 presidential campaign, see Justin Randolph Gage, "Vote as You Pray: The 1928 Presidential Election in Washington County, Arkansas," *The Arkansas Historical Quarterly* 68, no. 4 (Winter 2009): 388–417.

20. Telegram from J. Frank Norris to Senator Pat Harrison, October 14, 1928, J. Frank Norris Papers, Southern Baptist Historical Society and Archive (hereafter cited as Norris Papers), A.R. 124, Box 40, Folder 1799.

21. See Norris Papers, A.R. 124, Box 40, Folder 1799, item 24562; "Pat Harrison Answers Quiz of Dr. Norris," *Dallas Morning News*, October 19, 1928, news clipping, Norris Papers, Box 40, Folder 1799; and J. Frank Norris letter to Pat Harrison, October 21, 1928, Norris Papers, Box 40, Folder 1799.

22. J. Frank Norris to Glenn L. Gill, October 15, 1928, Norris Papers, Box 16, Folder 723.

23. Mrs. H. R. Duncan, Fort Worth, to J. Frank Norris, October 21, 1928, Norris Papers, Box 9, Folder 435.

24. Miss Sarah B. Balfour to J. Frank Norris, October 29, 1928, Norris Papers, Box 2, Folder 65.

25. For a brief history of the unlikely friendship of two men who initially opposed each other (and for evidence that J. Michael Utzinger's work on ecclesiology and fundamentalism merits another look) see J. Kristian Pratt, "From 'Funnymentalist' to Friend: The Evolving Relationship of Ben M. Bogard and J. Frank Norris," *Baptist History and Heritage* 42, no. 2 (March 2007): 105–13.

26. Ben M. Bogard, "Negro Equality and Al Smith," *Baptist and Commoner*, September 19, 1928, 3. Capitals in original.

27. "Ben M. Bogard's Speech in City Park, Little Rock, on Al Smith-Joe Robinson Issue," *Baptist and Commoner*, August 1, 1928, 5.

28. Ben M. Bogard, "What We See in Tammany Hall," *Baptist and Commoner*, October 10, 1928, 2. Bogard placed a similar article next to the photo, in case any of his readers had missed the points made below the fold. See "Shall We Have a Negro in the President's Cabinet?" *Baptist and Commoner*, October 10, 1928, 2.

29. Ben M. Bogard, "Beat Smith, The Wet Catholic Tammany Bolter, and Save Southern Democracy," *Baptist and Commoner*, October 31, 1928, 9.

30. L. J. Fowler, "The Missionary Outlook," *Grace and Truth*, January 1927, 1.

31. Josiah Strong, *Our Country* (1886; reprint, Cambridge: The Belknap Press of Harvard University Press, 1963), 201–2.

32. A. M. Moore, "Negro and White Man: A Great Address by a Great Leader," *The Baptist*, July 24, 1920, 913.

33. W. D. Powell, DD, "Negro Work in the South," *The Watchman-Examiner*, May 18, 1916, 638.

34. While the *Watchman-Examiner* was not a fundamentalist publication, per se, Laws kept the publication on a tack of conformity with fundamentalist thought.

35. John W. Bradbury, "Curtis Lee Laws and the Fundamentalist Movement," *Foundations* 5, no. 1 (January 1962): 52.

36. Howard Wayne Smith, DD, "Northern Migration of Negroes," *The Watchman-Examiner*, March 1, 1917, 266.

37. A. T. Robertson, "Negro Baptists as an Asset in Kingdom Work," *The Watchman-Examiner*, April 19, 1917, 498. Robertson contributed such articles often. See Robertson, "Memphis a Southern City," *The Watchman-Examiner*, March 16, 1922, 329–30; Robertson, "Southern Baptist Growth," *The Watchman-Examiner*, November 16, 1922, 1459–60; and Robertson, "Odds and Ends in a Hot Summer," *The Watchman-Examiner* August 21, 1930, 1073.

38. American Baptist Home Missionary Society advertisement, "America the Spiritual Granary of the World," *The Watchman-Examiner*, May 8, 1919, 573.

39. Frank L. Sullivan, "Sundays in Chicago," *The Watchman-Examiner*, March 9, 1922, 318.

40. Curtis Lee Laws, "American Blood in 1975," *The Watchman-Examiner*, March 14, 1918, 329.

41. Homer DeWilton Brookins, "The Northern Baptist Convention, Washington, District of Columbia, May 25–30," *The Watchman-Examiner*, June 3, 1926, 687.

42. For additional information on Riley, see William Vance Trollinger Jr., *God's Empire: William Bell Riley and Midwestern Fundamentalism* (Madison: University of Wisconsin Press, 1990).

43. William Bell Riley Collection, University of Northwestern (hereafter cited as W. B. Riley Papers), Scrapbook 39, p. 37.

44. Ibid.

45. William Bell Riley, "Fundamentalists! Attention!" *The Christian Fundamentalist*, May 1932, 348.

46. William Bell Riley, "Ho! For Columbus!" *The Christian Fundamentalist*, June 1932, 410.

47. William Bell Riley, "The Columbus, Ohio, Convention," *The Christian Fundamentalist*, July–August 1932, 4.

48. W. B. Riley, "Fundamentalists Association," *The Watchman-Examiner*, July 7, 1932, 856.

49. "Religion: Brothers and Sisters," *Time*, July 4, 1932, 32.

50. Mark Rogers, "End Times Innovator: Paul Rader and Evangelical Missions," *International Bulletin of Missionary Research*, 37, no. 1 (January 2013): 17.

51. *The Colored Quintette: A Narrative of God's Marvelous Dealings with the Cleveland Gospel Quintette and Their Personal Testimony* (Kilmarnock, Scotland: John Ritchie, Ltd., 1937), 3–49. A small mention of the Quintette also appears in Frederick Burton, *Cleveland's Gospel Music* (Charleston, SC: Arcadia Publishing, 2003), 10.

52. "Unusual Opportunities," *The Pilot*, December 1930, 68.

53. "Program of the Dallas Bible School, May 23–30," *The Sword of the Lord*, May 7, 1937, 1.

54. "Dallas Bible School Going Gloriously: Tindley, McCarrell and Springer Sensations Thus Far," *The Sword of the Lord*, May 28, 1937, 1–2.

55. "Dallas Bible School 11 Glorious Days, Nov. 21–Dec. 1," *The Sword of the Lord*, October 21, 1937, 1. Capitals original.

56. Sonnet Retman has argued that, during the Great Depression, Americans sought out "folk" performers in a search for authenticity. While Rice's use of Tindley during this period appears to support her contention, the use of black musicians predates the Great Depression. See Sonnet Retman, *Real Folks: Race and Genre in the Great Depression* (Durham: Duke University Press, 2011), 1–10.

57. Curtis Lee Laws, "The Editor Afield: Morehouse College and Spelman Seminary," *The Watchman-Examiner*, March 8, 1917, 298–9.

58. Advertisement, "Dr. French E. Oliver Announces! Famous Negro Sermons!" *Moody Bible Institute Monthly*, February 1928, 282. *The Christian Fundamentalist* ran a similar advertisement on its back cover of the April 1928 issue. "Dr. French E. Oliver Announces!" advertisement, *The Christian Fundamentalist*, April 1928, back cover.

59. French Earl Oliver, *Famous Negro Sermons* (Hollywood, CA: The Oliver Press, 1927), 7, 20, 31, and 50. In the unpaginated introduction, Oliver claimed that he had shown "some of the sermons to internationally famous ministers, professors in universities and platform celebrities, who literally commanded me to give the results of my labors to the public." His intent in publishing the book was "to let the people know that the sermons were and are just as inspiring as the songs." n.p.

60. Advertisement, "Seven Unanswerable Books," *Moody Bible Institute Monthly*, March 1929, 348.

61. For a discussion of Shadduck's books, see Ronald Numbers, *Darwinism Comes to America* (Cambridge: Harvard University Press, 1998), 118–9.

62. "It May Be Dey Am Right," *The Christian Fundamentalist*, December 1928, 31.

63. William Bell Riley, "What is the Meaning of Modernism?" *The Christian Fundamentalist*, July 1930, 34.

64. A. T. Robertson, "Odds and Ends in a Hot Summer," *Watchman-Examiner*, August 21, 1930, 1073.

65. Curtis Lee Laws, "Make Yourself Understood," *Watchman-Examiner*, January 2, 1930, 8.

66. "Just for Fun," *Watchman-Examiner*, January 9, 1930, 53.

67. Curtis Lee Laws, "About 'Amos and Andy,'" *Watchman-Examiner*, July 31, 1930, 969.

68. J. Frank Norris to J. H. Bradley, June 23, 1928, Norris Papers, Box 2, Folder 65.

69. J. Frank Norris to Jane Hartwell, December 28, 1928, Norris Papers, Box 19, Folder 853.

70. William Bell Riley, "The Editor's Trip Across Texas," *The Christian Fundamentalist*, March 1931, 324.

71. "When the Negro Loses His Religion," *Moody Bible Institute Monthly*, April 1931, n.p., in W. B. Riley Papers, Scrapbook 38.

72. "When the Negro Loses His Religion," W. B. Riley Papers.

73. J. Frank Norris telegram to Senator Tom Connally, May 5, 1930, Norris Papers, Box 5, Folder 237. Connally acknowledged receipt of Norris's telegram, but told him that he "could not comply with your request." Connally to Norris, May 8, 1930, Norris Papers, Box 5, Folder 237.

74. Curtis Lee Laws, "Negro Education," *The Watchman-Examiner*, February 13, 1930, 200.

75. Curtis Lee Laws, "A Little Journey to the Sunny South," *The Watchman-Examiner*, March 23, 1922, 363.

76. Curtis Lee Laws, "The Negro and Roman Catholicism," *The Watchman-Examiner*, February 26, 1931, 265.

77. See, for example, Grace Elizabeth Hale's discussion of the white obsession with black mammies in *Making Whiteness*, 85–120. Unlike Hale's subjects, the white fundamentalists making this argument were male, indicating that both white women and white men saw a value in constructing a loyal black domestic helper to contend with the challenges of the post–Civil War South.

78. Helen Cadbury Dixon, *A. C. Dixon*, 18–19, 26–27.

79. Powell, "Negro Work in the South," *Watchman-Examiner*, May 18, 1916, 637.

80. "Split is Expected When 5,000 Baptist Delegates Convene," W. B. Riley Papers, Scrapbook 39, p. 56. The article appears to be from the *Washington Post* but is torn.

81. Norris himself claimed the mantle of friend of the black man. In a heated exchange with the National Association of Colored People, Detroit Branch, Norris wrote to the branch director, the Reverend Robert L. Bradby Jr., that "I am the best friend of the Negro race, and everybody in the South knows that." J. Frank Norris to the Reverend Robert L. Bradby Jr., March 15, 1947, Norris Papers, Box 2, Folder 79.

82. "Educating the Negro," *The Watchman-Examiner*, December 10, 1925, W. B. Riley Papers, Scrapbook 40, p. 5; "The Southern People and the Negroes," *Southern Methodist*, June 26, 1929, p. 175, W. B. Riley Papers, Scrapbook 38, p. 175.

83. Curtis Lee Laws, "Race Prejudice," *The Watchman-Examiner*, February 5, 1925, 165–6.

84. Curtis Lee Laws, "The Progress of the Negro," *The Watchman-Examiner*, March 19, 1925, 359.

85. Curtis Lee Laws, "Negroes and White People," *The Watchman-Examiner*, October 15, 1931, 1321.

86. C. Allyn Russell, *Voices of American Fundamentalism: Seven Biographical Studies* (Philadelphia: The Westminster Press, 1976), 48–50.

87. John Roach Straton to John F. Hylan, December 5, 1922, John Roach Straton Papers, American Baptist Historical Society (hereafter cited as Straton Papers), RG 1075, Box 9, Folder Ku Klux Klan.

88. John Roach Straton, "How to Fight the Negroes, the Foreigners, the Catholics, and the Jews—The More Excellent Way," sermon dated December 10, 1922, Straton Papers, RG 1075, Box 9, Folder Ku Klux Klan.

89. Quoted in Hillyer H. Straton, "John Roach Straton and the Ku Klux Klan," *Andover Newton Quarterly* 9, no. 2 (November 1968): 129. H. H. Straton's apologetic explanation of his father's actions includes an argument that his father got involved in a group known as "The Supreme Kingdom," which turned out to be a Klan-sympathizing group, because "he trusted [people] until proved otherwise" if those people "spoke his language." (132) The news of his work in his new city reached African Americans in Norfolk, one of whom wrote to him expressing "special appreciation of the very daring but necessary thing you have recently done in exposing some of the rottenness of the underworld in America's great metropolis." Richard H. Bowling, pastor of the First Baptist Church, Colored, of Norfolk, added, "I am sending you a clipping from one of our colored papers showing you how one of our colored writers thinks about the matter." Unfortunately, no clipping remains with Preacher Bowling's letter. Richard H. Bowling to John Roach Straton, April 22, 1920, Straton Papers, RG 1075, Box 11, Folder Shackleford Suit.

90. Hale, *Making Whiteness*, 17.

91. Kimberly Wallace-Sanders, *Mammy: A Century of Race, Gender, and Southern Memory* (Ann Arbor: University of Michigan Press, 2008), 94.

92. John Roach Straton, "The Menace of Skepticism, Worldliness, and Lawlessness," *National Baptist Voice*, October 14, 1922, 2. He added that "there were three boys in our family and the prayers of this Negro mammy had a great influence in the molding and directing of our lives. . . . Those times between the white people and the black people in Dixie are the things that will save the race."

93. Untitled sermon, Straton Papers, Box 10, Folder Negro. Grace Elizabeth Hale has documented how widespread the practice of "conflat[ing] individual and regional childhoods" was among white southerners. Hale, *Whiteness*, 53–55.

94. Straton Papers, Box 16, Folder Straton, John Roach, Biographical; and John Roach Straton, "A Life-Changing Business," *Christian Herald*, December 28, 1929, in Straton Papers, Box 16.

95. John Roach Straton, "Will Education Solve the Race Problem?" *The North American Review* 170, no. 523 (June 1900): 800. Ironically, Straton freely employed the idea of racial "evolution," even relying on Darwin's theory of evolution for his argument for Anglo-Saxon superiority. By the early 1920s, he would be among those fighting biological Darwinism at every turn.

96. Gordon Reynolds Mumford, president of Southern Bible Institute from 1971 to 2006, credits the start with black men hearing students of white Dallas Theological Seminary (then called Evangelical Theological Seminary) street preach. See Gordon Reynolds Mumford, *Southern Bible Institute: The History*

from 1927–1998 (PhD diss., Tyndale Theological Seminary, 1998), 2. Another dissertation, *The Historical Development and Future of the Southern Bible Institute*, by Michael Cooks, depends largely on the account given in Mumford, but pamphlets reprinted in Cooks's appendix stress the outstanding need for training, rather than black initiative. Michael J. F. Cooks, *The Historical Development and Future of the Southern Bible Institute* (EdD diss., University of North Texas, 2008), University of North Texas Digital Library, accessed July 18, 2012, http://digital.library.unt.edu/ark:/67531/metadc6121/.

97. Quoted in Mumford, *Southern Bible Institute*, 4.

98. Quoted in Mumford, *Southern Bible Institute*, 5.

99. Cooks, *Historical Development*, 34.

100. "Helping to Solve a Great Problem: A Projected Bible Institute for the Colored People of the South," reproduced in Cooks, *Historical Development*, 124.

101. "Dallas Colored Bible Institute," *Christian Fundamentalist*, June 1929, 216–7.

102. Michael Cooks, "The History and Future of the Southern Bible Institute: A Post-Secondary School of Biblical Studies for African Americans," *Christian Higher Education* 9, no. 2 (April–June 2010): 156.

103. E. Schuyler English, *H. A. Ironside: Ordained of the Lord* (New York: Loizeaux Brothers, 1946), 259–60.

104. Southern Bible Institute website, accessed September 3, 2014, http://www.southernbible.org/index.cfm/PageID/1672/index.html.

105. "Perplexing Questions," *The Pilot*, March 1930, 191.

106. Stephen R. Haynes, *Noah's Curse: The Biblical Justification of American Slavery* (New York: Oxford University Press, 2002), especially 65–104.

107. "Perplexing Questions," *The Pilot*, July 1930, 303. Above the Ham question was a related inquiry, "Were the Egyptians, who held the children of Israel in bondage, negroes?" Apparently "B.M., Minneapolis, Minn." was looking for evidence either that blacks had held slaves or that blacks bore some responsibility in the captivity of the Israelites.

108. Haynes, *Noah's Curse*, 114–21. For a more detailed history of how Benjamin Palmer, Presbyterian minister, developed the Curse of Ham theology after the Civil War, see Stephen R. Haynes, "Race, National Destiny, and the Sons of Noah in the Thought of Benjamin M. Palmer," *Journal of Presbyterian History* 78, no. 2 (Summer 2000): 125–43. For an examination of how Calvinists in general handled the issue of Noah, Ham, Canaan, and the curse, see David Whitford, "A Calvinist Heritage to the 'Curse of Ham': Assessing the Accuracy of a Claim about Racial Subordination," *Church History and Religious Culture* 90, no. 1 (2010): 25–45. Another white fundamentalist, Donald Grey Barnhouse, also embraced the Curse of Ham as an explanation for black suffering. See Sutton, *American Apocalypse*, 136. Barnhouse drew rebuke from at least one former slave turned preacher. See Walter H. Brooks, "Did God Curse Black People?" *National Baptist Voice*, August 20, 1932, 3.

Chapter 2

1. "Colored vs. White," *National Baptist Union-Review* (hereafter cited as *NBUR*), April 21, 1917, 9.

2. William R. Hutchison, *The Modernist Impulse in American Protestantism* (Durham: Duke University Press, 1992), 2.

3. Clarence M. Wagner, *History of the National Baptist Convention, U.S.A., Inc.* (Decatur, GA: Tru-Faith Publishing Company, 1993), 40–44. Evelyn Brooks Higginbotham also sides with the publishing board thesis. See Higginbotham, *Righteous Discontent*, 164.

4. Lillian B. Horace, *"Crowned with Glory and Honor": The Life of Rev. Lacey Kirk Williams*, ed. L. Vencheal Booth (Hicksville, NY: Exposition Press, 1978), 166–7. The total membership of the NBC around the time of the split was over 2.9 million, and black Baptists accounted for 61 percent of all black churchgoers, according to statistics cited by both Evelyn Brooks Higginbotham and Paul Harvey. See Higginbotham, *Righteous Discontent*, 6; and Paul Harvey, "Black Protestantism: A Historiographical Appraisal," in *American Denominational History: Perspectives on the Past, Prospects for the Future*, ed. Keith Harper (Tuscaloosa: The University of Alabama Press, 2008), 129.

5. Bobby L. Lovett, *How It Came to Be: The Boyd Family's Contribution to African American Religious Publishing from the 19th to the 21st Century* (Nashville: Mega Publishing Corporation, 2007), 58.

6. In a tantalizing comment within a speech to the Baptist Ministers' Conference in 1925, W. H. Moses listed two factions in the debate over publishing but then added a third group—a "liberal group of cooperative-independents"—and named within that group the men who would go on to lead the National Baptist Convention, Incorporated, the body that had the more liberal denominational paper and that would have a complicated relationship with the Southern Baptist Convention over the administration of the American Baptist Theological Seminary. See W. H. Moses, "The Need of a United Negro Baptist Family: Historic Tendencies for It," *National Baptist Voice* (hereafter cited as *NBV*), March 21, 1925, 1.

7. "To Confer Toward Uplifting of the Negro," *Washington Bee*, September 5, 1908, America's Historical Newspapers database.

8. See N. Barnett Dodson, "Educational Interest: Advisory Board of National Religious Training School Begins Work," *Broad Axe* (Chicago, IL), October 22, 1910, America's Historical Newspapers database; George F. King, "Uplift of the Negro: Representative Whites Lend Ability to Great Institution," *Washington Bee*, October 22, 1910, America's Historical Newspapers database; and "An Institution for Race Up-Liftment," *Savannah Tribune*, October 22, 1910, America's Historical Newspapers database. The stories in the *Bee* and the *Tribune* were identical with the exception of title and George King's byline.

9. "Dr. James E. Sheppard: Religious Training School," *Washington Bee*, April 15, 1911, America's Historical Newspapers database.

10. "Two Prominent Clergymen Speak on Riot," *Chicago Defender*, August 9, 1919, America's Historical Newspapers database. Straton also received attention from the *New York Amsterdam News* for his denunciation of lynching and the KKK. See "Straton Denounces Lynching: Lynching and Ku Klux Klan Are Denounced by Southern Born Minister," *New York Amsterdam News*, April 1, 1925, America's Historical Newspapers database.

11. Michael Lienesch, *In the Beginning: Fundamentalism, the Scopes Trial, and the Making of the Antievolution Movement* (Chapel Hill: University of North Carolina Press, 2007), 183. For a defense of Straton by his son, see Hillyer H. Straton, "John Roach Straton and the Ku Klux Klan," *Andover Newton Quarterly* 9, no. 2 (November 1968): 124–34.

12. "Can't Purify Dance, Dr. Straton Says; Preacher Speaks of it as 'Bait of the Devil,'" *A.M.E. Christian Recorder*, September 16, 1920, 6.

13. John Roach Straton, "The Menace of Skepticism, Worldliness, and Lawlessness," *NBV*, October 14, 1922, 1, 2. The next week, the same publication ran an exposition of "The Mercy Seat," written by Dallas minister and friend of J. Frank Norris, A. Reilly Copeland. See A. Reilly Copeland, "The Mercy Seat," *NBV*, October 21, 1922, 2.

14. "Church and Klan Going Hand in Hand: Ku Kluxism Invading White Christian Pulpit: Donations Win Ministerial Support," *The Appeal* (St. Paul), December 2, 1922, America's Historical Newspapers database.

15. For a detailed examination of how uplift influenced African American ministers immediately following the Civil War, see Edward L. Wheeler, *Uplifting the Race: The Black Minister in the South, 1865–1902* (Lanham, MD: University Press of America, 1986).

16. Higginbotham, *Righteous Discontent*, 10.

17. Untitled article, *The Kansas City Advocate*, November 28, 1919, America's Historical Newspapers database.

18. "The Western Baptist Convention in Session," *The Kansas City Advocate*, July 24, 1925, America's Historical Newspapers database.

19. "A 'Kaiser Jesus,'" San Jose *Evening News*, April 25, 1922, America's Historical Newspapers database.

20. "The World is Lining Up," *Cleveland Gazette*, June 6, 1925, America's Historical Newspapers database.

21. For more on white secular media's coverage of the white fundamentalist movement, see Mathews, *Rethinking Zion*.

22. W. J. Walls, "A Clash in the Christian Family," *Star of Zion*, May 10, 1923, 4.

23. Joseph A. Booker, DD, "Northern Baptist Convention," *NBV*, July 1, 1922, 1, 12.

24. For a discussion of the tensions among fundamentalists over whether to reform or leave denominations, see Carpenter, *Revive Us Again*, 43–53.

25. Robert A. Ashworth, DD, "The Rift in the Baptist Lute," *NBV*, July 1, 1922, 3.

26. *Minutes of the Forty-fifth Annual Session of the National Baptist Convention of America* (Nashville: National Baptist Publishing Board, 1925), 17.

27. See also *Proceedings of the Forty-sixth Annual Session of the National Baptist Convention of America* (Nashville: National Baptist Publishing Board, 1926), 24; and *Proceedings of the Forty-seventh Annual Session of the National Baptist Convention of America* (Nashville: National Baptist Publishing Board, 1927), 27–8.

28. "Southern White Baptists," *NBUR*, March 17, 1928, 4.

29. "The World Baptist Congress," *NBUR*, April 21, 1928, 4. Frank seemed never to tire of discussing modernism. See also "Miracles," *NBUR*, November 2, 1929, 4; and "Big Business," *NBUR*, November 30, 1929, 4.

30. "The Old Order Passing," *Star of Zion*, October 4, 1923, 4.

31. The Rev. A. Ellison, "Mirrors of Zion—Has Christianity Lost Its Place in These Modern Times?" *Star of Zion*, February 7, 1924, 7.

32. Bishop W. J. Walls, "Change the Law and the Star Will Grow," *Star of Zion*, January 10, 1924, 4.

33. "Is Protestant Christianity in a Schism, a Battle, or a Split?" *Star of Zion*, January 2, 1924, 4.

34. "Baptists in Name Only," *NBUR*, February 16, 1918, 8.

35. Untitled editorial, *NBUR*, April 13, 1918, 9.

36. Sheldon Avery, *Up from Washington: William Pickens and the Negro Struggle for Equality, 1900–1954* (Newark: University of Delaware Press, 1989), 95; and "White Infidels Organize," *NBUR*, February 6, 1926, 4.

37. "The Infidels," *NBUR*, April 3, 1926, 4.

38. "Infidels Fighting the Preachers," *NBUR*, September 3, 1927, 4.

39. Historian Barbara Dianne Savage argues, however, that Miller was unfairly label as anti-Christian and that he believed that "African Americans were in fact the only true American Christians." See Savage, *Your Spirits Walk Beside Us*, 29.

40. "White Baptists," *NBUR*, April 17, 1926, 4.

41. "White Baptists," *NBUR*, July 10, 1926, 4.

42. "Northern Baptists," *NBUR*, August 21, 1926, 4.

43. "Nothing Between," *NBUR*, February 16, 1929, 4.

44. "Among White Baptists," *NBUR*, May 7, 1927, 4.

45. See Savage, *Your Spirits Walk Beside Us*, especially chap. 1; and Curtis Evans, *The Burden of Black Religion* (New York: Oxford University Press, 2008), 9–10.

46. "Among White People," *NBUR*, November 19, 1927, 4.

47. "White Baptists at War," *NBUR*, November 12, 1927, 4.

48. "Along the White Baptist Line," *NBUR*, February 4, 1928, 4.

49. "Along the White Baptist Line," 4. The "(smile)" is in the original. Frank used emoticons before they were even invented.

50. "What is the Matter with White Baptists?" *NBUR*, January 19, 1929, 4.

51. "Preachers Ought to Stop It," *NBUR*, November 30, 1929, 4; "What Fools

These Mortals Be," *NBUR*, September 21, 1929, 4; and "The Judas Kiss: 'Betrayeth thou the Son of man with a kiss?'" *NBUR*, August 3, 1929, 4. Capitals original.

52. "Whose Baby is It?" *NBUR*, February 11, 1933, 1. Capitals original.

53. "Is Civilization Sinking?" *Star of Zion*, November 23, 1922, 4.

54. Untitled editorial, *Star of Zion*, January 8, 1925, 4.

55. "The Fruits of Modernism," *Star of Zion*, January 9, 1930, 4.

56. "The Reason Why," *Star of Zion*, July 31, 1930, 4.

57. "Old Time Religion," *Star of Zion*, February 12, 1931, 4.

58. "Iconoclasm," *Star of Zion*, December 15, 1932, 4.

59. L. G. Jordan, "Our Historian Heard from Again," *NBV*, July 18, 1925, 7.

60. Ashworth, "Rift," *NBV*, 3–4.

61. "New Year's Day," *NBV*, January 1, 1921, 8.

62. R. F. Horton, DD, "The New Note in Christianity," *NBV*, January 1, 1922, 7, 10.

63. See, for example, Walter Rauschenbusch, "The Kingdom of God," in *The Social Gospel in America, 1870–1920*, ed. Robert T. Handy (New York: Oxford University Press, 1966), 264–7. The Social Gospel's impulses, however, would continue to be felt in American religious circles for decades to come. See, for example, Brantley W. Gasaway's work, *Progressive Evangelicals and the Pursuit of Social Justice* (Chapel Hill: University of North Carolina Press, 2014).

64. Ashworth, "Rift," *NBV*, July 1, 1922, 4.

65. "Missionary Mass Meeting," *NBV*, October 16, 1926, 9.

66. See Lillian B. Horace's biography, *"Crowned with Glory and Honor"*.

67. Lacey K. Williams, "The Third Annual Address of Dr. L. K. Williams, President: Delivered Before the Forty-fifth Annual Session of the National Baptist Convention, September 1925, at Baltimore, Maryland," *NBV*, October 17, 1925, 1, 14–15.

68. *Minutes of the Forty-third Annual Session of the National Baptist Convention (Unincorporated)* (Nashville: National Baptist Publishing Board, 1925), 11.

69. "Preacher Kills Man," *NBV*, August 28, 1926, 4.

70. George W. Slater, E. H. McDaniel, and P. H. Jackson, "The State of the Church," *A.M.E. Christian Recorder*, November 6, 1924, 13, 15.

71. Rev. I. W. L. Roundtree, "Do We Need a Reformation in the A.M.E. Church? If So, To What Extent?" *A.M.E. Christian Recorder*, January 29, 1925, 10.

72. "Report of the Committee on State of the Country," *A.M.E. Christian Recorder*, November 26, 1925, 2–3.

73. R. R. Wright Jr., "Neighborliness: The Good Samaritan," *A.M.E. Christian Recorder*, November 20, 1924, 1.

74. R. R. Wright Jr., "The Raising of Lazarus," *A.M.E. Christian Recorder*, December 4, 1924, 1.

75. Richard R. Wright Jr., *87 Years Behind the Black Curtain: An Autobiography* (Philadelphia: Rare Book Company, 1965), 37–49.

76. "How to Study the Bible," *NBUR*, March 27, 1926, 4.

77. See "Authority," *NBUR*, January 19, 1929, 4; and "The Fatherhood of God," *NBUR*, February 9, 1929, 4.

78. "Undergraduates Fortunate," *Star of Zion*, April 5, 1928, 4.

79. "Banning the Tardy," *Star of Zion*, September 11, 1930, 4.

80. See "'Both ** And,'" *Star of Zion*, March 8, 1928, 4; and the Reverend Joseph Fort Newton, "What the Church Can Do Today (The Sermon of the Month, Rev. James Gordon Gilkey, DD,)" reprint of *McCall's Magazine* article, *Star of Zion*, January 23, 1930, 1.

81. Rev. D. E. Thompson, "The Church Needs Rebels," *Star of Zion*, January 2, 1930, 7.

82. "The Breaking of Dawn," *NBV*, April 21, 1934, 2.

83. "The Social Gospel," *NBV*, October 13, 1934, 2.

84. "Dr. Fosdick and Modernism," *NBV*, November 30, 1935, 2.

Chapter 3

1. W. A. Taylor, "Is There a Need for a Restatement of Baptist Doctrines and Polity," *NBV*, July 20, 1935, 1, 8.

2. For Ernest Sandeen, fundamentalism was a doctrinal battle with deep roots in the nineteenth century. See Sandeen, *The Roots of Fundamentalism*. George Marsden painted a picture of fundamentalists as more concerned about American culture and its effects on religion. See Marsden, *Fundamentalism and American Culture*. While Marsden has been the prevailing standard in the field of American religious studies, Matthew Avery Sutton has challenged his reliance on culture wars and his focus on World War I as the impetus for so many fundamentalist battles. Sutton also revives the doctrinal argument. See Sutton, *American Apocalypse*. My own reading of the fundamentalists and the historiography seeks to combine these two disparate notions—culture and doctrine—into a more comprehensive understanding of the various fundamentalist movements. Culture and doctrine cannot be divorced from each other, and, moreover, it is folly to argue that one mattered more than the other. Fundamentalists and their sympathizers saw them as a piece, not as two distinct concepts. Cultural changes fostered adaptations of religious doctrine, but changes in religious doctrine also influenced reception of culture.

3. Timothy P. Weber, *Living in the Shadow of the Second Coming: American Premillennialism, 1875–1925* (New York: Oxford University Press, 1979).

4. For an underappreciated discussion of white southern resistance to premillennial teachings, see Glass, *Strangers in Zion*. Glass makes a cogent case against including premillennial belief in any definition of fundamentalism. Glass, *Strangers in Zion*, 19–24. Christopher Z. Hobson confirms my observation that premillennialism was rare among African American prophetic discourse. See Hobson, *The Mount of Vision*, 120.

5. Ronald L. Numbers, *Creationism in Twentieth-Century America: A Ten*

Volume Anthology of Documents, 1903–1961, vol. 1, *Antievolutionism Before World War I* (New York, Garland Publishing, Inc.: 1995), xiii. See also Mathews, *Rethinking Zion*, 83–88.

6. "Three Types of Baptists," editorial, *NBUR*, January 13, 1917, 8. The parenthetical "whatever that may mean" is in the original.

7. See R. A. Torrey, A. C. Dixon, et al., eds., *The Fundamentals: A Testimony to the Truth* (Los Angeles, CA: Bible Institute of Los Angeles, 1917; reprint, Grand Rapids, MI: Baker Books, 2000).

8. "Both Unchristian and Unscientific," *NBUR*, June 8, 1918, 8.

9. "The Editor in Chicago," *NBUR*, April 20, 1918, 8.

10. "Inspired," *NBUR*, May 19, 1928, 4.

11. "What is the Bible and How to Make Use of It," *NBUR*, March 12, 1932, 1.

12. "When the Convention Meets in Norfolk, VA," *NBUR*, March 16, 1929, 4.

13. "Among the White Baptists," *NBUR*, May 7, 1927, 4.

14. "During and After the War," *NBUR*, July 6, 1918, 8.

15. Untitled editorial, *NBUR*, August 17, 1918, 9.

16. "The Truth Makes Free," *Star of Zion*, March 15, 1928, 4.

17. "The Truth," *A.M.E. Christian Recorder*, April 30, 1925, 4.

18. "Report of the Committee on State of the Country," *A.M.E. Christian Recorder*, November 26, 1925, 3.

19. E. George Biddle, "The Fundamentals," *Star of Zion*, September 8, 1921, 1.

20. E. George Biddle, "Divinely Inspired Scriptures," *Star of Zion*, February 27, 1930, 1.

21. E. George Biddle, "The Mysteries of the Kingdom," *Star of Zion*, April 21 1932, 1.

22. E. George Biddle, "Holy Spirit Begotten," *Star of Zion*, November 18, 1937, 1. Biddle was a prolific author, and the bulk of his contributions to the *Star of Zion* and to the *A.M.E. Quarterly* explicated traditional Protestant doctrine. See, for example, "Knowing Christ and His Unsearchable Riches," *A.M.E. Zion Quarterly Review* 35, no. 3 (June–September 1924): 9–12; "The Recognition of Christ Jesus as Almighty God," *A.M.E. Zion Quarterly Review* 36, no. 1 (January–March 1925): 10–12; "The Creator and the Created: Who? When" How? Why?" *A.M.E. Zion Quarterly Review* 39, no. 4 (Fourth Quarter 1928): 5–9; and "The Restoration of All Things," *A.M.E. Quarterly* 39, no. 3 (July–September 1928): 3–5.

23. Dr. E. D. W. Jones, "Shaking the Plum Tree: Old Fundamentals Need to Be Re-instated," *Star of Zion*, May 8, 1919, 1.

24. Bishop G. C. Clement, "Quadrennial Address of the Bishops," *Star of Zion*, May 10, 1928, 1.

25. E. C. Morris, "Negroes' Loyalty to Church and State," *NBV*, January 15, 1921, 1, 9, 12.

26. Dr. R. B. Roberts, "Six Steps to the Throne," *NBV*, January 15, 1921, 3, 6.

27. Matthew Avery Sutton has recently reignited the debate over the essential

inclusion of premillennialism as a key part of fundamentalism and, as such, has placed emphasis on the malleable nature of this form of apocalyptic thought. I am arguing here that when African American Baptists and Methodists meant to be premillennial, they were; when they described the need for conversion, they meant that alone. Sutton's work is admirable, necessary, and informs my own, but sometimes in Christianity and especially for these writers, a conversion is just a conversion. See Sutton, *American Apocalypse.*

28. Dr. A. J. Stokes, "John's Wonderful Figurative Vision," *NBV*, January 29, 1921, 1, 4.

29. Dr. A. J. Stokes, "A New Heaven and a New Earth," *NBV*, February 12, 1921, 7, 10.

30. "Is the World Growing Worse?" *Star of Zion*, August 28, 1924, 4. The biblical quotation is from Matthew 7:12.

31. *Proceedings of the Forty-Sixth Annual Session of the National Baptist Convention of America Held with the Baptists of Indianapolis, Ind., in Tomlinson Hall, September 8–12, 1926, J. E. Wood, Pres. C. P. Madison, Sec."* (Nashville: 1926), 24.

32. Untitled editorial, *Star of Zion*, July 14, 1927, 4.

33. Dr. A. Reilly Copeland, "Imminency of Our Lord's Return is Greatly Enhanced by the Rapid Occurrence of World Events in the Light of Prophecy," reprint of *Tabernacle Voice* article in *NBUR*, October 7, 1933, 4. The *National Baptist Voice* also ran at least one of Copeland's premillennial columns. See A. Reilly Copeland, "The Bible and Science," *NBV*, May 7, 1927, 4–6, 10–12.

34. T. W. Callaway, "Evangelism, Hastening the Second Coming of Christ," reprint of *Western Recorder* article, *NBUR*, December 1, 1934, 2.

35. Untitled editorial, *Star of Zion*, February 12, 1925, 4.

36. For more on Biddle's long and rich career, see James Walker Hood, *One Hundred Years of the African Methodist Episcopal Zion Church, or the Centennial of African Methodism* (New York: A.M.E. Zion Book Concern, 1895), 480–82; and William J. Walls, *The African Methodist Episcopal Zion Church: Reality of the Black Church* (Charlotte, North Carolina: A.M.E. Zion Publishing House, 1974), 455.

37. Elder E. George Biddle, "Pre-Millennialism: Or the Doctrine that the Second Coming of Christ Precedes the Millennium," *Star of Zion*, August 24, 1922, 2, 8–9; and Elder E. George Biddle, "Pre-Millennialism: Or the Doctrine that the Second Coming of Christ Precedes the Millennium," *Star of Zion*, September 7, 1922, 5. Unfortunately, while the article ends with "to be continued," no copy exists of the September 14, 1922, edition of the *Star of Zion*. Timothy P. Weber, "Premillennialism," in *The Variety of American Evangelicalism*, eds. Donald W. Dayton and Robert K. Johnston (Knoxville: University of Tennessee Press, 1991), 6.

38. Elder E. George Biddle, "The Restoration of All Things," *Star of Zion*, February 10, 1927, 1, 5.

39. Biddle, "Restoration of All Things," 5.

40. E. George Biddle, "The Infallible Word," *Star of Zion*, June 30, 1932, 1.

41. T. C. Dunham, "A Layman on King James versus Moffatt," *Journal of Bible and Religion* 14, no. 2 (May 1946): 107–10.

42. See, for example, Rev. E. George Biddle, DD, "Patiently Waiting for Results," *Star of Zion*, October 31, 1929, 1, 6; and Rev. E. George Biddle, DD, "Perfection of Character, *Star of Zion*, April 10, 1930, 1.

43. Rev. E. George Biddle, DD, "Our Invisible Defenders," *Star of Zion*, September 26, 1929, 1, 5.

44. Carpenter, *Revive Us Again*, 6. In 1932, Biddle quoted Charles Spurgeon's "reflections" on Psalm 50. See E. George Biddle, "The Answered Prayer," *Star of Zion*, December 22, 1932, 1.

45. Sandeen, *The Roots of Fundamentalism*, 144.

46. See Margaret Lamberts Bendroth, *Fundamentalists in the City: Conflict and Division in Boston's Churches, 1885–1950* (New York: Oxford University Press, 2005), especially 86–98.

47. See E. George Biddle, letter to the editor, *Star of Zion*, September 9, 1921, 4; "Christian Manhood," *Star of Zion*, April 12, 1928, 1; "The Deity of Jesus Christ," *Star of Zion*, December 31, 1931, 1; and "Our Marvelously Constituted Body," *Star of Zion*, December 3, 1931, 1.

48. Rev. E. George Biddle, "Nonconformity," *Star of Zion*, February 9, 1928, 1, 8.

49. "Inventory," *Star of Zion*, January 5, 1928, 4. For more on the Religious Book Club and its influence on Protestant theology, see Matthew S. Hedstrom, *The Rise of Liberal Religion: Book Culture and American Spirituality in the Twentieth Century* (New York: Oxford University Press, 2013), 52–79.

50. E. George Biddle, "Beliefs that Matter," *Star of Zion*, July 31, 1930, 1.

51. See Eric D. Anderson, "Black Responses to Darwinism, 1859–1915," in *Disseminating Darwinism: The Role of Place, Race, Religion, and Gender*, eds. Ronald L. Numbers and John Stenhouse (Cambridge: Cambridge University Press, 1999), 247, 254.

52. See, for example, Savage, *Your Spirits Walk Beside Us*; and Evans, *The Burden of Black Religion*, for a discussion of how black sociologists debated African American religious tendencies and organizations.

53. See Jeffrey P. Moran, "Reading Race into the Scopes Trial: African American Elites, Science, and Fundamentalism," *Journal of American History* 90, no. 3 (December 2003): 891–2; and Jeffrey P. Moran, "The Scopes Trial and Southern Fundamentalism in Black and White: Race, Region, and Religion," *Journal of Southern History* 70, no. 1 (February 2004): 100–105.

54. "'Dishonest Scoundrels'" *Star of Zion*, May 28, 1925, 4.

55. See Michael Lienesch, *In the Beginning: Fundamentalism, the Scopes Trial, and the Making of the Antievolution Movement* (Chapel Hill: University of North Carolina Press, 2007), esp. 8–33.

56. Thomas Walker Wallace, "Bits of Comment," *Star of Zion*, July 2, 1925, 5.

57. "Bryan Speaks to Darwin," *Star of Zion*, July 9, 1925, 4.

58. "Darwinism, Mr. Bryan, and the Legislators," editorial, *Star of Zion*, February 23, 1922, 4. See also Mathews, *Rethinking Zion*, 84–85.

59. "A Monkey in the Pulpit," *A.M.E. Zion Quarterly Review* 25, no. 4 (October–December 1924): 42–43.

60. "Evolution Before the Law," *A.M.E. Christian Recorder*, May 29, 1925, 4.

61. "Evolution and Life," *A.M.E. Christian Recorder*, July 16, 1925, 4–5.

62. "Let the Evolutionist Talk," *A.M.E. Christian Recorder*, July 23, 1925, 4.

63. "Your Fool Religion," *Star of Zion*, July 23, 1925, 4.

64. "Evolution in the School Room," *Star of Zion*, February 19, 1925, 4.

65. The National Baptist Convention, U.S.A., Inc., website has a brief history of the Laymen's Movement and indicates that John L. Webb was the first organizer and that he spoke to an assembly in Baltimore in September 1925. Accessed July 1, 2014, http://www.nationalbaptist.com/departments/laymen/history.html.

66. "Moderator's Annual Address," *NBV*, September 12, 1925, 9, 12.

67. The Reverend F. C. Van Buren, "Why I am not an Evolutionist," *Star of Zion*, August 6, 1925, 7.

68. "Unsafe," *NBUR*, September 14, 1929, 4.

69. "Preaching Evolution," *A.M.E. Christian Recorder*, September 17, 1925, 4.

70. "The Limitations of Science," *NBUR*, January 20, 1926, 4.

71. "The Creation of the World, *A.M.E. Christian Recorder*, April 1, 1926, 1.

72. "Religion and Science," *A.M.E. Christian Recorder*, June 16, 1927, 5.

73. "Anti-Evolutionists Lag Behind Negroes Declares Bishop Jones in Pittsburgh," *Star of Zion*, July 9, 1931, 4.

74. "Science and Religion Discussed: Dr. N. A. Peyton Presents His Views on the Subject," *NBUR*, November 13, 1926, 1. For more on this understanding of science, see Ronald L. Numbers, *The Creationists: From Scientific Creationism to Intelligent Design*, expanded edition (Cambridge: Harvard University Press, 2006), 65–66.

75. See "Science Supporting Religion," *NBUR*, September 3, 1927, 1; and Mamie Bays, "Asserts Bible is History of Facts," *NBUR*, September 3, 1927, 1.

76. A. W. Pitzer, "The Wisdom of This World: Is There Any Real Conflict Between God's Word and True Science? False Philosophies," reprint of *King's Business* article, *NBUR*, May 12, 1928, 1, 3.

77. George McCready Price, "Modern Science Now Conforming to Scriptures: How the Discovery of Radioactivity Has Affected the Hypothesis That Matter is Eternal," reprint of *Sunday School Times* article, *NBUR*, April 26, 1930, 4. For more on Price, see Numbers, *The Creationists*, 88–119.

78. "Science: The False Messiah," *Star of Zion*, July 28, 1927, 4.

79. "Science and the New Era," *NBUR*, October 6, 1927, 4.

80. The Rev. E. George Biddle, "A Three Fold Work of God," *Star of Zion*, January 26, 1928, 1.

81. The Rev. E. George Biddle, "Futile Scientific Remedies for Sin," *Star of Zion*, November 17, 1932, 1, 5.

Chapter 4

1. "The Seventh Annual Address of Dr. L. K. Williams, President of the National Baptist Convention: Delivered Before the Forty-ninth Annual Session of the National Baptist Convention, September 4–9, 1929, Kansas City, Missouri," *NBV*, September 21, 1929, 5.

2. For the leading voice in discussing fundamentalism's militant anti-modernism, see Marsden, *Fundamentalism and American Culture*. Subsequent monographs have largely confirmed Marsden's categorization of the movement's opposition to modernity's social changes. See, for example, Carpenter, *Revive Us Again*. For an examination of how fundamentalists fared in the national press, see Mathews, *Rethinking Zion*, 67–79.

3. Higginbotham, *Righteous Discontent*, 193.

4. See Butler, *Women in the Church of God in Christ*, 14.

5. Susan K. Cahn, *Sexual Reckonings: Southern Girls in a Troubling Age* (Cambridge: Harvard University Press, 2007), 31.

6. Martin, *Preaching on Wax*, 32–61.

7. J. C. Austin, "The Church and the Social Life of Youth," *NBV*, July 13, 1935, 3.

8. For examples of articles that specifically condemned gambling, see "Church Lotteries," *NBV*, August 27, 1932, 2; "'Gambler's Fever,'" *Star of Zion*, February 25, 1933, 4; and "The Unseen Peril," *Star of Zion*, December 9, 1937, 4.

9. Cahn, *Sexual Reckonings*, 255.

10. "Dancing of the Doctors," *Star of Zion*, August 8, 1918, 4. The "Shim me-Shi Wabble" likely refers to "Shimmie Sha Wabble," a ragtime song by Spencer Williams, and a dance popularized in the Jazz Age, in which the dancer shakes her upper torso and arms. See Chadwick Hansen, "Jenny's Toe: Negro Shaking Dances in America," *American Quarterly* 19, no. 3 (Autumn 1967): 559–61; and David A. Jasen and Gene Jones, *Spreadin' Rhythm Around: Black Popular Songwriters, 1880–1930* (New York: Schirmer Books, 1998), 168–71.

11. W. E. Watson, "The Modern Dance," *A.M.E. Christian Recorder*, October 27, 1927, 2–3.

12. "Ten Reasons vs. Dancing," *Exchange* article reprint, *NBUR*, October 19, 1918, 6.

13. Pastor R. C. Campbell, "Evils of Modern Dance," reprint from *Western Recorder*, *NBUR*, April 14, 1934, 4.

14. "A Borrowed Editorial," reprint of *World Evangel*'s editorial, "'The Conscience and the Dance,'" *Star of Zion*, May 26, 1932, 4.

15. Dr. J. V. Jemison, "An Argument Against Dancing," *NBV*, July 16, 1927, 9.

16. The Reverend S. T. Hawkins, "Is It Right for Christians to Dance?" *Star of Zion*, January 9, 1929, 3.

17. "A Dance Hall and A Methodist Church," reprint from *World Evangel*, *Star of Zion*, June 21, 1928, 2.

18. "Not Dancing, But Recreation in Christian Plan," *Star of Zion*, January 24, 1924, 4.

19. "The Fight Looming on Dancing," *Star of Zion*, March 20, 1924, 4; "The Dancing War," *Star of Zion*, March 27, 1924, 4.

20. "The War Against Vice," *NBUR*, September 7, 1918, 8.

21. "Fleshly Lust!" *NBUR*, September 28, 1918, 5. For more on the Public Health Service's efforts, see Alexandra M. Lord, *Condom Nation: The U.S. Government's Sex Education Campaign from World War I to the Internet* (Baltimore: The Johns Hopkins Press, 2010), 25–47.

22. Christina Simmons, "African Americans and Sexual Victorianism in the Social Hygiene Movement, 1910–1940," *Journal of the History of Sexuality* 4, no. 1 (July 1993): 53–55.

23. "Sex Education," *NBUR*, November 24, 1917, 9.

24. "The Children," *NBUR*, January 4, 1919, 8.

25. "Sex Knowledge," advertisement, *NBUR*, January 4, 1919, 4.

26. "America's Greatest Peril," reprint of California *Advocate* article, *Star of Zion*, December 8, 1927, 1.

27. Bishop W. T. Manning, "The Call to Christians in These Distracted Days," reprint in *Star of Zion*, February 16, 1935, 4.

28. "The Seventh Annual Address of Dr. L. K. Williams," *NBV*, September 21, 1929, 5.

29. "Bishop Alleyne Assails Divorce," reprint of *Watertown* (New York) *Daily Times*, *Star of Zion*, April 1, 1937, 1, 5. In a small mention in the jump, the original article also noted that "Bishop Alleyne said the consciousness of God as a personal father was the answer to the problems of human suffering," but did not elaborate.

30. Miss Mary L. Jones, "Thousands Worship at Antioch—Dr. Goodall Stirs Houston," *NBUR*, January 16, 1932, 2.

31. "The Sanctity of the Marriage Vow," *Star of Zion*, March 25, 1937, 1, 8.

32. The Reverend W. F. Lovelace, "Is It Right to Divorce and Marry Again?" *NBV*, September 12, 1925, 4.

33. "The Meeting of Sex Experts," *Star of Zion*, October 3, 1929, 4.

34. "Vile Affections," *Star of Zion*, February 26, 1931, 4.

35. George Chauncey, *Gay New York: Gender, Urban Culture, and the Making of the Gay Male World, 1890–1940* (New York: Basic Books, 1994), 254–5.

36. "Birth Control," *Star of Zion*, March 26, 1931, 4.

37. The Reverend H. C. McDonald, "Birth Control Versus Christianity," *Star of Zion*, July 2, 1931, 2.

38. Deets Picket, "In Defense of American Women," letter to the editor, *Star of Zion*, June 25, 1931, 3.

39. Andrea Tone, *Devices and Desires: A History of Contraception in America* (New York: Hill and Wang, 2001), 4, 13.

40. Lord, *Condom Nation*, 17.

41. "Red Women of the Bible," *A.M.E. Zion Quarterly Review* 35, no. 4 (1924): 23.

42. "'The Model Woman' Sermon Preached by Rev. W. S. Ellington, DD, Pastor, First Baptist Church, East Nashville—Large Audience Present," *NBUR*, December 1, 1917, 2.

43. The Reverend M. D. Dickson, "Temperance," *NBV*, July 30, 1927, 6–7.

44. R. A. Adams, "Why Do Women Laugh At Insults?" *Star of Zion*, November 24, 1932, 5.

45. "Ashamed of Her," *NBUR*, June 9, 1917, 9.

46. Jeannette M. Freeman, "This Modern Generation," *Star of Zion*, October 22, 1931, 2.

47. Drusilla Dunjee Houston, "Parents Today Are to Blame," *NBUR*, January 12, 1935, 8.

48. See, for example, Thomas Pegram, *Battling Demon Rum: The Struggle for a Dry America* (Chicago: Ivan R. Dee, 1998); and Joe L. Coker, *Liquor in the Land of the Lost Cause: Southern White Evangelicals and the Prohibition Movement* (Lexington: The University Press of Kentucky, 2007).

49. See Richard Hofstadter, *The Age of Reform* (New York: Vintage, 1955); Jack S. Blocker, *Deliver Us from Evil: An Interpretation of American Prohibition* (New York: W. W. Norton, 1976); and Pegram, *Battling Demon Rum.*

50. Nancy J. Weiss, *Farewell to the Party of Lincoln: Black Politics in the Age of FDR* (Princeton: Princeton University Press, 1983), xv, 4–6.

51. See Lisa G. Materson, "African American Women, Prohibition, and the 1928 Presidential Election," *Journal of Women's History* 21, no. 1 (Spring 2009): 63–86.

52. See Rev. M. D. Dickson, "Temperance," *NBV*, July 30, 1927, 6; "Alcohol and the Body," *NBUR*, December 29, 1917, 11; "Gospel Temperance," *NBUR*, December 29, 1917, 2; and "Bishop Clement at the Citizenship Conference," *Star of Zion*, October 18, 1923, 4.

53. J. H. Larimore, "Prohibition and the Negro," *NBV*, February 12, 1927, 10, 11, 14, 15.

54. "The Negro and Prohibition," *Star of Zion*, August 25, 1927, 1. For a discussion of how southerners constructed railroad-related segregation, see Grace Elizabeth Hale, *Making Whiteness*, 125–38.

55. "Prohibition," *NBUR*, January 21, 1928, 4.

56. See James Billington, *The Protestant Crusade* (New York: Macmillan, 1938), and Charles R. Morris, *American Catholic: The Saints and Sinners Who Built America's Most Powerful Church* (New York: Vintage, 1998).

57. "Beware," *NBUR*, January 5–12, 1918, 8.

58. "What is the Matter with White People'" *NBUR*, March 12, 1927, 4. Frank mentioned his concerns about Smith's ring-kissing propensities in at least three other editorials: "That Roman Catholic Display," *NBUR*, September 4, 1926, 4; "What Do You Think of It?" *NBUR*, November 26, 1927, 4; and "Roman Catholics," *NBUR*, April 7, 1928, 4.

59. "Roman Catholics," *NBUR*, April 7, 1928, 4.

60. "Romanism," *NBUR*, November 26, 1927, 4

61. "Considering Colored Americans," *NBUR*, June 30, 1928, 4.

62. "A Bit Political," *NBUR*, September 29, 1928, 4.

63. "Democratic Subterfuge," *Star of Zion*, June 28, 1928, 4.

64. See "Early Democratic Desperation," *Star of Zion*, July 19, 1928, 4; and "A Time for Cool Heads," *Star of Zion*, July 26, 1928, 4.

65. "Mr. Hoover Accepts," *Star of Zion*, August 16, 1928, 4.

66. "The Power of Appointment," *Star of Zion*, October 18, 1928, 4.

67. "Gov. Smith at Oklahoma City," *Star of Zion*, September 27, 1928, 4.

68. Bishop George C. Clement, "Why Support Governor Smith," *Star of Zion*, October 11, 1928, 1, 8.

69. The Reverend James T. Gaskill, "Why Support Hoover," *Star of Zion*, October 25, 1928, 1.

70. B. J. Davis, "Ministers Have a Place in Politics," *NBUR*, October 6, 1928, 1.

71. Untitled editorial, *NBV*, November 17, 1928, 8.

72. "Victory," *Star of Zion*, November 8, 1928, 4.

73. William H. Ferris, "Bishop E. D. W. Jones Against Prohibition," reprint from *Louisville Leader*, October 8, 1931, 1.

74. "Bishop Jones and Prohibition," *Star of Zion*, October 8, 1931, 4.

75. See "Nationally Known Dry Leaders Call for the Re-Election of Mr. Hoover," *Star of Zion*, October 27, 1932, 1; and "Nationally Known Dry Leaders Call for the Re-Election of Mr. Hoover," *NBUR*, November 5, 1932, 1.

76. "Going to the Polls," *Star of Zion*, October 27, 1932, 4.

77. "The Church and Prohibition," *NBV*, June 11, 1932, 2–3.

78. "Political Orphans," *NBV*, June 19, 1932, 2.

79. "The Pot and the Kettle," *NBV*, November 19, 1932, 2.

80. "Governor Roosevelt Triumphs," *Star of Zion*, November 10, 1932, 4.

81. "Is It Too Early?" *Star of Zion*, December 15, 1932, 4.

Chapter 5

1. "Unprecedented Crime Waves," *NBV*, January 1, 1921, 8.

2. See Edward J. Blum and Paul Harvey, *The Color of Christ: The Son of God and the Saga of Race in America* (Chapel Hill: The University of North Carolina Press, 2012), 141–69.

3. For an understanding of the racial situation in the United States in the early twentieth century, see Leon Litwack, *Trouble in Mind: Black Southerners in the Age of Jim Crow* (New York: Vintage, 2010); and Isabel Wilkerson, *The Warmth of Other Suns: The Epic Story of America's Great Migration* (New York: Vintage, 2010).

4. Albert J. Raboteau's groundbreaking work on slave religion introduced a generation of scholars to slave interpretations of Paul's words. Raboteau, *Slave Religion: The "Invisible Institution" in the Antebellum South* (New York: Oxford University Press, 1978).

5. Other scholars have noted the tendency of black evangelicals to combine biblical admonitions with political efforts to integrate the United States. See, for example, Sandy Dwayne Martin, *For God and Race: The Religious and Political Leadership of A.M.E.Z. Bishop James Walker Hood* (Columbia: University of South Carolina, 1999); and Stephen W. Angell and Anthony B. Pinn, eds., *Social Protest Thought in the African Methodist Episcopal Church, 1862–1939* (Knoxville: The University of Tennessee Pres, 2000).

6. "Nordics and Negroes," *Star of Zion*, July 11, 1929, 4.

7. See Christopher Z. Hobson, *The Mount of Vision: African American Prophetic Tradition, 1800–1950* (New York: Oxford University Press, 2012). Hobson's excellent analysis makes use of a number of African American religious leaders and biblical texts. The general strands he describes do appear in my sources, if not in the exact format described in his important book. Rather than parse black Baptist and Methodist participation in prophetic language, I seek to demonstrate how they used these themes to frame an ecclesiology that excluded many white Americans.

8. Hale, *Making Whiteness*, 199–239.

9. "We Will Continue to Pray," *NBUR*, July 21, 1917, 8.

10. "Kirwin, Texas," editorial, *A.M.E. Christian Recorder*, May 18, 1922, 4.

11. "Report of the Committee on State of the Country," *A.M.E. Christian Recorder*, November 26, 1925, 2–3.

12. "South's Lynching Diabolism," *NBV*, January 8, 1921, 6.

13. "'Vox Populi, Vox Dei,'" *NBV*, February 5, 1921, 6. The *NBV*'s concern over the state of American "civilization" was a common theme in news outlets covering lynching. See Mathews, *Rethinking Zion*, 15–17.

14. See "Bloody Old Georgia's Diabolism," *NBV*, February 26, 1921, 1; "The Power of the South, Like the Power of the Nation, Its Womanhood, Is Awakening to the Demoralizing Effects of Lynching and its Accompanying Diabolical Atrocities," *NBV*, February 11, 1922, 1; and "Civilization Toppling," *NBV*, June 3,1922, 8.

15. "The Mark of the Beast," *Star of Zion*, January 6, 1927, 1.

16. "Racial Discrimination and Lynching," *Star of Zion*, October 31, 1929, 4.

17. Kelly Miller, "Kelly Miller Says: Let Us Pray," *Star of Zion*, May 29, 1930, 1, 2. For information on the Sherman Courthouse Riot, see Edward Phillips, "The Sherman Courthouse Riot of 1930," *East Texas Historical Journal* 25, no. 2 (September 1987): 12–19.

18. See Nancy MacLean, *Behind the Mask of Chivalry: The Making of the Second Ku Klux Klan* (New York: Oxford University Press, 1994).

19. "Ku Klux Klan in the North," *A.M.E. Christian Recorder*, January 20, 1921, 1.

20. "The Negro and the Klan," *Star of Zion*, July 3, 1924, 4.

21. Untitled editorial, *Star of Zion*, July 19, 1924, 4. For an extended defense of Simon of Cyrene as black, see Boykin Sanders, "In Search of a Face for Simon the Cyrene," in *The Recovery of Black Presence: An Interdisciplinary*

Exploration, Essays in Honor of Dr. Charles B. Copher, eds. Randall C. Bailey and Jacquelyn Grant (Nashville: Abingdon Press, 1995), 51–63.

22. "The Battling South," *Star of Zion*, March 29, 1925, 4.

23. "Klan's Power On Decline: Civil Liberties Union Reports: Factional Disputes, Loss of Dues, Political Defeats Fatal to Klan," *Star of Zion*, April 23, 1925, 1.

24. Bishop G. C. Clement, "Quadrennial Address of the Bishops," *Star of Zion*, May 10, 1928, 5. Clement's belief that the Klan was dead was certainly wrong. In 1937, the *Star* was still chastising public figures for their alleged KKK involvement. See E. A. Abbott, "Psychologically Speaking: Black and the Ku Klux Klan," *Star of Zion*, November 4, 1937, 6. For more on the Klan and white Christians, see Kelly J. Baker, *The Gospel According to the Klan: The KKK's Appeal to Protestant America, 1915–1930* (Lawrence: University Press of Kansas, 2011).

25. "The Handwriting on the Wall," *Star of Zion*, July 11, 1929, 4.

26. "The Negro Problem in Theory and Practice," *NBUR*, August 25, 1917, 8.

27. "Southern White Baptists," *NBUR*, March 17, 1928, 4.

28. "Segregation in Church," *A.M.E. Christian Recorder*, December 29, 1921, 5.

29. "'The Race Question,'" *A.M.E. Christian Recorder*, March 11, 1926, 1, 4.

30. A. W. Jackson, BD, DD, "Does Your Present-Day Protestantism Conform to the Program of Jesus Christ?—Christ's Program," *A.M.E. Christian Recorder*, June 16, 1927, 12–13.

31. "When the Negro Moves Away," *Star of Zion*, November 12, 1931, 4.

32. "'Jesus Was Not White,'" *Star of Zion*, February 6, 1930, 4. See Blum and Harvey for a discussion of African Americans who did portray Christ as black. Blum and Harvey, *The Color of Christ*, 194–204.

33. "A Suggestion to Negroes," *Star of Zion*, March 15, 1928, 4.

34. Mornay Williams, "A Prayer for Freedom from Race Prejudice," *NBV*, May 9, 1931, 8.

35. The Rev. S. T. Hawkins, "'Why Sit Here Until We Die?'" *Star of Zion*, October 22, 1931, 2.

36. Hawkins's use of Joel 1 illustrates how different writers could use different sections of prophetic texts. Christopher Hobson notes repeated use of Joel 2 (which discusses the Day of the Lord) to demonstrate that God will work for justice, but Hawkins instead focused on the preparations for the day and the need for repentance. This variation adds another rich layer to Hobson's work. See Hobson, *The Mount of Vision*.

37. Kelly Miller, "White and Black Hypocrites," *Star of Zion*, October 3, 1929, 1.

38. "The Color Line and Christianity," reprint from *Pittsburgh Courier*, *Star of Zion*, October 10, 1929, 5.

39. "Poor God," *Star of Zion*, October 17, 1929, 4.

40. "Pastor Blackshear's Black Sheep," reprint from the *Pittsburgh Advocate*, *Star of Zion*, October 17, 1929, 5. Many of the arguments made in the above

coverage of Blackshear are reflected in William Edward Burghardt DuBois's commentary on the same matter. See William Edward Burghardt DuBois, "The Color Line and the Church," in *DuBois on Religion*, ed. Phil Zuckerman (Willow Creek, CA: AltaMira Press, 2000), 169–71, accessed July 16, 2013, http://books. google.com/books?id=xsMszzLoPccC&pg=PA169&lpg=PA169&dq=black-shear+st.+matthew%27s+church+brooklyn&source=bl&ots=UAGalnPzO-J&sig=1CyirSshSbRXuc4PQtd0JRGW3Bs&hl=en&sa=X&ei=foXlUbqKFo-jkywH_hIDICQ&ved=0CEcQ6AEwBg#v=onepage&q=blackshear%20st.%20 matthew%27s%20church%20brooklyn&f=false.

41. "Colored Americans Not Wanted," *NBUR*, December 7, 1929, 4.

42. "Discrimination at the Altar," *Star of Zion*, June 12, 1930, 4.

43. C. C. Coleman, "'Let the Niggers Trust Their God,'" *Star of Zion*, August 18, 1932, 1, 8.

44. Francis J. Grimke, "Dr. Grimke Writes [illegible] Warning Regarding the Negro's Attitude Toward Christianity," reprint from the *Southern Workman*, *NBUR*, January 5, 1935, 1.

45. "The Negro, The Goat," *Star of Zion*, November 3, 1932, 4.

46. The Reverend William E. Guy, DD, "What the Black Man Thinks of the White Man's Religion," in *Social Protest Thought in the African Methodist Episcopal Church, 1869–1939*, eds. Stephen W. Angell and Anthony B. Pinn (Knoxville: The University of Tennessee Press, 2000), 179.

47. "Inter-Racial Co-Operation," *A.M.E. Christian Recorder*, September 16, 1926, 4.

48. Richard R. Wright Jr., "Amos Pleads for Justice. Amos 5:1, 2, 10–15, 21–24," *A.M.E. Christian Recorder*, October 27, 1927, 1.

49. "No Race Line with Jesus' Service," *Star of Zion*, July 14, 1927, 1.

50. The Reverend R. J. Drummond, DD, "The Principles of Christ as Applied to Industrial and Social Problems," *NBV*, February 25, 1922, 10.

51. The Reverend T. Nelson Baker, "The Negro and His Friends," *A.M.E. Christian Recorder*, January 7, 1926, 6.

52. "White Baptists," *NBUR*, July 10, 1926, 4.

53. "Billy Sunday's Opportunity," reprint of *Atlanta Independent* article, *NBUR*, November 24, 1917, 1.

54. "New Year's Day," *NBV*, January 1, 1921, 8.

55. Untitled editorial, *NBV*, July 7, 1934, 2.

56. Roland T. Heacock, "Jim Crow Christianity," reprint from the *Advance*, *NBV*, July 28, 1934, 2.

57. "The Black Man Stood Pat," reprint from Chicago *Herald Examiner*, *NBUR*, January 4, 1919, 1.

58. "A Race Crisis," *NBV*, January 15, 1921, 3.

59. The Reverend J. Q. Johnson, "Eloquent Speech of Bishop Jones at Federal Council of Churches, Meeting in Boston," *NBV*, January 8, 1921, 1, 4. Information on denominational affiliation of Bishop Jones from *Year Book of the Churches, 1921–1922*, ed. E. O. Watson (Washington, DC: The Federal Council of Churches of Christ in America, 1922), 261, accessed July 17, 2013, http://books.

google.com/books?id=DAInK0AMQVAC&pg=PA261&lpg=PA261&dq=bishop+j.h.+jones+federal+council+of+churches&source=bl&ots=kqf5bdsgSj&sig=wn4-GZw7AhsIW16uoBhUg9eZwi8&hl=en&sa=X&ei=Ls7mUeCAG-6fuyQHb3IGwCw&ved=0CC4Q6AEwAQ#v=onepage&q=bishop%20j.h.%20jones%20federal%20council%20of%20churches&f=false.

60. "Annual Address of Edward Perry Jones, BS, DD, President of the National Baptist Convention of the U.S., Delivered at New Orleans, LA. Sept. 8, 1921," *Journal of the National Baptist Convention, 41st* (Nashville: National Baptist Publishing Board, 1922), 88.

61. Dr. E. C. Morris, "Negroes' Loyalty to Church and State," *NBV*, January 15, 1921, 1, 9.

62. William G. Jordan, *Black Newspapers and America's War for Democracy, 1914–1920* (Chapel Hill: University of North Carolina Press, 2001), 36–37. Historian Henry Justin Ferry made similar observations. See Henry Justin Ferry, "Patriotism and Prejudice: Francis James Grimke on World War I," *Journal of Religious Thought* 32, no. 1 (Spring/Summer 1975): 86–94.

63. Untitled editorial, *NBUR*, May 17, 1919, 8.

64. "The Negro's Contribution to the Religious Life of America: Opening Address at Interdenominational Ministers' Conference, Held at Fisk University, Delivered by Bishop L. W. Kyles, On the Evening of June 25, 1928," *NBV*, September 8, 1928, 1, 5.

65. "Negroes to Pray That God Trouble the Conscience of White America," *NBV*, April 23, 1921, 10.

66. "The Negro—Most Important Factor in America," *A.M.E. Christian Recorder*, November 26, 1925, 1, 4.

67. "'America's Race Problem,'" *Star of Zion*, March 29, 1925, 4.

68. "Godless Russia," *NBV*, February 16, 1935, 2.

69. Kelly Miller, "The Power of Moral Protest," *NBUR*, April 15, 1933, 8.

70. Kelly Miller, "Race Prejudice in Germany and in Georgia," *NBUR*, July 1, 1933, 3.

71. "The Religious Press and Germany," *NBV*, August 10, 1935, 2.

72. "To Our Jew Friends," *NBV*, November 4, 1933, 2.

73. "President Williams Delivers Key-Note Message at the Louisville Meeting," *NBV*, December 16, 1933, 3.

74. Untitled editorial, *Star of Zion*, August 6, 1936, 4.

75. "Christ For Every Crisis," reprint from *Church School Herald-Journal*, *Star of Zion*, July 22, 1937, 4.

76. "The Responsibility of the Present Day Church: Annual Message Delivered by President W. H. Jernagin to Sunday School and B.Y.P.U. Congress Delegates at Dayton, Ohio, Thursday, June 20, 1935," *NBV*, June 29, 1935, 1.

Conclusion

1. "The White Man has Religion but His Religion is Unchristian Religion," *NBUR*, May 17, 1941, 4.

2. "War Goes on in Europe, Asia, and Africa, and Lynch Murders Goes [*sic*] In America," *NBUR*, May 31, 1941, 4.

3. See Savage, *Your Spirits Walk Beside Us*, 20–55.

4. For more on Mays, see Randall Maurice Jelks's excellent biography, *Benjamin Elijah Mays: Schoolmaster of the Movement, a Biography* (Chapel Hill: University of North Carolina Press, 2012).

5. "Atlanta Baptist Ministers Union Questions the Orthodoxy of Rev. B. E. Mays, President Morehouse College as a Baptist Minister," *NBUR*, July 26, 1941, 5; and "Like Peter Denied Christ in the Hour of Peril, A Servant Denied His Baptism in the Hour of Danger," *NBUR*, August 2, 1941, 4.

6. Wallace Best, "The Right Achieved and the Wrong Way Conquered": J. H. Jackson, Martin Luther King, Jr., and the Conflict over Civil Rights," *Religion and American Culture: A Journal of Interpretation* 16, no. 2 (Summer 2006): 195–226.

Bibliography

Primary Sources

Newspapers

A.M.E. Christian Recorder
A.M.E. Quarterly Review
A.M.E. Zion Quarterly Review
A.M.E. Zion Star of Zion
Appeal (St. Paul)
Baptist
Baptist and Commoner
Broad Axe (Chicago)
Chicago Defender
Christian Fundamentalist
Cleveland Gazette
Evening News (San Jose)
Grace and Truth
Journal of the National Baptist Convention
Kansas City Advocate
The Moody Bible Institute Monthly
Minutes of the National Baptist Convention, Unincorporated
National Baptist Union-Review
National Baptist Voice
New York Amsterdam News
New York Times
North American Review
Pilot
Proceedings of the National Baptist Convention of America
Savannah Tribune

Sword of the Lord
Washington Bee
Watchman-Examiner
Western Recorder

Collections

Papers of A. C. Dixon, Southern Baptist Historical Library and Archive
Papers of J. C. Massee, American Baptist Historical Society
Papers of J. Frank Norris, Southern Baptist Historical Society and Archive
Papers of W. B. Riley, University of Northwestern—St. Paul
Papers of John Roach Straton, American Baptist Historical Society

Books

DuBois, William Edward Burghardt. "The Color Line and the Church." In *DuBois on Religion*, edited by Phil Zuckerman, 169–71. Willow Creek, CA: AltaMira Press, 2000.

Oliver, French Earl. *Famous Negro Sermons*. Hollywood, CA: The Olvier Press, 1927.

Strong, Josiah. *Our Country*. 1886. Reprint, Cambridge: The Belknap Press of Harvard University Press, 1963.

Torrey, R. A., A. C. Dixon, et al., eds. *The Fundamentals: A Testimony to the Truth*. Los Angeles, CA: Bible Institute of Los Angeles, 1917. Reprint, Grand Rapids, MI: Baker Books, 2000.

Watson, E. O., ed. *Year Book of the Churches, 1921–1922*. Washington, DC: The Federal Council of Churches of Christ in America, 1922.

Wright, Richard R., Jr. *87 Years Behind the Black Curtain: An Autobiography*. Philadelphia: Rare Book Company, 1965.

Secondary Sources

Anderson, Eric D. "Black Responses to Darwinism, 1859–1915." In *Disseminating Darwinism: The Role of Place, Race, Religion, and Gender*, edited by Ronald L. Numbers and John Stenhouse, 247–66. Cambridge: Cambridge University Press, 1999.

Anderson, Theo. "Back Home Again (and Again) in Indiana: E. Howard Cadle, Christian Populism, and the Resilience of American Fundamentalism." *Indiana Magazine of History* 102, no. 4 (December 2006): 301–38.

Angell, Stephen W., and Anthony B. Pinn, eds. *Social Protest Thought in the African Methodist Episcopal Church, 1862–1939*. Knoxville: The University of Tennessee Pres, 2000.

Avery, Sheldon. *Up from Washington: William Pickens and the Negro Struggle for Equality, 1900–1954*. Newark: University of Delaware Press, 1989.

Baker, Kelly J. *The Gospel According to the Klan: The KKK's Appeal to Protestant America, 1915–1930*. Lawrence: University Press of Kansas, 2011.

Bendroth, Margaret Lamberts. *Fundamentalists in the City: Conflict and Division in Boston's Churches, 1885–1950*. New York: Oxford University Press, 2005.

Best, Wallace. "The Right Achieved and the Wrong Way Conquered": J. H. Jackson, Martin Luther King, Jr., and the Conflict over Civil Rights." *Religion and American Culture: A Journal of Interpretation* 16, no. 2 (Summer 2006): 195–226.

———. *Passionately Human, No Less Divine: Religion and Culture in Black Chicago, 1915–1952*. Princeton: Princeton University Press, 2007.

Blum, Edward J. *Reforging the White Republic: Race, Religion, and American Nationalism, 1865–1898*. Baton Rouge: Louisiana State University Press, 2005.

———. *W. E. B. DuBois: American Prophet*. Philadelphia: University of Pennsylvania Press, 2007.

Blum, Edward J., and Paul Harvey. *The Color of Christ: The Son of God and the Saga of Race in America*. Chapel Hill: The University of North Carolina Press, 2012.

Borland, James. "Mordecai Ham: A Thorn in the Devil's Side." *The Fundamentalist Journal* 3, no. 2 (February 1984): 44–46.

Bowman, Matthew. *The Urban Pulpit: New York City and the Fate of Liberal Evangelicalism*. New York: Oxford University Press, 2014.

Bradbury, John W. "Curtis Lee Laws and the Fundamentalist Movement." *Foundations* 5, no. 1 (January 1962): 52–58.

Bradley, David Henry. *A History of the A.M.E. Zion Church*. 2 vols. Nashville, TN: The Parthenon Press, 1970.

Brereton, Virginia Lieson. *Training God's Army: The American Bible School, 1880–1940*. Bloomington: Indiana University Press, 1990.

Burton, Frederick. *Cleveland's Gospel Music*. Black America Series. Charleston, SC: Arcadia Publishing, 2003.

Butler, Anthea. *Women in the Church of God in Christ: Making a Sanctified World*. Chapel Hill: The University of North Carolina Press, 2007.

Cahn, Susan K. *Sexual Reckonings: Southern Girls in a Troubling Age*. Cambridge: Harvard University Press, 2007.

Carpenter, Joel. *Revive Us Again: The Reawakening of American Fundamentalism*. New York: Oxford University Press, 1997.

Chauncey, George. *Gay New York: Gender, Urban Culture, and the Making of the Gay Male World, 1890–1940*. New York: Basic Books, 1994.

Coker, Joe L. *Liquor in the Land of the Lost Cause: Southern White Evangelicals and the Prohibition Movement*. Lexington: The University Press of Kentucky, 2007.

Colored Quintette, The: A Narrative of God's Marvelous Dealings with the Cleveland Gospel Quintette and Their Personal Testimony. Kilmarnock, Scotland: John Ritchie, Ltd., 1937.

Cooks, Michael. "The History and Future of the Southern Bible Institute: A Post-Secondary School of Biblical Studies for African Americans." *Christian Higher Education* 9, no. 2 (April–June 2010): 151–65.

Cooks, Michael J. F. *The Historical Development and Future of the Southern Bible Institute*. Denton, TX: University of North Texas Digital Library. Accessed July 18, 2012, http://digital.library.unt.edu/ark:/67531/metadc6121/.

Dailey, Jane. "Sex, Segregation, and the Sacred after *Brown*." *The Journal of American History* 91, no. 1 (June 2004): 119–44.

DeRemer, Bernard R. "H. A. Ironside: Archbishop of Fundamentalism." *Fundamentalist Journal* 3, no. 8 (September 1984): 45–47.

Dickerson, Dennis C. "African American Religious Intellectuals and the Theological Foundations of the Civil Rights Movement, 1930–1955." *Church History* 74, no. 2 (June 2005): 217–35.

———. *African American Preachers and Politics: The Careys of Chicago*. Jackson: University Press of Mississippi, 2010.

Dixon, Helen C. A. *A. C. Dixon: A Romance of Preaching*. New York: G. P. Putnam's Sons, 1931.

Dunham, T. C. "A Layman on King James versus Moffatt." *Journal of Bible and Religion* 14, no. 2 (May 1946): 107–10.

Dvorak, Katharine L. *An African-American Exodus: The Segregation of Colored Churches*. Brooklyn, NY: Carlson Publishing, Inc., 1991.

English, E. Schuyler. *H. A. Ironside: Ordained of the Lord*. New York: Loizeaux Brothers, 1946.

Evans, Curtis. *The Burden of Black Religion*. New York: Oxford University Press, 2008.

Ferry, Henry Justin. "Patriotism and Prejudice: Francis James Grimke on World War I." *Journal of Religious Thought* 32, no. 1 (Spring/Summer 1975): 86–94.

Gage, Justin Randolph. "Vote as You Pray: The 1928 Presidential Election in Washington County, Arkansas." *The Arkansas Historical Quarterly* 68, no. 4 (Winter 2009): 388–417.

Gasaway, Brantley W. *Progressive Evangelicals and the Pursuit of Social Justice*. Chapel Hill: University of North Carolina Press, 2014.

Glass, William R. *Strangers in Zion: Fundamentalists in the South, 1900–1950*. Macon, GA: Mercer University Press, 2001.

Gregg, Robert. *Sparks from the Anvil of Oppression: Philadelphia's African Methodists and Southern Migrants, 1890–1940*. Philadelphia: Temple University Press, 1993.

Guterl, Matthew Pratt. *The Color of Race in America, 1900–1940*. Cambridge: Harvard University Press, 2002.

Hale, Grace Elizabeth. *Making Whiteness: The Culture of Segregation in the South, 1890–1940*. New York: Pantheon Books, 1998.

Handy, Robert T., ed. *The Social Gospel in America, 1870–1920*. New York: Oxford University Press, 1966.

Harvey, Paul. "Black Protestantism: A Historiographical Appraisal." In *American Denominational History: Perspectives on the Past, Prospects for the Future*, edited by Keith Harper, 120–45. Tuscaloosa: University of Alabama Press, 2008.

———. *Redeeming the South: Religious Cultures and Racial Identities Among Southern Baptists, 1865–1925.* Chapel Hill: University of North Carolina Press, 1997.

Haynes, Stephen R. *Noah's Curse: The Biblical Justification of American Slavery.* New York: Oxford University Press, 2002.

———. "Race, National Destiny, and the Sons of Noah in the Thought of Benjamin M. Palmer." *Journal of Presbyterian History* 78, no. 2 (Summer 2000): 125–43.

Hedstrom, Matthew S. *The Rise of Liberal Religion: Book Culture and American Spirituality in the Twentieth Century.* New York: Oxford University Press, 2013.

Higginbotham, Evelyn Brooks. *Righteous Discontent: The Women's Movement in the Black Baptist Church, 1880–1920.* Cambridge: Harvard University Press, 1993.

Hobson, Christopher Z. *The Mount of Vision: African American Prophetic Tradition, 1800–1950.* New York: Oxford University Press, 2012.

Hood, James Walker. *One Hundred Years of the African Methodist Episcopal Zion Church, or the Centennial of African Methodism.* New York: A.M.E. Zion Book Concern, 1895.

Horace, Lillian B. *"Crowned with Glory and Honor": The Life of Rev. Lacey Kirk Williams.* Edited by L. Vencheal Booth. Hicksville, NY: Exposition Press, 1978.

Hutchison, William R. *The Modernist Impulse in American Protestantism.* Durham: Duke University Press, 1992.

Jelks, Randall Maurice. *Benjamin Elijah Mays: Schoolmaster of the Movement, a Biography.* Chapel Hill: University of North Carolina Press, 2012.

Jordan, William G. *Black Newspapers and America's War for Democracy, 1914–1920.* Chapel Hill: University of North Carolina Press, 2001.

Kazin, Michael. *A Godly Hero: The Life of William Jennings Bryan.* New York: Alfred A. Knopf, 2006.

Levine, Lawrence W. *Defender of the Faith: William Jennings Bryan, the Last Decade, 1915–1925.* New York: Oxford University Press, 1965.

Lienesch, Michael. *In the Beginning: Fundamentalism, the Scopes Trial, and the Making of the Antievolution Movement.* Chapel Hill: University of North Carolina Press, 2007.

Litwack, Leon. *Trouble in Mind: Black Southerners in the Age of Jim Crow.* New York: Vintage Books, 2010.

Lora, Ronald, and William Henry Longton, eds. *The Conservative Press in Twentieth-Century America.* Westport, CT: Greenwood Press, 1999.

Lord, Alexandra M. *Condom Nation: The U.S. Government's Sex Education Campaign from World War I to the Internet.* Baltimore: The Johns Hopkins University Press, 2010.

Lovett, Bobby L. *How It Came to Be: The Boyd Family's Contribution to African American Religious Publishing from the 19th to the 21st Century.* Nashville:

Mega Publishing Corporation, 2007.

Luker, Kristin. *When Sex Goes to School: Warring Views on Sex—and Sex Education—Since the 1960s*. New York: W. W. Norton and Company, 2006.

MacLean, Nancy. *Behind the Mask of Chivalry: The Making of the Second Ku Klux Klan*. New York: Oxford University Press, 1994.

Marsden, George M. *Fundamentalism and American Culture: The Shaping of Twentieth-Century Evangelicalism, 1870–1925*. New York: Oxford University Press, 1980.

Martin, Donald L., Jr. "A. C. Dixon's Views on Immigration and Race." *Baptist History and Heritage* 26, no. 4 (October 1991): 44–51.

Martin, Lerone A. *Preaching on Wax: The Phonograph and the Shaping of Modern African American Religion*. New York: New York University Press, 2014.

Martin, Sandy Dwayne. *For God and Race: The Religious and Political Leadership of A.M.E.Z. Bishop James Walker Hood*. Columbia: University of South Carolina Press, 1999.

Materson, Lisa G. "African American Women, Prohibition, and the 1928 Presidential Election." *Journal of Women's History* 21, no. 1 (Spring 2009): 63–86.

Mathews, Mary Beth Swetnam. *Rethinking Zion: How the Print Media Placed Fundamentalism in the South*. Knoxville: University of Tennessee Press, 2006.

Miller, Albert G. "The Construction of a Black Fundamentalist Worldview: The Role of Bible Schools." In *African Americans and the Bible: Sacred Texts and Social Textures*, edited by Vincent L. Wimbush, 712–27. New York: Continuum Press, 2000.

Montgomery, William E. *Under Their Own Vine and Fig Tree: The African-American Church in the South*. Baton Rouge: Louisiana State University Press, 1993.

Moore, Moses Nathaniel. "Orishatauken Faduma and the New Theology." *Church History* 63, no. 1 (March 1994): 60–80.

Moran, Jeffrey P. "Reading Race into the Scopes Trial: African American Elites, Science, and Fundamentalism." *The Journal of American History* 90, no. 3 (December 2003): 891–911.

———. "The Scopes Trial and Southern Fundamentalism in Black and White: Race, Region, and Religion." *The Journal of Southern History* 70, no. 1 (February 2004): 95–120.

Mumford, Gordon R. "Southern Bible Institute: The History from 1927 to 1998." PhD diss., Tyndale Theological Seminary, 1998.

Newport, Kenneth C. G. "Premillennialism in the Early Writings of Charles Wesley." *The Wesleyan Theological Journal* 32, no. 1 (March 1997): 85–106.

Numbers, Ronald L. *The Creationists: From Scientific Creationism to Intelligent Design*. Expanded edition. Cambridge: Harvard University Press, 2006.

———. *Creationism in Twentieth-Century America: A Ten-Volume Anthology of Documents, 1903–1961*. Vol. 1, *Antievolutionism Before World War I*. New York, Garland Publishing, Inc., 1995.

———. *Darwinism Comes to America*. Cambridge: Harvard University Press, 1998.

Pegram, Thomas. *Battling Demon Rum: The Struggle for a Dry America*. Chicago: Ivan R. Dee, 1998.

Phillips, Edward. "The Sherman Courthouse Riot of 1930." *East Texas Historical Journal* 25, no. 2 (September 1987): 12–19.

Pratt, J. Kristian. "From 'Funnymentalist' to Friend: The Evolving Relationship of Ben M. Bogard and J. Frank Norris." *Baptist History and Heritage* 42, no. 2 (March 2007): 105–13.

Retman, Sonnet. *Real Folks: Race and Genre in the Great Depression*. Durham, NC: Duke University Press, 2011.

Rogers, Mark. "End Times Innovator: Paul Rader and Evangelical Missions." *International Bulletin of Missionary Research* 37, no. 1 (January 2013): 17–24.

Russell, C. Allyn. *Voices of American Fundamentalism: Seven Biographical Studies*. Philadelphia: The Westminster Press, 1976.

Sandeen, Ernest A. *The Roots of Fundamentalism: British and American Millenarianism, 1800–1930*. Chicago: University of Chicago Press, 1970.

Sanders, Boykin. "In Search of a Face for Simon the Cyrene." In *The Recovery of Black Presence: An Interdisciplinary Explorations: Essays in Honor of Dr. Charles B. Copher*, edited by Randall C. Bailey and Jacquelyn Grant, 51–69. Nashville: Abingdon Press, 1995.

Savage, Barbara Dianne. *Your Spirits Walk Beside Us: The Politics of Black Religion*. Cambridge: The Belknap Press of Harvard University Press, 2008.

Sawyer, Mary R. "Black Protestantism as Expressed in Ecumenical Activity." In *Re-Forming the Center: American Protestantism, 1900 to the Present*, edited by Douglas Jacobsen and William Vance Trollinger, 284–99. Grand Rapids: William B. Eerdmans Publishing Company, 1998.

Simmons, Christina. "African Americans and Sexual Victorianism in the Social Hygiene Movement, 1910–1940." *Journal of the History of Sexuality* 4, no. 1 (July 1993): 51–75.

Singleton, George A. *The Romance of African Methodism: A Study of the African Methodist Episcopal Church*. New York: Exposition Press, 1952.

Smith, Timothy L. "The Evangelical Kaleidoscope and the Call to Christian Unity." *Christian Scholar's Review* 15, no. 2 (1986): 125–40.

Smith, Willard H. "William Jennings Bryan and Racism." *Journal of Negro History* 54, no. 2 (April 1969): 127–69.

Sommerville, Raymond R., Jr. *An Ex-Colored Church: Social Activism in the CME Church, 1870–1970*. Macon, GA: Mercer University Press, 2004.

Straton, Hillyer H., "John Roach Straton and the Ku Klux Klan." *Andover Newton Quarterly* 9, no. 2 (November 1968): 124–34.

Sutton, Matthew Avery. *American Apocalypse: The History of Modern Evangelicalism*. Cambridge: The Belknap Press of Harvard University Press, 2014.

Tone, Andrea. *Devices and Desires: A History of Contraception in America*. New York: Hill and Wang, 2001.

Trollinger, William Vance, Jr. *God's Empire: William Bell Riley and Midwestern Fundamentalism*. Madison: University of Wisconsin Press, 1990.

Utzinger, J. Michael. *Yet Saints Their Watch Are Keeping: Fundamentalists, Modernists, and the Development of Evangelical Ecclesiology, 1887–1937*. Macon, GA: Mercer University Press, 2006.

Wagner, Clarence M. *History of the National Baptist Convention, U.S.A., Inc.* Decatur, GA: Tru-Faith Publishing Company, 1993.

Walls, William J. *The African Methodist Episcopal Zion Church: Reality of the Black Church*. Charlotte, NC: A.M.E. Zion Publishing House, 1974.

Weber, Timothy P. *Living in the Shadow of the Second Coming: American Premillennialism, 1875–1925*. New York: Oxford University Press, 1979.

———. "Premillenniallism." In *The Variety of American Evangelicalism*, edited by Donald W. Dayton and Robert K. Johnston, 5–22. Knoxville: University of Tennessee Press, 1991.

Weiss, Nancy J. *Farewell to the Party of Lincoln: Black Politics in the Age of FDR*. Princeton: Princeton University Press, 1983.

Wheeler, Edward L. *Uplifting the Race: The Black Minister in the South, 1865–1902*. Lanham, MD: University Press of America, 1986.

Whitford, David. "A Calvinist Heritage to the 'Curse of Ham': Assessing the Accuracy of a Claim about Racial Subordination." *Church History and Religious Culture* 90, no. 1 (2010): 25–45.

Wilkerson, Isabel. *The Warmth of Other Suns: The Epic Story of America's Great Migration*. New York: Vintage Books, 2010.

Williamson, Joel. *The Crucible of Race*. New York: Oxford University Press, 1994.

Index

Abyssinian Baptist Church, 110
Adams, R. A., 114
Advance, 144
Africa, 138
African Americans: dialect of, 22, 25–28; paternalism toward, 11–12, 15, 21, 32–33, 36; patriotism of, 21, 145–47, 154; violence toward, 46, 128–31, 153; white "expertise" about, 2–3, 31–39, 137–38. *See also* African Americans, stereotypes about; race; white fundamentalists, relationship to African Americans
African Americans, stereotypes about, 2, 6, 34–35; as credulous, 31; as drunks, 116–17; as emotional, 25; as hyper-religious, 86–87; as hyper-sexual, 18–19, 101, 111; as justification for slavery, 36; as musically exceptional, 22–25
African Methodist Episcopal Church (AME), 8–9, 45; founding of, 74; tenets of, 62. *See also A.M.E. Christian Recorder*
African Methodist Episcopal Zion (AMEZ), 8–9, 48; *A.M.E. Zion Quarterly Review*, 89–90, 112–13; founding of, 74. See also *Star of Zion*
Alabama State Baptist Convention, 103

Alexander, Charles T., 29–30
Alleyne, Cameron C., 108
amalgamation, 134
AME. *See* African Methodist Episcopal Church
A.M.E. Christian Recorder: on American values, 148; on biblical interpretation, 75, 94; on dancing, 45, 101–2; on evolution, 90–91; on fundamentalist/modernist debate, 61–64; on Ku Klux Klan, 131; on lynching, 129; on segregation, 133–35; on social justice, 140–41; traditionalism of, 74. *See also* African Methodist Episcopal Church
American Baptist Home Missionary Society, 21
AMEZ. *See* African Methodist Episcopal Zion
A.M.E. Zion Quarterly Review, 89–90, 112–13
Amos, Book of, 140–41
Anderson, Eric D., 86
Anderson, J. Harvey, 57, 101
Antichrist, 81, 130
apocalypticism. *See* premillennialism
Appeal, 45
Ashworth, Robert A., 49, 59
Associated Negro Press, 115

Atlanta Baptist Ministers' Union, 154
Atlanta Independent, 143–44
Austin, J. C., 100
Avery, Sheldon, 53

Baker, T. Nelson, 142
Baltimore Sun, 88
baptism, 154–55
Baptist and Commoner, 18–19
Baptist Bible Union, 32
Baptists, 43–44, 59, 169nn4, 6. See also
    National Baptist Union-Review;
    National Baptist Voice
Baptist World Alliance, 149–50
Baptist Young Peoples Union Con-
    gress, 100
Barbour, R. C., 66, 144, 149–50
Barton, Bruce, 55
Bendroth, Margaret Lamberts, 84
Benedict College, 30
Best, Wallace, 155
Bible: on alcohol, 116; as divinely in-
    spired, 2, 43, 75, 89; social customs
    and, 99–100, 102; social justice in, 4,
    127, 140–41, 155; traditional wom-
    en's roles and, 112–13; translations
    of, 84. *See also* biblical interpreta-
    tion/criticism
Bible Institute of Los Angeles, 96–97
biblical interpretation/criticism, 12; his-
    toricity, 64–65; infallibility/inerrancy,
    4, 51, 55, 69–70, 72–73, 83, 92, 155;
    private vs. institutional, 51; tradition-
    alist vs. fundamentalist, 79, 85–86;
    traditionalist vs. modernist, 73–75
Biddle, Eli George, 75, 82–86, 96
birth control, 110–11
"Birth of a Nation," 34
Bishop College, 149
Blackshear, William, 136–38
Blackwell, W. A., 150
Bleak House (Dickens), 148
Blum, Edward J., 5, 12, 127
Bogard, Ben, 16–19
Bond, James A., 117–18
Booker, Joseph A., 48–49

Bowman, Matthew, 159n2
Boyd, Richard H., 43
Bradbury, John W., 20
Broad Axe, 44
Broadus, John A., 27
Brookins, Homer DeWilton, 21–22
Browder, Earl, 124
Bryan, William Jennings, 88, 91
Butler, Anthea, 8, 10, 100

Cahn, Susan K., 101
California, 1
California *Advocate*, 107
Callaway, T. W., 81–82
Calvary Baptist Church, 33–34, 45
Calvin, John, 16
Campbell, R. C., 102
Canada, 55
Canadian Baptist Convention, 55
Carpenter, Joel, 12, 84
Carroll, Richard Alexander, 76
Catholicism. *See* Roman Catholicism
Chauncey, George, 110
Chicago Defender, 45
Christian and Missionary Alliance, 24
Christian Century, 148
Christian Fundamentalist, 23, 26–27,
    29, 38
Christianity: conversion, 11, 13, 20,
    32, 69–70, 81; evangelization,
    20–22, 51, 82, 90; missionaries, 138,
    147–48; Mormonism, 156; Pente-
    costalism, 9–10, 38–39, 72; salva-
    tion, 78, 144–45, 149; traditional-
    ism, 7, 69–71, 77, 86, 142–43. *See
    also* African Methodist Episcopal
    Church (AME); African Methodist
    Episcopal Zion (AMEZ); Baptists;
    Bible; conversion; ecclesiology; fun-
    damentalism; Jesus Christ; Roman
    Catholicism; theology; tradition-
    alism
Christian Realist movement, 85
Christian Recorder. See *A.M.E. Chris-
    tian Recorder*
Christian Scientists, 72

Christian Work, 60

Church of Jesus Christ of Latter-Day Saints, 156

Church School Herald-Journal, 151

civil rights movement, 5, 154–55

Civil Service Commission, 17

Civil War, 21

Clarendon Street Baptist Church, 84

class, 15, 35, 101, 136–37

Clement, George C., 76, 121–22, 132

Cleveland Colored Quintette, 21–22

Cleveland Gazette, 47

Coleman, C. C., 139

Communist Party, 124

Comstock Act of 1873, 111

conservatism, 7, 73–74

conversion: as civilizing force, 20; eschatological imagery and, 81; social issues and, 13; stories of, 11, 32; traditionalism and, 69–70. *See also* evangelization

Copeland, A. Reilly, 81

Crenshaw, J. D.: on crime, 126; on lynching, 129–30; Social Gospel language of, 59–60; on social justice, 144

Crozer Theological Seminary, 20

Dallas Bible School, 24–25

Dallas Colored Bible Institute, 37–39

dancing, 100–105

Darby, John Nelson, 70, 77

Darrow, Clarence, 91, 142

Darwin, Charles. *See* evolution

Davenport, William H.: on birth control, 110; on eschatology, 80–82; on evolution, 88–89, 91, 96; on fundamentalist/modernist debate, 51–52, 57–58, 74–75; on homosexuality, 109–10; on Ku Klux Klan, 132; on prohibition, 120–21; on Roman Catholicism, 138–39; on segregation, 135–37; on theory vs. practice, 140; on voting, 124–25; on women, 156

Davis, Benjamin Jefferson, 122–23, 153–54

Dayton, 88

DCBI (Dallas Colored Bible Institute), 37–39

Democratic National Convention, 119

Democratic Party, 17–20, 118–23. *See also* 1928 presidential election

Denver Bible Institute, 20

Deuteronomy, 141–42

Dickens, Charles, 148

Dickerson, Dennis, 5

Dickson, M. D., 113–14

dispensationalism. *See* premillennialism

divorce, 108–9

Dixon, Amzi Clarence, 2, 14–16, 32

Dixon, Helen Cadbury, 16, 31–32

Does Civilization Need Religion? (Niebuhr), 85

Douglass, Frederick, 16

Drummond, R. J., 141–42

DuBois, W. E. B., 4–6

Dunham, T. C., 84

ecclesiology, 6, 126–52; foreign vs. domestic injustice and, 148–51; Ku Klux Klan and, 131–32; lynchings and, 128–31; patriotism and, 145–47; segregation and, 132–39; social justice and, 139–45

Eddy, Mary Baker, 72

education: Baptist vs. Methodist, 57; manual labor and, 15–16; of ministry, 37–38, 63; modernism and, 29–31; racial uplift and, 31, 46, 86–87; religious doubt and, 91–92; Scopes trial, 86–92; segregation and, 135; sex education, 106–7; Social Gospel and, 65; universities, 29–31; voting rights and, 15

Eichelberger, James W., Jr., 141

Eighteenth Amendment. *See* Prohibition

Ellington, W. S., 113

Elmer Gantry, 55

English, E. Schuyler, 38

eschatology. *See* premillennialism

evangelicalism: anti-Catholicism of,

118–19; conservative/liberal terms and, 7; construction of, by African Americans, 2, 6, 8, 151–52; vs. fundamentalism, 3–4, 69, 74, 77; science and, 89. *See also* Baptists; evangelization; fundamentalism/fundamentalists; Methodists; traditionalism

evangelization: to African Americans, 20–22; biblical inerrancy and, 90; missionaries, 138, 147–48; as reaction to modernism, 51; Second Coming and, 82. *See also* conversion

Evans, Curtis, 55

Evening News, 47

evolution, 12; free inquiry and, 59; mockery of, 22–24, 26–27; racial implications of, 87, 167n95; Scopes trial, 86–92; study of, 63; theological opposition to, 71, 93

Federal Council of Churches of Christ in America (FCC), 110, 146

feminism, 84

Fisk University, 148

Florida Avenue Baptist Church, 68

Foley, C. W., 39

Ford, James W., 124

Fosdick, Harry Emerson, 51, 57, 65–66

Fowler, L. J., 20

Frank, Jonathan H.: on evolution, 93–94; on fundamentalist/modernist debate, 41, 50, 52–56, 64–65, 71–74; on Jim Crow, 133; on missionaries, 147–48; on prohibition, 118; on Roman Catholicism, 119; on science and religion, 95–96; on traditionalism, 71–74; on women, 156

Freeman, Jeannette M., 115

fundamentalism/fundamentalists, 1–10, 68–97; definition of, 3–4, 65, 69, 75, 173n2, 174n27; early history of, 11–12, 47, 173n2; intolerance and, 59; as racialized term, 5–6, 159n3; on science, 63; self-identification as, by African Americans,

75–76; traditionalism and, 69–74, 77, 86, 155. *See also* evolution; modernism; premillennialism; white fundamentalists, relationship to African Americans

Fundamentals, The, 6, 42, 71–72, 86

Gaines, A. L., 62

Galatians (St. Paul), 127

gambling, 100–101

Gaskill, James T., 122

gender: gender roles, 111–12; of God, 83–84; masculinity, 106; parenting and, 108; privilege and, 99–100. *See also* women

Genesis, 39

Georgia, 149

Germany, 73, 145, 147, 149–50

Gilkey, Charles Whitney, 65

Gilkey, James Gordon, 65

Glass, William R., 70

God, 83–84. *See also* Jesus Christ

Goodall, T. J., 108

Gordon, Adoniram J., 84

Grace and Truth, 20

Gray, James, 37

Great Depression, 123, 125, 165n56

Great Migration, 21, 33

Grimke, Francis, 139–40

Guy, William E., 140

Haldeman, I. M., 47

Hale, Grace Elizabeth, 35, 128, 167n93

Harlem, 110

Harris, Joel Chandler, 27

Harrison, Pat, 17–18

Harvey, Paul, 127

Hatcher, William, 15

Hawkins, S. T., 103, 136, 183n36

Haynes, Stephen R., 39

Heacock, Ronald T., 144

Heard, W. H., 62

Hedstrom, Matthew S., 85

Herald Examiner, 145

Higginbotham, Evelyn Brooks, 46, 99–100

Hobson, Christopher Z., 4, 128, 141, 183n36
Hodges, H. D., 24
Holy Spirit, 84
homosexuality, 109–10
Hoover, Herbert, 17–18, 100, 118–24
Horace, Lillian B., 43–44
Horton, R. F., 60
Houston, Drusilla Dunjee, 115
Hovey, George Rich, 31
Hutchison, William R., 42
Hylan, John F., 34

Independent, 122
Interdenominational Ministers' Conference, 148
International Workers of the World (IWW), 145
Ironside, Edmund H., 36–38
Ironside, Harry A., 24, 36–37
Islam, 29

Jackson, A. W., 134–35
Jackson, J. H., 155
Jackson, P. H., 62
Jasper, John, 15, 162n11
Jelks, Randall Maurice, 5
Jemison, J. V., 103
Jernagin, W. H., 151
Jesus Christ: race of, 126–27, 135–36, 139; social justice and, 139–40, 143–44
Jesus or Christianity—A Study in Contrast (Page), 130
Jews/Judaism, 149–50
Jim Crow, 12, 37, 46, 117, 133
Johnson, James Weldon, 138
Jones, E. D. W., 75–76, 95, 123
Jones, Edward Perry, 146–47
Jones, J. H., 146
Jones, Mary L., 108
Jones, Spurgeon R., 24
Jordan, George W., 154
Jordan, J. G., 58–59
Jordan, William G., 147

Kansas City Advocate, 47

Kentucky Interracial Commission, 117
Kingdom of God, 60, 65–66, 143
King James Bible, 84
King, Martin, Sr., 154
King, Martin Luther, Jr., 154–57
King's Business, 96
Ku Klux Klan, 34, 45–46, 131–33
Kyles, L. W., 148

Lacy, Floyd H., 24
Lake Geneva Student Conference, 141
Landmark Baptists, 18
language, 22, 26–28
Laws, Curtis Lee, 20–21, 25, 27, 30–31, 33, 49, 163n34
Leader, 123
League of Nations, 81, 83
Lewis, Sinclair, 55
liberalism, 7. *See also* modernism; progressivism
Lienesch, Michael, 45
Living Word, 15
Love, Mia, 156
Lovelace, W. F., 109
Lovett, Bobby L., 44
Lowry, Henry, 129
Luther, Martin, 51
lynching, 46, 128–31, 153

Machen, J. Gresham, 65
Man Nobody Knows, The (Barton), 55
Manning, W. T., 107
manual labor, 15–16
marriage: adultery and, 107–9; dancing and, 103; divorce, 108–9; gay marriage, 1; interracial, 16–17; prostitution and, 105–6; traditional structure of, 111–12
Martin, Lerone A., 8–9, 100
masculinity, 106
Massee, Jasper Cortensus, 14, 31, 44–45, 49
materialism, 65
Mathews, Shailer, 52, 64
Matthew (NT gospel), 127
Matthews, M. C., 47

McDaniels, E. H., 62
McDonald, H. C., 110–11
Mercer University, 33
Methodists. *See* African Methodist Episcopal Church (AME); African Methodist Episcopal Zion (AMEZ)
migration/migrants, 12, 19, 21, 33, 145
Miller, Kelly, 4–5, 53, 130, 136–37, 149
minstrelsy, 22–23
missionaries, 138, 147–48. *See also* evangelization
Missions, 31
modernism, 3–4; biblical interpretation and, 73–75, 89, 92; compromise/diplomacy about, by African Americans, 58–66; consequences of, 29–31, 57–58, 63–64; definition of, 42; education and, 37–38; evolution and, 87–88; as non-Christian, 159n2; social justice and, 143; as white phenomenon, 4, 42–43, 47–48, 53–57, 66, 155. *See also* fundamentalism/fundamentalists; modernism, social changes relating to; progressivism
modernism, social changes relating to, 7–8, 98–125, 155; birth control, 110–11; dancing, 100–105; marriage/divorce, 107–9; sex education, 106–7; sexually transmitted diseases and, 105–6; women's traditional roles/behavior and, 111–16. *See also* Prohibition
Moffat Bible, 84
Moody, Dwight L., 12, 84
Moody Bible Institute Monthly, 26, 29
Moore, Moses Nathaniel, 5
Moran, Jeffey, 87
Morehouse College, 25, 154
Mormons, 156
Morris, Elias Camp, 43, 77–78, 147
Morton, Ferdinand, 17, 19
Mullins, E. Y., 54

National Association for the Advancement of Colored People (NAACP), 95, 138, 148

National Baptist Convention, Incorporated, 9–10, 43–44, 169n6. See also *National Baptist Voice*
National Baptist Convention, Unincorporated, 9–10, 43–44. See also *National Baptist Union-Review*
National Baptist Laymen's Movement, 92
National Baptist Union-Review: on biblical infallibility, 72–73; as conservative, 73–74; criticism of other Baptists by, 71–72; on dancing, 102; on domestic vs. foreign injustice, 149; on eschatology, 73–74, 81–82; on evolution, 94; on fundamentalist/modernist debate, 41, 44, 50, 52, 54–55; on Jim Crow, 133; on lynchings, 128–29; on marriage, 106–7; on ministers' political involvement, 122–23; on missionaries, 138, 147–48; on patriotism, 145; on Prohibition, 118, 123–24; on prostitution, 105–6; on racial equality, 143–44; on Roman Catholicism, 118–20; on sex education, 106–7; traditionalism of, 71; on white hypocrisy, 139–40, 153; on women's traditional roles, 113–15
National Baptist Voice: on crime, 126; on dancing, 45, 103; on diversity in Bible, 136; on evolution, 92; on fundamentalist/modernist debate, 44, 48, 58–61, 65–66; on lynchings, 129–30; on marriage, 107–9; on Nazi Germany, 149–50; on 1928 presidential election, 123; on patriotism, 145–46; on premillennialism, 77–80; progressivism of, 71; on Prohibition, 117, 124; on social justice, 65–66, 141–42, 144, 148; on voting, 124–25
National Law Enforcement Conference, 35, 45
National Religious Training School, 44
National Sunday School, 100
NBUR. See *National Baptist Union-Review*

Niebuhr, Reinhold, 85
1919 Washington riots, 45
1928 presidential election, 16–20, 118–23
Norris, J. Frank, 14, 16–17, 28–32, 60–61, 166n81
North American Review, 36
North Carolina Central University, 44
Northern Baptist Convention, 59
Northern Baptists, 20–22, 59
Northwestern Bible College, 39
nostalgia, 31, 58
Numbers, Ronald L., 26, 71

Obama, Barack, 1
Olivet Baptist Church, 21, 155
Ottoman Empire, 81
Our Country (Strong), 20
Owens, Jesse, 150

Page, Kirby, 130
Palmer, Benjamin M., 39, 168n108
Parker, J. W., 24
patriotism, 21, 145–47, 154
Pentecostalism, 9–10, 38–39, 72
Pickens, William, 53
Pickett, Deets, 111
Pilgrim Baptist Church, 147
Pilgrim Holiness Church, 26
Pilot, 11, 24, 39, 162n11
Pittsburgh Advocate, 137–38
Pittsburgh Christian Advocate, 130
Pittsburgh Courier, 137–38
politics: 1928 presidential election, 16–20, 118–23; rights, 16; voting, 15, 116–17, 124. *See also* progressivism; Prohibition; segregation; social justice
Powell, Adam Clayton, 110
Powell, W. D., 20
premillennialism, 3, 37, 49, 174n27; as nontraditional, 86; opposition to, 2, 70, 73–74, 77–80, 155; support for, 81–82
Price, George McCready, 96
progressivism, 2, 7–9; Baptist schism and, 43, 71; biblical support for, 127,

151–52; Prohibition and, 121; on racial issues vs. social customs, 7–8, 143–44, 155–56; science and, 96–97. *See also* modernism; traditionalism
Prohibition, 100, 116–25; benefits of, 117–18, 121; disenfranchisement and, 116–17; 1928 presidential election and, 118–23
prophecy. *See* premillennialism
Proposition 8, 1
prostitution, 103, 105
Protestantism, 20, 110, 157. *See also* Baptists; fundamentalism/fundamentalists; Methodists

Quarterly Review. See *A.M.E. Zion Quarterly Review*

race: definition of, 134; interracial marriage, 16–17; of Jesus, 126–27, 135–36, 139; modernism and, 42–43, 47–48, 53–57, 66; orthodoxy and, 52–54; race consciousness, 22; racial difference, 13–16, 18–19, 22, 39. *See also* African Americans; racial difference; racial uplift; racism; white people
racial difference, 13–16; dialect and, 22; education and, 15–16; religious justification for, 14, 39; sexuality and, 18–19; voting rights and, 15
racial uplift, 8; as anti-modernist, 93; class and, 136–37; politics and, 125; prohibition and, 116, 118; science and, 86–87; social behavior and, 46, 98–99, 101; women's roles and, 115–16
racism: consequences of, 44; eschatology and, 80, 83; lynching, 46, 128–31; prevalence of, 33. *See also* African Americans, stereotypes about; segregation; slavery; Social Gospel
Rader, Paul, 23–24
Rapture, 82
Recorder. See *A.M.E. Christian Recorder*
religion: Islam, 29; Judaism, 149–50;

science and, 4–5, 63, 88–91, 94–97. *See also* Christianity

Republican Party: African American support for, 117, 121, 123–25, 156; during 1928 presidential election, 17–20, 118–23

Rice, John R., 24–25

Richmond Christian Advocate, 134

Richmond College, 20

Rightly Dividing the Word (Scofield), 37

rights, 16. *See also* civil rights movement; progressivism; social justice

Riley, William Bell, 11, 22–24, 27, 29, 31–32, 49, 162n11

Roberts, R. B., 78–79

Robertson, A. T., 21, 27

Roman Catholicism: dancing and, 104; danger to American democracy, 118–20; modernism and, 51–52; racism in, 138–39; of Al Smith, 17, 116; tenets of, 63

Roosevelt, Franklin Delano, 153

Roosevelt, Theodore, 16

Roundtree, I. W. L., 62–63

Russell, C. Allyn, 14

Russia, 149

salvation, 78, 144–45, 149

Sandeen, Ernest, 84, 173n2

Savage, Barbara Dianne, 5, 55, 154

Savannah Tribune, 44

Sawyer, Mary R., 7

SBC. *See* Southern Baptist Convention

science: limitations of, 94; racial uplift and, 86–87; religion and, 4–5, 63, 88–90, 94–97; scientific racism, 16. *See also* evolution

Scofield, Cyrus, 37, 84

Scofield Reference Bible, 84

Scopes trial, 86–92

Scottish realism, 89

Second Coming, 81–82

secularism. *See* modernism

segregation, 7–8, 12–20; of churches, 2, 136–38; evolution and, 95; hypocrisy of, 132–36; justification for,

12–16, 36; 1928 presidential election and, 16–20; in Tennessee, 90; World War II and, 154. *See also* Social Gospel

seminaries, 31, 37–39, 57

sex/sexuality: dancing and, 102–5; homosexuality, 109–10; interracial, 134; sexually transmitted diseases, 105–7; stereotypes about, of African Americans, 18–19, 101, 111

Sherman Courthouse Riot, 130

Shields, T. T., 55

Simmons, Christina, 106

Slater, George W., Jr., 62

slavery: African Americans, stereotypes about, and, 34–35; American values and, 146; justification for, 36, 39, 168n108; legacy of, 46; nostalgia about, 11; prohibition and, 121

Smith, Al, 17, 118–23

Smith, Dean, 149

Smith, Eugene E., 21–22

Smith, Howard Wayne, 21

Social Gospel: biblical basis of, 141–42; opposition to, 82–83; support for, 44, 60, 64–66, 70, 141, 143–44

social justice, 4, 128, 140, 143–45. *See also* progressivism; segregation; Social Gospel

sola scriptura, 110

Southern Baptist Convention (SBC), 50, 55–56, 169n6

Southern Baptist Theological Seminary, 33

Southern Bible Institute. *See* Dallas Colored Bible Institute

Star of Zion, 9; on adultery, 107; on biblical interpretation, 74–75; on birth control, 110–11; on dancing, 101–4; on eschatology, 80–83; on evolution, 88–89, 93; on fundamentalist/modernist debate, 48, 50–52, 56–58; on gambling, 100–101; on homosexuality, 109–10; on Ku Klux Klan, 131–32; on lynching, 130; on marriage, 108–9; on 1928 election,

120–22; on Jesse Owens, 150; on prayer, 136; on Prohibition, 117–18, 123–24; on Roman Catholicism, 138–39; on segregation, 135–38; self-identification of, as fundamentalist, 75; on theory vs. practice, 128, 140, 148; traditionalism of, 71; on voting, 124–25; on white hypocrisy, 128
Stealey, Clarence P., 55
Stewart, Lyman, 6, 42
Stires, Ernest M., 138
St. Matthew's Protestant Episcopal Church, 136
Stokes, A. J., 79
Straton, John Roach, 2, 31, 33–36, 45, 49, 51, 167nn89, 95, 170n10
Strong, Josiah, 20
Sullivan, Frank, 21
Sunday, Billy, 143
Sutton, Matthew Avery, 173n2, 174n27
Synthetic Bible Studies, 37

Tabernacle Baptist Church, 103
Tabernacle Voice, 81
Talbert, Alexander E., 24
Tammany Hall, 17
Taylor, W. A., 68
Ten Commandments, 129
theology: of fundamentalism, 43–44, 93; lynchings and, 128–30; orthodoxy, 70; vs. practical action, 63–64, 78–79, 128, 140, 148; racial uplift and, 46; vs. science, 87; sola scriptura, 110. See also Social Gospel
Thompson, D. E., 65
Time, 23
Tindley, Elbert T., 24–25, 165n56
Tone, Andrea, 111
Toronto Mail and Empire, 22
traditionalism, 7; definition of, 69–71; vs. fundamentalism, 77, 86; social justice and, 142–43. See also evangelicalism; progressivism

Union-Review. See National Baptist Union-Review

United States: foreign policy of, 147–48; ideals of, 21, 146–48; patriotism, 21, 145–47, 154
US Constitution, 16, 117, 119, 129. See also Prohibition
US House of Representatives, 156
US Public Health Service, 105
universities, 29–31
University of Chicago, 64, 75
University of Pennsylvania, 64
University of Richmond, 20

Van Buren, F. C., 93
Virgin Birth, 69, 75
Voice. See National Baptist Voice
Volstead Act, 120
voting: civil rights and, 124–25; disenfranchisement, 116–17; education and, 15; 1928 presidential election, 16–20, 118–23

Wagner, Clarence M., 43
Wallace-Sanders, Kimberly, 35
Walls, W. J., 48, 50, 89, 104
Washington, Booker T., 16
Washington Bee, 44
Watchman-Examiner, 20–21, 23, 25, 27, 32, 163n34
Watson, W. E., 102
WCFA (World Christian Fundamentalist Association), 22
Webb, John L., 92
Weber, Timothy, 70, 79, 82
Weiss, Nancy J., 117
Wells, H. G., 56–57
Western Baptist Convention, 47
Western Recorder, 29–30, 81–82, 102
white fundamentalists, relationship to African Americans, 2–3, 11–40, 155; evangelization, 20–22; marginalization, 22–28; modernism and, 6, 28–31; racial "expertise" and, 31–39, 137–38; segregation, 12–20. See also segregation
white people: emulation of, 46, 99, 101; modernism and, 4, 42–43, 47–48,

53–57, 66, 155; Roman Catholicism and, 119; as unchristian, 153.
See also African Americans; race;
racism; white fundamentalists, relationship to African Americans
Williams, Lacey Kirk: on divorce,
107–8; on domestic vs. foreign
injustice, 150–51; on fundamen-
talist/modernist debate, 60–61; on
National Baptist Convention split,
43–44; on social changes, 98
Wilson, Woodrow, 148
women: dancing and, 102–3; feminism, 84; in leadership roles, 47;
mammies, 31–32, 35–36, 166n77,
167n92; parenting by, 108; paternalism toward, 19; sex education and,
106–7; traditional roles of, 111–16;
women's liberation, 105, 111, 156.
See also gender
Wood, J. Edmund, 49–50, 81

Woodson, Carter, 6
World Baptist Alliance, 50
World Christian Fundamentalist Asso-
ciation, 22
World Evangel, 57, 103–4
World's Christian Fundamentalist
Conference, 47
World War I: African American patri-
otism during, 21, 145–47; sexually
transmitted diseases during, 105–6;
Social Gospel and, 60; traditional-
ism and, 12
World War II, 154–55
Wright, Richard R., Jr.: on biblical
literalism, 63–64; on Ku Klux Klan,
131–32; on lynchings, 129; on
science, 90–91, 94–95; on social
justice, 140–41; traditionalism of, 75

Young People's Society for Christian
Endeavor, 151